To Roy,

Best Regards,

9/25/94

REHEARSALS FOR GROWTH

Theater Improvisation
for Psychotherapists

A NORTON PROFESSIONAL BOOK

REHEARSALS
FOR GROWTH

Theater Improvisation
for Psychotherapists

_____

Daniel J. Wiener, Ph.D.

W · W · NORTON & COMPANY

NEW YORK · LONDON

For further information on Rehearsals for Growth, contact:

Rehearsals for Growth
c/o Daniel J. Wiener, Ph.D.
1 East 28th Street
New York, NY 10016
(212) 684-6776

Copyright © 1994 by Daniel J. Wiener

All rights reserved.

Printed in the United States of America

First Edition

Composition by Bytheway Typesetting Services, Inc.
Manufacturing by Haddon Craftsmen, Inc.

Library of Congress Cataloging-in-Publication Data

Wiener, Daniel J.
    Rehearsals for growth : theater improvisation for psychotherapists
/ Daniel J. Wiener.
        p.   cm.
    "A Norton professional book."
    Includes bibliographical references and index.
    ISBN 0-393-70187-5
    1. Improvisation (Acting) — Therapeutic use.   I. Title.
RC489.P7W52   1994
616.89′165 — dc20   94-20894   CIP

W. W. Norton & Company, Inc., 500 Fifth Avenue, New York, NY 10110
W. W. Norton & Company, Ltd., 10 Coptic Street, London WC1A 1PU

                1   2   3   4   5   6   7   8   9   0

CONTENTS

PART III

Pragmatics: Applying Improv to Clinical Practice and Training

ACKNOWLEDGMENTS

I FIRST WISH to express deepest appreciation and affection for the personal support, incalculable help, and abiding love of Gloria Jean Maddox, my spouse, without whom this work could have neither begun nor developed. Her participation has spanned the roles of teacher, colleague, helpful critic, and playful partner.

I am profoundly grateful to Keith Johnstone, who in both concept and spirit has laid the foundation for my use of improvisation in psychotherapy and who has modelled for me the roles of keen observer and inspirational teacher.

Thanks also to Thelma Jean Goodrich, Howard Seeman, and Carole Douglis, wonderful colleagues whose careful reading and thoughtful comments greatly assisted me in preparing the manuscript.

Finally, this work could not have been developed without the participation of the numerous stage improvisers, student therapists, and clients who have participated with me in rehearsals, performances, classes, workshops, and therapy sessions over the past nine years. To all of you, great thanks!

Daniel J. Wiener

INTRODUCTION

T HEATER IMPROVISATION (improv) is a method of stage-acting in the moment, using minimal prearranged structures (such as scripts, plots, or props). One version of improv that was developed by Keith Johnstone (1981) has influenced my work in using improv for relationship enhancement workshops, clinical practice, and the training of therapists. Since 1989 I have been calling my methods Rehearsals! for Growth (RfG).

RfG is not a complete therapy or theory but an approach that can be used for a variety of therapeutic purposes, particularly that of improving relationships and relationship skills. Beyond its utility, there is an alluring quality to improvising, a challenging encounter with immediacy that can be appreciated fully only when experienced personally. Based upon my experience with training mental health professionals, improv offers at least as much to the person of the therapist as to his or her clients.

HOW I CAME TO THIS WORK

My wife, actress/acting teacher/director Gloria Maddox, had been trained by Keith Johnstone in improvisational theater. When she offered theater improvisation training for nonactors in 1984 I became Gloria's pupil, later performing team improvisational comedy for six years. From the first, I found improv valuable for personal enjoyment and emotional release. About a year after beginning to perform on stage I realized that the principles of good improvising and good relationship functioning overlapped considerably. As I had previously employed action techniques and psychodrama, it was not long before I began to utilize some of the improv exercises and games in my clinical practice with individuals, groups, couples, and families. As a psychologist who has trained mental health professionals in family therapy at three postgraduate programs since 1981, I began in 1986 to employ improv in my family therapy training work. Currently, I present RfG training workshops (usually coworking with Gloria or one of the therapists we have trained) to therapists and educators as well as laypersons interested in enhancing their relationships.

WHY IMPROVISE? FACING FEAR THROUGH FUN

Fun? Horrors! As I sit down to write this introduction, I fantasize that I stand in front of a vast, critical audience. I can't speak — I must write on an overhead projector where every mistake, every clumsy phrase, every inaccuracy is there for everyone to see. Not only that, I can't take anything back — erasures are not permitted. The audience is impatient. They want a show . . . Now . . . **Now!** . . . **NOW!!!!!** I am improvising on the brink of disaster — and to my surprise, I love it!

This fearful fantasy is just like improvising at first, before we step into the world of play. In so-called real life, we constantly rearrange our lives to insure that we always know who we are to be, what the situation is, and how to meet others' expectations so that we will be seen as worthy. When improvising, this comfortable familiarity is stripped away, replaced by a fear of being noticed by others while being unable to control our performance. Often, this fear stops us from taking action and amplifies a self-judging critical voice in us, warning of disaster. "Being, acting, creating in the moment without props and supports, without security, can be supreme play, and it can be very frightening, the very opposite of play" (Nachmanovitch, 1990, p. 23). Which it is to be, delightful or terrifying, depends on whether we can give ourselves over completely to the moment while seeing through our own preconception of the awfulness of failing to meet our idea of the expectations of others. As Nachmanovitch points out:

> When we drop the blinders of our preconceptions, we are virtually propelled by every circumstance into the present time and the present mind: the moment, the whole moment and nothing but the moment. This is the state of mind taught by improvisation . . . to be an improviser you have to . . . go out on a limb and take risks, perhaps occasionally fall flat on your face. In fact, what audiences

love most is for you to go ahead and fall. Then they get to see how you manage to pick yourself up and put the world together again. (p. 22)

Once we are able to relax our fearful vigilance, open up our imaginations, and give ourselves over to the absorbing intensity of being in the moment, we are open to the delights of play.

Just as social interaction develops and assumes meaning out of a basic agreement regarding what is real, important, ethical, etc., improv is founded on the basic agreement that "this is play." Once this premise is accepted the participants (players) are freed to a great extent from the constraints, sanctions, and consequences of prevailing social reality and may explore alternate realities. Note that improv does not constitute an escape from reality so much as permission to create and explore new realities, to experience imagined truth as present truth. Improvising is a way of returning to the immediacy of childhood play — fortunately, most of us remember that play was enormously satisfying, even though we have lost our easy access to it. With practice, players experience the shift in and out of the play context and thereby learn (or, in the case of most adults, relearn) access to the play context. In itself, this access is useful, particularly in the case of overly rigid, serious individuals and relationship systems.

While improv arose in the context of training actors, improv itself should be distinguished from acting in that each session is a new performance with no necessary continuity of character to any previous one. By contrast, in acting the actor develops a character in great depth, exploring that character in subsequent rehearsals. In so-called "real life," people ordinarily are not self-consciously playing character, but present sides of themselves in accordance with the immediate social context. Some observers, such as sociologist Erving Goffman, view all real-life interaction as a dramatic production (Goffman, 1959), equating social roles with dramatic ones.

Since 1985 Gloria and I have worked (or played) with people who are in psychotherapy and those who are not, with trained actors, and with professional therapists. Fundamentally, we are all the same. My focus is not on performance, but on self-growth. Yes, some people are better improvisers than others, but everyone can play, become involved, and grow from the experience. Even in performance, experienced improvisers will occasionally fall apart and rank beginners will sometimes create a gem on the spot.

The basic principles of improvisation may be narrowed down to the following: accepting offers, paying attention to others, advancing the action, and supporting others to look good. These principles are taught through the use of certain exercises and games that bring the participants into fuller awareness of the present moment and erode the habits of a lifetime which wrap us like the cloth of a mummy in a restrictive illusion of power and safety. A seeming paradox of RfG is that the safety of being not-ourselves in improv leads to taking greater risks as we free our imaginations and explore underused impulses. Gradually, as we incorporate these principles into our lives and work, having learned and practiced them in the safe and receptive atmosphere of a workshop or in therapy, we experience greater freedom of expression, a deeper kind of power based in cooperation, intuition, insight, a sense of adventure and the potential for pleasant surprises.

ADVANTAGES OF USING IMPROVISATION

Accessing Playfulness

Karl Buhler, a pioneer in child development research, coined a German word, *funktionlust*, which means the pleasure of doing, of producing an effect, as distinct from the pleasure of attaining the effect of having something. Play in the form of improv is *funktionlustig* since it consists more of pleasurable discovery and doing than of anything found or a result obtained.

Most adults and some children have limited access to their own playfulness due largely to fears that emerge when they anticipate or begin playing. RfG provides both a safe, nonjudgmental context and sufficient structure for people to "face fear through fun" (the RfG motto). The games and techniques used can be selected and modified to match the level of challenge and support optimal for the emergence of the client's playfulness.

Expanding Interpersonal Trust

The distinctive feature of the Johnstone method of improv that is the foundation of RfG is the principle of putting aside one's willfullness, defensive overcontrolling, and competitive attention to others in order to attend fully and receptively to one's partner(s). By doing so under the socially stressful conditions of improvising, one discovers that the scene will only work when each one is trying to make the others "look good," in contrast to the cultural value of "looking out for Number One." Yet this is not the same thing as passively conceding all initiative to others; there is little satisfaction and less artistry in fading into the background or in shutting oneself down. Rather, one both permits and actively risks being fully in the moment together with the other(s), without capacity to know or control the future. Even when one experiences this only momentarily it has a powerful effect in opening up the possibility of learning to trust others in real life and expanding one's trust of self. Nachmanovitch (1990) makes a similar point:

> The shared reality we create brings up even more surprises than our individual work. In playing together there is real risk of cacophony, the antidote to which is discipline. But this need not be the discipline of "let's agree on a structure in advance." It is the discipline of mutual awareness, consideration, listening, willingness to be subtle. Trusting someone else can involve gigantic risks, and it leads to the even more challenging task of learning to trust yourself. (pp. 96–97)

Because there is a sense of being "on the edge" of danger when improvising, people who improvise together share an adventure. This provides a social bonding experience that permits enjoyment, friendship, and trust for further adventuring. Keith Johnstone observes that if you enjoy working with someone, they're a good improviser.

Opening to Creativity

> Improvisation, as playful experiment, is the recovery in each of us of the savage mind, our original child-mind. . . . Full-blown artistic creativity takes place when a trained and skilled grown-up is able to tap the source of clear, unbroken play-consciousness of the small child within. (Nachmanovitch, 1990, pp. 47–48)

Play is the creative mind in action. Most adults habitually censor their imaginations, usually without realizing the extent to which they do so. In RfG exercises, clients encounter their self-censorship and are encouraged to experiment with play that unfetters the imagination, even to "split off" from a censoring subpersonality or part of self. Improv can also be used in a way that outraces the censoring process; when the client allows herself or himself to experience this, she or he frequently opens to increased vitality and pleasure in being more fully creative. Accessing our childlike playfulness through improv activates creativity. In improv, as with other play forms, there is a giving over to, an immersion or absorption in play, which shifts the context of adult mindfulness and allows inspiration, or "something wonderful right away" in the words of the book title by Jeffrey Sweet (1987).

Experiencing Spontaneity

Spontaneity can be defined both as an ability to experience and express fully, without inhibition, and as an ability to respond externally to new situations in an immediate, creative, and appropriate manner. Yet spontaneity can also be thought of not so much as an ability as a state of being, the presence of the timeless present. Nachmanovitch (1990) points out that improvisation is synonymous with extemporization, which has the meanings of "outside of time" and "from the time":

> In improvisation, there is only one time: This is what computer people call real time. The time of inspiration, the time of technically structuring and realizing

the [performance], the time of playing it, and the time of communicating with the audience, are all one. Memory and intention (which postulate past and future) and intuition (which indicates the eternal present) are fused. The iron is always hot. (p. 18)

Viola Spolin (1963) makes a similar point:

> The intuitive can only respond in immediacy—right now. It comes bearing its gifts in the moment of spontaneity . . . Spontaneity is the moment of personal freedom when we are faced with a reality and see it, explore it and act accordingly . . . It is the time of discovery, of experiencing, of creative expression. (p. 4)

The major obstacle to being in the present moment is the controlling tendency of the mind to shape or avoid the future. This survival-adaptive tendency is aroused particularly when there is uncertainty or the possibility of present but nonimmediate danger. In improv, although there is no physical peril, being "on the spot" to respond without knowing what will come next is experienced by the mind as danger, with the result that the improviser's mind goes into "survival mode." Keith Johnstone (1981) observes that spontaneity is socially threatening because it reveals your natural self as opposed to the self you've been trained to present. Many of his methods were developed to bypass, trick, or confound the mind's habitual tendency to avoid psychological danger and exercise its controlling ways. In RfG, growth is the outcome of facing danger and overcoming fear; developing spontaneity is both a means and a result of facing the fear of what our imaginations might unleash.

Broadening Sensory, Emotive, and Movement Expressiveness

Face-to-face interpersonal communication is a multichannel phenomenon. In addition to the verbal content of our speech (itself decipherable on different levels), we are signalling to one another by our vocal inflection and intonation, the tension in our voice, nonverbal vocalizations, breath sounds and breathing, eye movents, body posture, physical gestures, facial expressions, body odors, and several rhythms that are combinations of some or all of these. Not only does signalling occur across all these channels, but a rich and varied dance of interaction is in constant process among all present. There is no disputing that nearly all of us possess the greatest degree of skill and precision in sending and receiving information via words. For a variety of reasons, psychotherapy has become a predominantly verbal enterprise, with the result that all other channels have been relatively neglected. RfG enactments redress this imbalance to some extent by attending to other communication channels of expression in performance. As a result, clients become more aware of and versed in the intentional use of multichannel communication.

Creating and Cocreating New Realities with Others

A common human experience is to be unsure of one's identity when called upon to assume an unfamiliar role (the "imposter syndrome"). RfG provides an opportunity for people to "stretch themselves" to incorporate other social roles into their social identities and even to select and try out possible roles by enacting them dramatically. In addition, such dramatic role rehearsals provide an opportunity for others to try on complementary identities in scenes which bring forth novel patterns of interaction. In this way, relationships can be expanded beyond their existing, habitual limits.

SOME COMMON MISCONCEPTIONS REGARDING IMPROVISATION

Improv is totally arbitrary, random activity.

> Improvisation is not "just anything"; it can have the same satisfying sense of structure and wholeness as a planned composition. But there is a case to be made for the opposite side. There is a time to do just anything, to experiment without fear of consequences, to have a play space free from fear of criticism, so that we can bring out our unconscious material without censoring it first. One such sphere is therapy, in which we enjoy perfect confidentiality that enables us to explore the deepest and most troubling matters in our lives. (Nachmanovitch, 1990, p. 69)

Sperber (1974) interviewed professionals and students in the fields of dance, music, and theater and draws the following conclusions regarding the value of improvisation in the performing arts: (1) free, unstructured, and unmotivated improv is not thought desirable or artistically viable—it should have purpose, form, and control; (2) one must master the techniques and discipline of one's art in order to improvise more skillfully and artistically; (3) in the improvisational adventure or experiment the performer must risk himself. I view the conduct of therapy (outside of certain protocols like test administration) as an improvisational enterprise to which the same criteria and standards apply as to artistic improvisation.

Improv is a specialized art form unfamiliar to most people. This misconception stems from a frame of reference that presupposes that deliberation and planning are natural to us, and that most of us are incapable of functioning outside of routines. However, everyday speech is unrehearsed and improvised; we play off of what others say with no more predetermined structure than jazz musicians use, doing so effortlessly. In fact, people find ways to improvise precisely to avoid the dulling effects of adhering to fixed routines; for instance, cooking (other than from rigidly adhered-to recipes) may be improvisational. The mind oscillates between liking variety and sameness, challenge and safety, involvement and quiescence; improvising is likely to occur whenever the mind swings toward the first-named of these quality pairs.

Improv has merit only when it utilizes great originality. Very nearly the opposite is true; the attempt to be original typically results in a disruption of spontaneity, while accepting the first thing that comes to mind, the obvious, contributes to the opening of others' imagination and promotes an absorbing connection to an audience. When an improviser cultivates a "being average" attitude she or he ceases a willful striving for effect and is able to be fully present and attentive to the moment. People habitually compensate for some self-perceived inadequacy by having to be "special"; by allowing a spontaneous "ordinariness" they learn self-acceptance and lessen anxiety regarding their self-image. Keith Johnstone (1993) points out, that, paradoxically,

> ideas that seem "original" are always "old hat" (or how would we recognize them as "original"?) but if [people] pursue the "obvious," and cultivate "effortlessness," then they will be perceived as original. Or, to put it another way, since everyone already is original (i.e., unique), why "try" to be? (p. 21)

A SUMMARY OF USES FOR
IMPROV IN THERAPY

1. Improv games and exercises shift the context of social reality to a more playful and fantastic mode, thus lessening fear of "real life" consequences of change and empowering exploratory behavior.
2. Improv games and exercises can be used both for assessment and intervention with individual clients, groups, couples, and families.
3. As with other nonverbal techniques, improv increases the participation of children by de-emphasizing verbal processing and heightening the use of physical movement during sessions.
4. Improv principles correspond with rules for healthy interpersonal functioning, particularly attending fully to others, aligning oneself with others (accepting offers), and supporting others to be right or look good. The practice of these principles in improv teaches these relationship skills.
5. Improv practice promotes a deeper grasp of societal norms and mirrors the client's social functioning and its effects on others.
6. RfG provides tools for promoting the restorying of individual and relationship narratives.

A SUMMARY OF THE BENEFITS OF
IMPROV TRAINING FOR THERAPISTS

1. Therapists sharpen their observational skills, particularly regarding nonverbal cues.
2. Status work opens powerful possibilities for promoting structural change via status shifts of the therapist.
3. Therapists learn to use self more effectively, trusting imagination, taking risks, and allowing spontaneity in sessions.
4. Therapists can compare assessment data derived from verbal responses with data from enactment performances.
5. A number of RfG games are useful in learning systemic thinking.
6. Therapists learn accurate empathy with clients' fears and their difficulties in making changes.

TERMINOLOGY

Role, when unmodified by "social" or "psychological," is used in this book as a dramatic part rather than as a socially prescribed pattern of behavior. *Character* refers to any particular interpretation of a role. I use *person* to refer to an individual who is not intentionally in role while *player* refers to an individual who knowingly is in role. Depending on the context, *client* may stand not only for an individual person but also for an entity in clinical treatment, such as an individual, couple, family, or group. I use *therapist/director* to stand for the therapist in the social role as a leader of improvisation exercises.

An *action technique* in therapy refers to any psychotherapeutic method that involves the client in physical movement. The distinction between dramatic and nondramatic action techniques rests upon whether the players are intentionally acting a nonself role or are unself-consciously acting as themselves (i.e., whether or not the action occurs within the "playspace," as defined in Chapter 1). *Enactment* is an action undertaken to carry out a task by means of assuming a role; as used here, enactment is a dramatic action technique, unlike the use of the term in structural family therapy. Improv is the dramatic action technique in which the client creates most of the choices of character and plot, and develops these in the present moment. *Endowment* refers to an attribute or characteristic (physical, attitudinal, or emotional) that is given to a player to help define that player's character. *Condition* refers to the defining circumstances or rules for enacting an improv scene, such as being given the location of the scene or speaking only in rhyming couplets (see Appendix B).

As noted above, I use the term *spontaneity* much as it was originally used by J. L. Moreno (1934), the founder of psychodrama, to convey both an ability to experience and express fully, without inhibition, and an ability to respond externally to new situations in an immediate, creative, and appropriate manner.

As also noted above, *improv* is shorthand for "theater improvisation." Improv *exercise* differs from improv *game* in that an exercise is an activity used to acquire a skill or experience, while a game has some dramatic structure and coherence both to its players and to an audience.

For the reader who has some acquaintance with theatrical improvisation, it may be helpful to note here that there is no standardization whatsoever in the names given to, or the precise description of, improv games and exercises. In large measure this is due to games and exercises being copied, modified, and (frequently) misunderstood by the loose, diverse, and unorganized world of improvisational theater. In that world, credit for the invention of a game or exercise is seldom given, nor is it possible to trace the chronology of its usage. For example, *Spoon River Game*, found in Chapter 6, is known as *Voices from the Grave* in Belgium and *Tapestries* in Finland. In some cases I have given both the name of the game or exercise as I have encountered it, as well as alternative names where I am aware of these. In other cases, the name I have given a game or exercise is my own invention, since I have modified it for clinical purposes or have classified it within the context of other, therapeutically-related games or exercises. Where known, I have credited the source from which I learned it.

PRINCIPLES AND TECHNIQUES OF IMPROVISATION

Good improvising consists of following interlinked principles and objectives. *Principles* are necessary elements for improv to work. The failure of any player to incorporate these principles will regularly result in tensions between players and a constricted esthetic experience for players and audience alike. Except when scenes are used for assessment, improv scenes in which the following principles are violated are best interrupted with coaching so that players can experience the contrast to what was not working previously:

- accepting offers
- paying attention to others
- advancing the action
- supporting others to look good

The following *objectives* are growth goals which when attained promote greater exploration of other parts of the self:

- freeing the imagination
- expanding emotional range

- encouraging spontaneity
- breaking conventional logic
- giving up overcontrol
- getting others into trouble playfully
- using voice and body fully
- utilizing narrative skills in cocreating adventures
- attending to status (power) transactions

After-session feedback and reenactment of scenes is appropriate for both enhancement of enjoyment and psychological growth.

Signs of Good Improvising

Clear boundaries   Players make and respect clear boundaries that define the play context and what is permissible in playing. Players are clear with themselves and one another regarding the distinction between player-as-person and player-as-character.

Balanced contribution   There is frequent contribution from each player and a balanced sense of contribution, an equality of give-and-take. Players are observant and responsive to the offers of one another; they listen and don't talk over one another.

Character acceptance   Players give and fully accept character, making others look good without imposing conditions for how they themselves appear (e.g., clever, heroic, sexy, high-status, central to the scene); they put developing the improv ahead of showing off or hiding out.

Wide expressive range   Players "physicalize" in a grounded way corresponding to the story; they fully use their expressive range, according to the spirit of the situation.

Strong character   Players stay in the present moment when they don't know what is happening or when their imagination is blank. They do not become defensively self-conscious or utilize familiar protective behavior (e.g., breaking character to apologize to the audience, panicking, quitting the scene, blaming other players) unless they playfully incorporate such actions into the scene.

Positive outcome   Players are often surprised and pleased by the outcome of the scene; they enjoy having cocreated and shared an adventure and like each other at the end of the improv. They accept and learn from what occurred and quickly let go of judgments of self and of others.

Spontaneous idea development   Players develop the first idea offered, make specific offers, are willing to allow both the obvious and the irrational or unconventional, and justify these offers, making them work in the scene (i.e., they do not censor or block the offers of their own imagination). Players are not planning ahead, but are making it up as they go; they remember where they have been and reincorporate previously-used story elements.

Improv Games and Enactments

The distinction between exercises and games, as noted on p. xviii, is that exercises are less complex, usually brief, warm-ups which are utilized to establish a playful context and encourage participation; games are lengthier enactments that involve advancing the action and narrative coherence.

There is considerable overlap in the principles and objectives embodied in the games and exercises described in this book, and there are many more examples of games and exercises (over 200 variations are known to have been used in performance improv). The ones described in Part II are a sample of those I have found to be the most useful in teaching and clinical application (see Appendix A for a comprehensive catalogue). My decision to include a certain game or exercise within a particular chapter is somewhat arbitrary and was often made on the basis of the main purpose for which I have used it. It is not necessary to know all or even most of these games in order to make effective use of any of them (provided the user understands the principles and objectives), although the experienced therapist will have the advantage of selectivity. Which one to use in any given situation is a skill that develops over time with experience in improvisation and familiarity with the body of work.

The guiding principles for therapist/directors in all improv work are: (1) to create a safe, playful atmosphere that facilitates exploration and spontaneity; (2) to accept whatever players do in the exercises while encouraging further stretching of their "comfort boundaries" by repetition of enactments and selective coaching (remember, it's a rehearsal, not a performance!); and (3) to remain open to the creative impulse that may lead to novel observations and insights, new variations, or even new improv games.

Anatomy of an Improv Exercise

While the more than 90 games and exercises described in this book differ along a number of dimensions (see the classification scheme in Appendix A), they all share the following properties.

Voluntary participation   Participation is always based on informed consent; that is, the game or exercise is explained first and the potential players are asked whether they are willing to play.

Unknown future   There are aspects of the narrative that unfold in a game that are unknown to the players at the outset and which are created during the scene (this is not the case for exercises, which have no story and consist only of present activity).

Explicit form/rules   There are rules which distinguish one game from another that take the form of certain limiting conditions that determine how the scene is to be played.

Accepting offers   The fundamental principle of improv is to accept all offers, except where the explicit rule of the game or exercise specifies a type of blocking.

Advancing action   In games, the scene is built moment-to-moment from offers made by the participants (which may include the audience or therapist/director) in the service of telling a story.

Reincorporation   In games, the narrative builds upon what has already been established.

How to Use This Book

While many readers will either read this book in the order written, or choose from the table of contents what is of particular interest to them, there are some choices and sequences that may help the reader select features of specific relevance.

If you wish to understand RfG in relation to other psychotherapies, start with Chapter 3 and then go back to the Introduction.

If you already understand the RfG approach and want to learn games and techniques, review the previous section, "Principles and Techniques of Improvisation"; next read the more detailed descriptions in Chapters 4 through 8, followed by Appendices A and B.

To read how RfG technique is applied in clinical cases, read Chapter 9 followed by Chapters 10, 11, 12, and 13 in any order. The bulk of cases described in this book are contained in these chapters. Specific games and exercises used in these cases are cross-referenced by page or the chapter in which they are described.

To learn how RfG is used in training therapists, first read Chapter 9 and then Chapter 14.

To place RfG and psychotherapy in a theatrical perspective, read Chapter 1 as well as the interview with David Shiner at the end of Chapter 2.

REHEARSALS FOR GROWTH

Theater Improvisation
for Psychotherapists

PART I

Overview

Drama is both a playground for the release of interpersonal tension and a laboratory for the safe anticipation of events. Even more importantly, it is the clarification of the structures which validate our experience of social living.

—Roger Grainger (1992, p. 165)

Both dramatists and therapists use some of the same techniques — paradox, staging, asides, scripting, creating catharsis. The similarity, however, goes deeper than the use of a related set of techniques. Both theatre and therapy share a common impulse — an attempt to go beyond the everyday forms of communication to shift people's basic notions of themselves and their world. Both represent a revolt against the normal use of discourse, an understanding of the natural limits of rhetoric, and a recognition that communication is at least as much an emotional phenomenon as a linguistic one.

—Edward Friedman (1984, p. 24)

CHAPTER 1

Theatrical and Therapeutic Reality

THE DISCIPLINES of theater and psychotherapy have long cross-fertilized one another. Interest in the interplay between reality and pretense that is at the core of the dramatic experience has led to considerable scholarship on stagecraft as a model for psychological process, particularly the connection between personality and social interaction. For example, Wilshire (1991), using phenomenological methods, takes the point of view that acting is more than role-playing; it is the process of creating the self. Actors attempt to display how we are already mimetically involved with others offstage; thus, theater is lifelike and life is theater-like.

THE PSYCHOLOGY OF DRAMA:
WHAT THERAPISTS LEARN FROM THE STAGE

Drama has itself undergone several transformations and cycles regarding its psychological paradigm. "Meta-theater," according to Kopp (1977), describes drama in which the characters know they are characters. Stage

3

characters at some point in the history of theater shifted from blindly reacting to circumstances to possessing the self-awareness to choose how to construe their (stage) reality. Characters in meta-theatrical works experience and act on their knowledge of the metaphors of life-as-(at least partial) illusion and behavior-as-(sometimes intentional) performance. The layered awareness that results from the shifting levels of perspectives on reality in the Luigi Pirandello play *Six Characters in Search of an Author* (1951) and R. D. Laing's recursive psychological poetry in *Knots* (1970) is quite similar.

Yet, the clear demarcation of the "fourth wall," which separates stage from spectator, is what permits audience members to experience stage reality vicariously, even in meta-theatrical works in which characters refer directly to the illusion of the present performance. As Hubert (1991), writing of such self-referential theater devices, puts it: "As spectators we need never suspend our disbelief, because all along we consciously indulge in, and react to, patently fabricated fictions" (p. 2). It is for this reason that some experimental theater creators, most notably Augusto Boal, have sought to break down the audience/actor distinction by developing such forms as "invisible theater," which involves the public in theatrical action without an awareness of their participation as theater; they become "spect-actors" rather than "spectators" (Boal, 1992).

One intriguing point of view, developed by Hubert (1991) primarily through his analyses of Shakespeare's plays, is that within a drama, stage characters (not the actors portraying them) may be assessed as successful to the extent that they play their roles well.

> [A] psychological or moral determination in a character invariably coincides with his or her *performative* failure or success as dramatist, director, player, spectator. . . . Macbeth provides . . . a compelling model of performative failure . . . the usurper fails as actor, for not only does he find the crown and royal robes of Scotland far too big for him, but in crucial circumstances he does not know how to cast himself in, and perform, a suitable part. He also fails as dramatist and director, for in every move he requires the promptings of the witches or of his wife. Finally, he fails as critical spectator, for, unlike Banquo, he takes at face value the deceptive show staged for his undoing by three untrustworthy hags. A skilled actor entrusted with this demanding role would obviously know how to take full advantage of of the performer's numerous performative lapses. Macbeth's various failures in performance correspond to, and transfer into, theatrical terms, ambition, usurpation, unworthiness, cruelty, and indecision — all of them crucial to the understanding of character and the unfolding of the plot, or in other words, to a plausible fictional narrative of the events. (pp. 7–8)

What Hubert notes as the performative failure or success of a dramatic character can also be a therapeutically productive viewpoint in understanding the problems of a client. That is, the client's difficulties may be seen as evidence that she or he is doing poorly in one or more of the above-mentioned "theatrical" functions. Psychological health, then, is the equivalent of being dramatically skilled.

A related point of view has been developed by Holt (1992), a Jungian and drama therapist. Often, therapists are dealing more with an awkwardly lived life (i.e., a socially maladaptive pattern) than with a person. He views "all behaviour as necessarily theatrical: necessarily, because theatre is *how* we are invested in reality" (p. 70). As does Goffman (1959), Holt considers insight and interpretation inadequate to account for what happens when we present action either in life or on a stage.

> When I step onto a stage I draw attention to myself. I do so in a way that includes the stage. Appearing before an audience on a stage, I point to myself being on-stage. A stage appearance poins at itself as being presented, shown, put forward. (p. 75)

It is this drawing attention to oneself that distinguishes theater from narrative.

Holt's insight, that the projection process operating in therapy as transference and counter-transference phenomena is the same process operating between actor and audience, leads him to observe that

> there is a gap between stage and audience which makes projection possible. In making projection possible it guarantees our investment in in the reality of what is happening. It both invites and sustains a certain suspension of disbelief. If that gap is crossed that suspension collapses. Yet, in that collapse, our understanding of plot is changed radically. It becomes participatory. It is energised by action rather than by observation. (p. 72)

In his "Dramatic Model" of everyday life and therapeutic intervention, Holt draws the two orthogonal dimensions of performance (horizontal) and narrative (vertical) as follows:

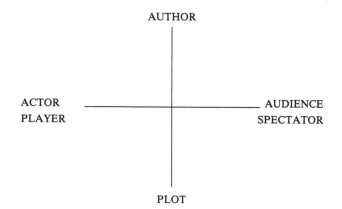

Expanding on Holt's model, I view many life problems as arising from an imbalance in the use of each of the four positions and the consequent curtailment of range in these two dimensions. Schematically, the absence of one of the four poles in the diagram leaves us confined to a triangle demarcated by the other three. When the *vertical dimension*, which represents the "given text" or fatedness of our lives, is curtailed we become stuck in either the lower triangle (which excludes the author position), unable to redirect (or "author") our lives, or in the upper triangle (which excludes the plot position), lacking a sense of historical grounding and living in the fragmented, shallow, expediency-dominated way described by Gergen (1991). When the *horizontal dimension*, which represents the "performance" component of life, is limited we become stuck in either the left triangle (which excludes the audience/spectator position), resulting in an egocentrism and incapacity to choose and see our drama from an outside position, or in the right triangle (which excludes the actor/player position), being reduced to passivity, watching ourselves live life rather than experiencing our agency. It is plausible to expect that different therapeutic approaches are effective for the problems brought on by limitation in either dimension. Problems associated with limitations of the vertical dimension would be attended to in narrative approaches to therapy; problems resulting from curtailment of the horizontal dimension would be dealt with by Gestalt therapists. RfG techniques are helpful in dealing with problems of both dimensions.

THERAPY AS THEATER:
A SURVEY OF PERSPECTIVES

Scripting, Miscasting, and Other Concepts

A number of psychotherapists have made use of theatrical metaphor to describe the origins of psychological identity formation. Kopp (1977), viewing psychotherapy itself as a theatrical form designed to counteract the unfortunate influence of "family-of-origin theater," takes a point of view similar to Hubert's:

> Too often, as children, we are encouraged to try to be something other than ourselves. It is demanded that we assume a character not our own, live out a life-story written by another. The plot-line is given. Improvisations are unacceptable, and the direction is an oppressive form of close-quarter tyranny. Neurosis is in part the result of being miscast into a scenario plotted out in accord with somebody else's unfilled dreams and unfaced anxieties.
>
> As a result of the personal unhappiness that comes of such miscasting, unconvincing performers such as these sometimes appear in that theatrical setting known as psychotherapy. They bill themselves as tragic figures and ostensibly they come to hire the therapist to rewrite their script, or at best to serve as

an acting coach. But in the psychotherapeutic montage of illusion and reality, patient and therapist take turns as performers, audience, director and play-wright, during their tumultuous limited engagement. (p. 4)

Kopp sees the resolution to miscasting as consisting of a learned ability to distinguish pretense from the spontaneous expressing of feeling as well as taking a more detached, even nihilistic, perspective, seeing "that parents are fallible, choosing comedy over tragedy and *holy* insecurity over faith in higher principles [and the] absurdity of life over [belief in a] Grand Design" (p. 29). Similarly, Schorr (1972) puts great emphasis on how the patient has been defined falsely by others (usually parents) and how he must set aside such idealized or despised self images in order to claim his true identity.

Drama therapist Landy, although using a metaphor similar to Kopp's, sees the client's problem as improved by a greater, not lesser involvement with pretense.

The client enters drama therapy as a novice actor, a burned-out performer, hopelessly typecast, or a bit-player in search, finally, of a leading role. The severely emotionally disturbed client, one locked into a single role of dependent child, fool, demon, or outcast, may initially present no role at all, simply an empty shell. In such a case, the drama therapist's job is to teach the basic skills of impersonation and play. (1991, p. 36)

On this issue, RfG stands in close agreement with drama therapy; the thera-peutic aim is to increase the client's ability to enter a playful state at will and to use pretense to explore and select from a broader range of role identities than he is currently and habitually using. In attaining such expan-sion of possibility, the client actually increases awareness of the boundary between play/pretense and consensual social reality.

The Hall of Mirrors: Pretense and Reality

Even infants during their first year appear capable of responding to the contrast of illusion and reality and of learning to create altered realities with others. For instance, Arthur Koestler (1964) observed that a tickled child "will laugh only if the tickling is perceived *as a mock attack*, a caress in a mildly aggressive disguise" (p. 80). Tickling will fail to produce laughter if the element of mock is too great (as when you attempt to tickle yourself) or where the element of attack is too great (as when the tickler is a stranger, rather than someone safely familiar to the child). Koestler concludes that the child becomes "a willing victim to the illusions of the Stage . . . the tickled child's laughter is the discharge of apprehensiveness recognized as unfounded by the intellect" (p. 81).

Riebel (1992) notes the paradox that for the client to experience the therapy as helpful and the therapist as trustworthy and authentic, the thera-pist must occasionally use stagecraft to create or sustain that illusion. Acting skills that the therapist may call on include: *illusion of the first time*, where the therapist responds with apparent spontaneity and interest to familiar circumstances; *reading of a line*, where the therapist intentionally selects the emotional tone and emphasis for therapeutic purposes; *keeping a straight face*, where the therapist behaves as though the absurd is normal or as though the therapist's actual feelings are other than what they are portrayed as; *playing the moment*, where the therapist improvises in the face of the unexpected, including the skillful handling of inadvertently *breaking character* and unexpected events that require *going on with the show*; and *eliciting the subtext*, where the therapist tunes into the meaning and patterns underlying the words and actions of the session. As Riebel summarizes:

> Therapy, like theater, is a rarefied, exotic, and paradoxical world in which the most artificial and unnatural setting and circumstances may bring forth the most authentic and profound aspects of human nature. . . . The capacity for maintaining the tightrope act, for balancing between perfect freedom and perfect control, unlimited emotional resonance and calculated technique, is what good actors, and therapists, strive to acquire, so that their "audience" — spectators or clients — can fully live in the theater of everyday life. (p. 37)

Riebel implies that the therapist and client cocreate a reality which calls for the therapist to take up the role of "that therapist which is needed in the moment." The skill and training of the therapist enable her or him to play that role, as opposed to playing her- or himself by choosing purely on the basis of self-interest in the moment. The character the therapist assumes to fulfill that role not only has personal stylistic features but is shaped by the language, assumptions, and methods of the therapist's orientation, which also includes a position on how much latitude in using the self is appropriate. Examples of therapeutic role-orientation include: game unmasker (transactional analysis), "one-who-remains-unanxious-and-stays-out-of-fusion-and-triangles" (Bowen family systems), "game-defeating-strategist" (early Milan School), etc. Even the Rogerian/humanistic approach, which emphasizes the authenticity and transparency of the therapist, does not transcend the paradox of being onself, since the therapist will still be left at times with the struggle to control antitherapeutic impulses (e.g., voicing or acting on feelings of disrespect toward the client, or wishing to withdraw attention from the session). Another implication, that of therapist as performer for a professional peer audience, is attended to in Chapter 13.

Johnson (1992) provides a useful term: the playspace, which is the context for establishing the characters and conditions that the therapist and client then enact.

> The playspace is an interpersonal field in an imaginative realm *consciously* [italics added] set off from the real world by the participants, in which any image, interaction and physicalisation has a meaning within the drama. The

> playspace is an *enhanced* space, where the imagination infuses the ordinary.
> . . . The playspace is summoned merely by the creation of the illusion of an
> alternative reality, without necessarily establishing with clarity what the roles
> are. In this sense, the playspace is a form of trance. (pp. 112–113)

Psychological health requires the capacity to enter and leave the playspace
at will. Therapies (such as RfG) that induct clients into the playspace develop that capacity as well as make use of the playspace to enhance and
expand the use of self. As an obvious corollary, the effective therapist must
also be adept in negotiating the playspace boundary.

Landy (1991) views the therapist as taking up one or more of a number
of universal dramatic role types. The therapist might take up the Dispatcher
role, whose function is to send the client on a journey; the Helper, whose
function is to move the client forward while guiding and nurturing; the
Donor, whose function is to give the client permission to play imagina-
tively; or the Trickster, whose function is to provoke and prod clients. Even
the traditional therapist, who functions as distanced observer, plays the role
of audience as critical parent or impartial judge. Landy observes:

> Drama therapists generally strive to find a balance between the part of them-
> selves that is actor-like, capable of conjuring up an excellent performance, and
> the part of themselves that is therapist-like, audience-like, observing the effects
> of the action and judging when and how to move it to another level of role-
> enactment and distance. In many ways, the aim is to become the consummate
> repertory player, a juggler of roles, a one-person masquerade. (p. 36)

To Pretend To Be—or Not To Pretend, But To Be

The psychotherapy field appears polarized regarding the desirability of
authenticity versus pretense, both for the client and for the therapist. In
part, this stems from disagreement concerning the social construction of
reality (which is discussed further under social constructivism in Chapter
3). Alan Watts (1966), in a chapter titled "How to be a Genuine Fake,"
insightfully penetrates the societal pretense about identity:

> Other people teach us who we are. Their attitudes to us are the mirror in which
> we learn to see ourselves, but the mirror is distorted. . . . Yet the very society
> from which the individual is inseparable is using its whole irrisistible force to
> persuade the individual that he is indeed separate! Society as we now know it is
> playing a game with self-contradictory rules. Just because we do not exist apart
> from the community, the community is able to convince us that we do—that
> each one of us is an independent source of action with a mind of its own. The
> more successfully the community implants this feeling, the more trouble it has
> in getting the individual to cooperate, with the result that children raised in such
> an environment are almost permanently confused. (pp. 64–65)

My view is that we're all acting, all the time, and are occasionally (self-
consciously) aware of our acting. We may label not being self-conscious
as "natural," but being natural is not necessarily functionally better nor

psychologically healthier. It is precisely in order to improve upon the outcome of being unself-conscious that we mobilize our conscious will to exert
influence over our performance and presentation of self (similar to Goffman, 1959). Yet, if we construe our self-awareness of our behavior-as-
performance as an indication of insincerity or inauthenticity, labelling ourselves as imposters or phonies, we attach a negative meaning to nothing less
than our capacity to choose our performance. Indeed, the majority of
problems brought to therapists stem from clients' experienced limitation or
failure to choose or change their performances: to handle social situations
more successfully, to "do the (morally) right thing," to feel better about
their lives.

An exhaustive elaboration of all the possible permutations of such vari-
ables as intentional pretense, self-deception, concern about the opinions of
others, other-influenced self-esteem, interest in testing others' detection of
pretense, risk of being believed in one's pretense, etc., lies beyond the scope
of this book and leads into the tangles and paradoxes that absorbed R. D.
Laing in *Knots* (1970). Regarding the choice of whether to enact a pretense
and the underlying motives informing this choice, I have identified four
frequently encountered positions:

1. "This is a me who I'm proud of (and I want to be seen this way)";
   therefore I display myself authentically, knowing my behavior is
   genuine.
2. "This isn't me, but whom I'm willing to be seen as"; therefore I
   display myself as authentic, although I know I'm pretending.
3. "This is a me but I don't want to be seen as this"; therefore I'll
   either (a) signal that I'm only pretending to be this, or (b) avoid
   being noticed.
4. "This isn't me and I don't want to be mistaken as being this";
   therefore I'll either (a) avoid being noticed, or (b) signal that my
   performance is a pretense.

There are, of course, other positions and response strategies when the
choice of "not caring what others think of the me I present" is included.
When improvising I offer others a performance that is patently not-me, yet
my performing carries the dangers of unintended self-revelation as well as a
performance judged as unsatisfactory by myself and/or others.

Catharsis in Drama and Therapy

In classical Greek drama, even more than in contemporary theater,
catharsis of all the emotions was valued; plays were judged for excellence
according to how much catharsis the audience experienced. The link between emotional release (catharsis) and mental health was explicit for
Greeks in the 5th century BC, who took note of the strong emotional effect

that drama exerted upon the audience. For Plato, drama was to be condemned when it aroused passions, for this might undermine the State; for Aristotle, ever in disagreement with his erstwhile mentor, drama may produce catharsis by purging the audience of pity and terror (as stated in his *Poetics*). If this dispute appears too remote from contemporary life, we might recall the recurrent controversy over the effects on mental health and public order of passions stirred up at rock music concerts or by certain films.

Within psychotherapy, catharsis was advocated as curative by Sigmund Freud, who collaborated with Joseph Breuer on his first eight psychotherapy cases. In these early cases Freud conceptualized catharsis as a discharge of "strangulated" affect in the service of healing. Only later did he opt for a more intellectualized and controlled approach that emphasized insight. (Freud, 1904). Later therapies (among them Reichian, Gestalt bioenergetic and primal therapies) returned to a cathartic approach.

Scheff (1979) believes catharsis to be a necessary condition for therapeutic change and regards drama and ritual as sharing with psychotherapy the power to induce catharsis. For Scheff, catharsis of the major emotional distresses (embarrassment, anger, fear, and grief) contains two components: (1) emotional content, signalled by physical processes like laughing and crying; and (2) optimal distancing, signalled *subjectively* by feelings of control, pleasure, and relief, and *objectively* by being in contact with the here and now of the immediate environment. For catharsis to operate effectively there needs to be an optimal distance, termed *aesthetic distance*, in which the theatrical audience, ritual participant or psychotherapy client is simultaneously and equally aware of being both participant and observer. By contrast, *overdistanced* drama (such as the emotionless drama of ideas typified by the plays of George Bernard Shaw or of socialist realism), "impoverished" modern rituals (such as most contemporary patriotic or religious ceremonies), and intellectualized, exclusively "surface-talk" therapies leave us hardly moved; *underdistanced* drama (such as "shock" theater or film that displays extreme and unrelieved violence, horror, or cruelty), ordeal-like rituals (such as hazing or fraternity initiation), or ventilative therapies (such as primal therapy) evoke raw emotion which, when unaccompanied by resolution, leads to distress, not catharsis.

Scheff considers many of the devices of classical theater, such as masks, stylized speech (rhyme and meter), asides, soliloquies, disruption of the time frame between scenes, mythical or unfamiliar settings, and comic relief (the insertion of comic scenes within a tragic play) as necessary reminders to the audience that the dramatic action is not real (p. 128). However, comedy makes use of the same devices, where such a reminder seems unnecessary, to increase emotional distance in the audience. Moreover, the absence of literal realism in drama (as in other art forms, playful activity, or psychotherapy) frequently heightens, not detracts from, the degree of involvement with the activity or presentation.* Moreno (1983) called the play context "surplus reality," referring to the way that dramatic presentation highlights and focusses the essential features of a situation in a way that mundane realism cannot. As Blatner and Blatner (1988) point out,

> using techniques that create surplus reality, the essential actions can be exaggerated and irrelevant ones eliminated. Furthermore, in the realm of surplus reality, people can interact with their fantasy, memory, and other roles existing in their mind. (p. 32)

Consequently, in therapy, part of the aesthetically distanced client's attention is in the past, absorbed in reliving and recounting a distressful experience that has been restimulated by the present context ("feeling it from the inside"); however, part of the client's attention is also in the present, taking the perspective of the therapist and realizing that there is no real threat ("seeing it from the outside").

As drama therapists move in and out of role enactment, they intentionally vary their own emotional distance with the roles they take up, thus occasionally (if temporarily) relinquishing the conventional overdistanced professional stance. For instance, the drama therapist may need to act underdistanced in playing a scene with an overdistanced client in order to evoke a response from that client. In effect, the drama therapist is the consummate actor whose underlying aesthetic balance permits her to acquire and use a broad repertory of roles with skill and mastery in shifting emotional distance. This capacity serves as a model for the client in learning "to expand his skills as a future performer in everyday life" (Landy, 1992, p. 103).

COMPARING ACTORS AND THERAPISTS:
AN INTERVIEW WITH GLORIA MADDOX†

DAN Over the years, as we've talked about our respective careers, I've been aware of intriguing parallels between your training actors and my doing supervision and therapy.

GLORIA Acting is an active research of human nature. When you train to be an actor, you learn how to let yourself embody a character who is living in specific circumstances. Training makes your voice, your body, your emotions accessible. Actors express the inner workings of a character through behavior in performance. Acting is pretending from an au-

---

*Although the devices for representing reality have varied widely from classical times to the present, theatrical audiences have always been drawn into accepting the dramatic illusion. See Jacobus (1989, pp. 3–6).
†Excerpted from Wiener & Maddox, 1992.

thentic place in yourself. Actors draw on their own imagination and experience of human nature to create characters.

DAN A major difference between actors and therapists appears to be that actors focus fully on themselves while therapists focus on the client. While assuming responsibility for treatment, therapists necessarily give up the option of being fully self-absorbed. The pity is that often they don't give themselves permission to explore self when "off-duty" and during training. Are actors apt to be too self-indulgent to notice and accomodate to other actors in a scene or play?

GLORIA My experience is that the stereotype of the self-indulgent actor is a myth. Actually, self-indulgent acting is bad acting; it's playing for emotion, rather than taking action. Good actors are very conscious of the other actors and what needs to be done in the play. While "off-duty" many actors go into therapy to help get their lives in order and free themselves for greater expression in their work.

DAN Are actors, by their personalities or their actor training, superior to nonactors as improvisers?

GLORIA Being an actor doesn't automatically make one a good improviser. Even so, actors have the advantages I spoke of before regarding access to body and emotions. One of the benefits of improv training for actors is that it develops greater observing and listening skills. Other benefits include becoming more spontaneous and taking risks, since the actor can't hide inside someone else's words.

DAN I see improv as benefiting therapists precisely for the same reasons. Many therapists are only capable of being deliberate, not spontaneous. They process self-awareness internally rather than "play the moment," and they attend to language but not to nonverbal information.

GLORIA When we do Rehearsals! for Growth workshops for therapists I notice that many of them are constricted in the use of their bodies and emotions. We call this work "Facing Fear Through Fun" because it is scary at times to venture into unknown territory.

DAN I'm all in favor of us therapists learning what it's like to take risks— after all, we're asking our clients to do just that! How do actors keep from getting overinvolved with the roles they play?

GLORIA Well, good actor-training teaches you to pick up a role and put it down. I am still amazed that during a production I would be spending all my time with a company of actors and we would be family to one another—such intensity, on-stage and off. I thought that these actors would be in my life forever. Repeatedly, I discovered that once the show closed those relationships would vanish—I could barely remember some of their names, or they mine. Because of this temporary full involvement, it's really vital for actors to have a nonstage life with outside supports and interests.

DAN What effects does living many roles have on the personal development of the actor?

GLORIA It could work either as a strengthening of self, exploring in ways that bring insight and deepening consciousness, or it could work as an escape of self. Which it is to be depends on the actor's personal development and hence what they're after from acting. Therapy for actors is definitely helpful in their making growthful choices.

DAN As an acting teacher, how do you select roles for your students?

GLORIA I suggest roles that are close to their everyday personae and also roles that exercise self in areas where they may be blocked and afraid of going.

DAN Quite similar to what therapists may do, in that the therapist initially joins with the client in a way that is familiar to the client's experience and later shifts the context of therapy to support growthful stretching.

GLORIA And improvising accomplishes that stretching through play.

DAN How does acting training go beyond the demands of improvising?

GLORIA There is more discipline involved in acting than in improvisation. Improv teaches talking and listening, while acting trains one to become a character that speaks and listens. Improv is a challenge on the moment but is seldom as deep as scripted acting; a good scripted piece has more complexity to it. At the core of a scripted performance, however, is a kind of lived improv that gives it interest and vitality.

IMPROVISATIONAL THEATER: SPONTANEITY AND STRETCHING

Keith Johnstone, playwright, director, and acting teacher is Professor of Theater at the University of Alberta in Calgary, Canada. Over the past 35 years he has acquired an international reputation as a creator of new theatrical forms, most notably Theatresports, an innovative fusion of team improvisational theater and athletic contests. Theatresports, played by both professional and amateur actors in numerous countries around the globe, is particularly popular with a young audience (ages 15 to 30).

Johnstone's approach to theater has been influenced by his keen observations of both audience and performer psychology. His ongoing efforts have been directed toward creating maximum involvement of the audience with the performer — who is at risk of failing in front of them. To heighten audience involvement, Theatresports has the format of a contest in which teams of players engage in a mock competition, akin to staged wrestling, rather than to earnest sporting events. At the same time, the improvising performers place themselves at risk by functioning publicly without many of their social defenses, chiefly that of looking good by playing it safe and concealing failure. For Johnstone, audience involvement stems from a combination of admiring performer skill and daring, feeling close to performers who fail good-naturedly, being interactively present at an unpredictable event, and being offered adventures in which collective fantasies are enacted.

The games devised by Johnstone stemmed from his interest in solving problems of stage improvisers. These games and exercises, many of which I have adapted to therapeutic purposes, prevent players from controlling the future; for him, a game without risk is not a game. As an example, consider a scene played with the condition "you lose if you say a word containing the letter R." If the players treat not-losing as paramount they will speak quite hesitantly, mentally screening their speech in order to avoid elimination. However, this produces a stilted result. What is more enjoyable and interesting for players and spectators alike is for the players, while still looking ahead, to plunge in and speak at a conversational pace, despite then being at risk of losing. This will inevitably result in a loss that is fun to all, provided the loser is gracious.

Johnstone sees an inevitable tension between the desires of the improvising performers (to remain safe and be admired for their competence and wit) and those of their audience (to witness risk and good-natured failure). In essence, this form of theater is the embodiment of narrative in which the hero is tormented. The improviser is simultaneously a potential hero and the storyteller, whose performance will either confirm or disconfirm the performer as heroic. If she or he controls the story to satisfy her or his own desires the audience will be disaffected; if she or he takes risks, they will reward the performer's vulnerability and daring.

Johnstone's implicit position is that our interest in theater derives from experiencing there what we lack in everyday life. In real life, we avoid danger and battle others for control. However, when we try to change others and avoid being changed by them, we miss adventure, spontaneity, danger, and fantasy. We project what we lack onto the stage and hope to live at risk vicariously. This is the function all human societies assign to the hero, which is part of all of us as individuals. At the same time that we, as audience, admire the hero for his courage, and pity him his suffering, we envy him for doing what we dare not. This can be seen in the way we treat real-life (i.e., nonstage) heroes; admiration and envy are intermingled. Our era appears to parallel this premise of creating and then tormenting the hero. In contrast to an earlier time, when heroism was established by achievement (exploration, invention, artistic creation, statesmanship, etc.) and sustained by the media even when discrepant "unheroic" personal details of the hero's private life were known, today's heroes are often famous merely by virtue of their incomes (entertainers, sports figures, or entrepreneurs) and are pilloried by the same media that created their celebrity whenever their lifestyles are exposed as unworthy of adulation. Today, a major reason for our interest in the private lives of celebrities is the desire to reassure ourselves that famous people are no different from the rest of us, while at the same time we hunger for heroes that model transcendence.

Theatresports, as Johnstone points out, is the opposite of "show business"; failure is invited, rather than hidden. In sports, by contrast, all interest would quickly atrophy if there were no mistakes or losses; the "agony of defeat" is bound up with the "thrill of victory" and the television camera is as readily trained on the dropped pass as on the successful first down.

The relevance of all of this to therapy is twofold: on the one hand, clients want to overcome the unheroic limitations of their lives, leading to restorying and struggling with the risky business of change; on the other hand, they want to attain success, feel better, and be treated nicer by others while avoiding change. RfG uses the context of play and the techniques of improv as the bridge to move clients from the stuckness of avoiding both danger and change to the challenging novelty of expanded possibility in their lives. In a familiar metaphor, the therapeutic venture is a hero's quest; in RfG, therapy prepares clients to perform heroically on the stage of life.

Some therapists have recently modified their practice away from a traditional overconcern for client confidentiality, feeling that it implies that there is something shameful and pathological about being in therapy. O'Hanlon (1993, p. 158) cites a conversation with David Epston in which Epston reported that he regularly invites therapy clients who have succeeded in resolving their concerns to record their success story, a practice founded on an approach to therapy in which clients appear as heroes in their own lives, often wanting their heroism publically acknowledged and celebrated.

An Interview with Keith Johnstone*

I have known Keith Johnstone since 1988 when he first conducted improvisation workshops in New York City. His is a freshly inventive mind aided by keen powers of observation. Midway through the writing of this book Gloria and I spent two intensive and absorbing weeks studying at his International Improvisation School. The following interview was conducted with a view to explicating Keith Johnstone's work in light of his personal experience in developing and teaching his approach over the past thirty-plus years.

DAN What were the personal reasons that attracted you to improvisation?
KEITH I think most people's talent for the arts closes down quite early. Mine closed down somewhere about age 23 or 24, by which time I'd

---

*The following interview was conducted by the author and Gloria Maddox at the Loose Moose Theatre in Calgary, Canada, on July 27, 1993.

already achieved some things and was well known. It became impossible to do anything—I had a total block. I'd seen actors improvise and I knew that every now and again they were wonderful. So, I believed that if I could investigate ways of having that happen more often with actors, by finding out what was screwing them up, I could probably apply it to myself. So I began teaching actors and it actually worked—it was very good thinking. At the time it was desperation, but it functioned well.

GLORIA So Keith, your beginning work with improv was a way of reawakening or releasing your own creativity.

KEITH Yeah, I wanted to find out how to make those people creative. I'd already been in a writer's group before that and had suggested that, to hold the group together, we shouldn't discuss anything that could be acted out. That was VERY successful. Anytime anybody brought up any point that could be dramatized, we would have to get up and do it. That decision, the avoidance of discussion, forced the writer's group to become an improvisation group for which there had been no tradition.

DAN I'd like to get into what improv games reveal about people both as performers and as audience. What do you see as being characteristic of people when they get on stage as performers?

KEITH Well, they defend, including the ones who aren't shy. To explain this, I see storytelling as basic to human behavior. I don't think you could be conscious without storytelling ability; very small children seem to understand exactly what stories are. Relating the past to the present is what makes this structure we call stories. A story is an enjoyable way of doing this relating for you, but the mind's doing something like that anyway. I mean, there are no stories; experience is a great mess which the brain filters and puts into the shape of stories.

People defend against being involved as heroes in life; normal human beings are desperately trying not to be involved as the hero of their life-story, even though they see it in story terms. So, whenever their life is going to go into a story, most people do something to prevent it, to make their life dull. Some people actually build a dull persona so that nothing ever happens.*

DAN What about the audience? What effect do stories have on the audience in terms of evoking fear, or emotion in general?

KEITH Well, I think laughter is therapeutic. I think it's also good for them to yell and shout and scream.

DAN So, you see the audience basically as having cathartic experiences . . .

KEITH Yeah, and yelling and jumping up and down. I'm trying to get a

---

*Another perspective on therapy suggested by Johnstone's answer is that effective therapy assists clients to meet the heroic challenge implicit in life, rather than provide "stress management" or support legitimizing a victim position.

sports audience in the theater. I think a sports audience is the right audience, not one that sits there being critical. Our theater audiences often accept the second-rate because they think if it's cultural, it's okay. I want the audience to be thrilled.*

DAN Can you have Theatresports when people in the audience are moved to terror, pity, or to some other less pleasurable emotion?

KEITH The problem is, that when you bring in that stuff, you have to put lots of padding in between. If you have a tragic scene you build to the tragic moment. Tragedies are only tragic for a short time. They involve you briefly and then they go away from strong negative emotion. In horror movies the day comes and everything's okay, but then the night arrives and vampires come out. But you need the day to calm it all down.

DAN Let me move along to a couple of other things. How do improvisors develop trust and sharing risk on stage? Most of what I hear you teaching has to do with handling individual problems rather than relationship problems.

KEITH Well, the guys I don't work closely with often use the confidence they get on the stage to become social bullies. They can become very arrogant and shine in public, or they can go to a cinema and make lots of noise because they're not scared like normal people are. . . . If I work a lot with the improvisers, the work does tend to make them what I would call more matured . . . they do tend to get a more balanced attitude.†

DAN I've noticed that it's far easier to see opportunities for good improv choices when in the audience than when performing. What happens to an improviser's skill level when she or he gets on stage?

KEITH In theory, a good improviser does see everything. A good improviser is aware of what's going on, but may not have been when she or he started improvising.

GLORIA Is improvisation training a training of one's awareness of what's going on?

KEITH Well, that happens when a training exercise works. For example, I had the actors try to add emotional sounds to a scene in such a way that the audience wouldn't be able to identify what was changed. They became more and more aware of where they were and of each other — it was like watching them become better actors or more solid people. Ordinarily, when they're improvising you don't get that. Often they're

---

*Note the parallel emphasis with classical Greek theater, cited earlier. Johnstone is attempting to develop a popular theater in which Everyman may experience catharsis.

†Johnstone frequently refers to the prosocial quality of good improvising. As he puts it, "If you enjoy working with someone, they're a good improviser."

walking around the stage like zombies without contact; then I'm often intruding into that, telling them to slow down and notice.

DAN What are the benefits to the performer of exposing, rather than hiding failure?

KEITH If people try to do their best, they screw themselves up. Because acting is a high-stress situation—just being watched is stressful—we have ways to defend against that, such as taking out transitions* and becoming uninteresting to be looked at. In bad improvisational theater you can see in every scene that no one's changed, since that would make the actors feel vulnerable.

DAN It seems that the unwillingness to go toward vulnerability in order to grow is the biggest impediment to an improviser's development.

KEITH That's right. But then, most people don't see that. The improvisation coach should be looking to see if one person is changed by the other. But you get distracted by the fact that it's very funny sometimes.

As I said before, my bias is totally toward storytelling, which implies being a hero and moving into trouble. Either we say we're training comedians which is, I think, a bit superficial, or we say we're training wonderful storytellers. And that's a very difficult task—like training opera singers, but more fun.

DAN Do you see a therapeutic function of theater? Beyond catharsis, do you see something that promotes healing and growth rather than just entertains?

KEITH Yeah. I see it in terms of getting more freedom. I mean, a shy person or an arrogant person is not functioning well. Somebody who's only a passenger, or only a director, is not functioning well.† People have to have some of both. I try to move improvisers into some sort of center state from which they can go in any direction. My image is of a wheel with lots of spokes—for me everything is visual—I want them in the middle. If they're way out on some spoke of the wheel, they're stuck. [Once they can get to the middle] I don't care which spoke they go out, which direction they go in—they take whichever is the easiest and if it gets difficult they try another one. You try to get them into a center position from where they can go places.‡

DAN Otherwise, they become specialists and only function in one place.

KEITH Right. They may always have a frown on their face. Or they may always have a stupid smile. And that's a sign of profound disturbance of the whole person. If you take the frown away, it's gonna cause disturbance.

---

*Transitions or "beats" are the choice points in a scene at which action or change occurs.
†Passengers are improvisers who don't take responsibility for full involvement with the scene; directors are those who refuse to share control with other players.
‡As in therapy, flexibility and equipotentiality are assets for improvisers.

DAN To what extent does improv training heal a disturbed person?

KEITH I don't know. I think these things should be tested but I'm not a scientist. I do know that people here have been thrown out of the group for being impossible to be with; I got them back in again, and they have emerged as very good improvisers and very different people. On the other hand, some people drop out and I don't see them again.

GLORIA I was in a workshop once where they went on the premise that the health of the group was shown by how they handled the scapegoat.

KEITH We have sometimes had very disturbed people here that we haven't been able to handle. Once a man ran around the Theatresports group saying he was our star improviser. I think he was deluded, actually. You know, mask teachers in other cultures say some people can't be worked with. In possession cults, some people don't get possessed right.

DAN In everything, I think.

KEITH Yeah. That's right.

DAN When you developed the Life Game [described in Keith's answer below] did you see a therapeutic value in dramatizing people's actual life stories?

KEITH Absolutely — because people are so scared of life stories. Why shouldn't you put somebody on stage and interview them and then act out bits of their life? It seems such a rational thing to do. But often there's such extreme anxiety in the audience. Once, when we tried the Life Game, a girl cried on the stage and the audience were so appalled. Why shouldn't we cry in public sometimes if we're tuned in to emotionally distressing material? The only damaging thing would be to somehow teach people that they shouldn't express their emotions and punish them if they did. But we're not therapists — we try not to work with people whose purpose is to work out material that distresses them. We try to say, "What was it like? What happened?" So, the Life Game was first called "How It Was."

GLORIA I wonder about men and women improvisers; do you see much difference between them?

KEITH I see a huge difference. To begin with, the kind of improvisation we're doing is kind of aggressive. And the problem I have is that women, in order to compete with the men, have to become kind of man-like. I try to get the women improvisers to work together 'cause women treat each other differently than men treat each other, and they treat each other differently in the presence of men. I discuss this with both the women and the men and I try to get the women protected to some extent. In some cases the men despise the women, or that's how they function. And that's not the real problem. The problem is, this is a very sexist society and if the men treat the women the way they treat each other, the women get very upset.

Really, I would like 50% women. We get situations like in Norway, where the men were at first too formal to do it, and so the women started Theatresports in Norway. But, now Norway is up to what it's like in any other country, nine men for one woman, and the women have to get tough. I don't know why this is—I just feel there is some gender difference in displayed behavior which is exploited in theater sports and public improvisation, and it does some bad things. But it's natural for the men to get on stage and shine.

DAN There's a lot of male preening behavior on stage?

KEITH Yes. Well, the women preen as well, but they do it differently. I think we're dealing with biological differences. I know that's very unpopular, and that, supposedly, women are just women because they've been trained to be women and we've been trained to be men. I think that's actually not true. But if we weren't careful, there'd be no women in Theatresports. They would all be deeply offended and they would move on. But the offending is often unintentional.

DAN Are you aware of people applying improv to different fields? What are some of the applications you have worked with?

KEITH I think this stuff works for anybody. I know it's been used in business. I've taught millionaires, the inheritors of masses of wealth. I've taught Women's Lib groups. The women were hard as nails; the men were incredibly sensitive. I've taught Zen people; I'll try anybody. I don't know any group of human beings who isn't grateful for this stuff. Even people who don't want to try it at first gradually get coaxed into doing it. It seems to offer people something they want. I'm just very cautious in making claims for any benefit.

DAN Have you seen any application to therapeutic problems?

KEITH No, but I've heard it's been very successful in treating neurotics in various countries and in controlling phobias. I've tried to teach improvisation to psychotics but it doesn't really seem to reach them.

You see, part of what makes this successful is the performance of the person teaching. I mean, I have a way of behaving that makes people think it'll be okay to stick their necks out. I realize I'm not entirely clear as to what I do regarding that. I don't know what it is, precisely, but I consciously try to build a persona that makes this happen.

DAN It seems to me that you have real caring for the people that you're working with. You're not just using them to demonstrate some point to others.

KEITH No. I'm interested in them. But also, I'm very playful. I'm a bit naughty.

To say there is no necessity for things to happen as they do is perhaps another way of saying that the world is play.

—Alan Watts (1961, p. 37)

CHAPTER 2

The Importance of Play

U NTIL FAIRLY RECENTLY psychologists and philosophers made a distinction between human thought process as *either* adult/mature/rational/logical/abstract/Freudian-secondary-process *or* childlike/immature/irrational/associative/concrete/Freudian-primary-process. Childlike thought might have been regarded as valuable in the service of artistic creativity, but in every other way adult thought was seen as superior. A more contemporary view, articulated by Bruner (1986), is that human thought and understanding operates in two general forms, each adaptive in its own domain: the predominantly verbal, sequential *paradigmatic mode*, useful for ordering experience through abstraction in the pursuit of truth; and the multisensory, nonsequential *narrative mode*, useful in organizing experience metaphorically for constructing a believable reality. These modes are complementary and irreducible to one another; mental health requires a balanced capacity to use both modalities.

Play is an important, perhaps even the central, activity of the mind in the narrative mode. That is, our unceasing attempts to make sense of our lives result in imaginative thoughts and acts that appear unrelated to any other functional purpose. Far from being manifest only in childhood, play is omnipresent, though in differing forms, throughout the life span. Theater improvisation, when entered into with a nonpurposive spirit, is a form of play well suited to exploring alternative stories and meanings, particularly those concerning human relationship. However, unlike fantasizing, or most unstructured play activities, it is also a form of play that draws the player into a world of immediacy, uncertainty, and emotional intensity while experiencing the risk of failing to meet performance expectations. Through examining the subject of play more closely the connection between narrative mode thinking and experiencing alternative realities is clarified.

WHAT IS PLAY?

A considerable diversity of scholarly thought has been directed to the at-once-familiar-yet-mysterious phenomenon of play. Millar (1972) points out that, since almost all the natural functions of an organism are used in play, play cannot be a special kind of activity. "A certain degree of choice, lack of constraint from conventional ways of handling objects, materials and ideas, is inherent in the concept of play. This is its main connexion with art and other forms of invention. Perhaps play is best used as an adverb; not as a name of a class of activities, nor as distinguished by the accompanying mood, but to describe how and under what conditions an action is performed" (p. 21).

Nachmanovitch (1990) emphasizes the power of play to bring novelty and stimulate variety.

> Play is always a matter of context. It is not what we do, but how we do it. Play cannot be defined, because in play all definitions slither, dance, combine, break apart, and recombine . . . In play we manifest fresh, interactive ways of relating with people, animals, things, ideas, images, ourselves. . . . Our actions take on novel sequences. To play is to free ourselves from arbitrary restrictions and expand our field of action. Our play fosters richness of response and adaptive flexibility. . . . By reinterpreting reality and begetting novelty, we keep from becoming rigid. Play enables us to rearrange our capacities and our very identity so that they can be used in unforeseen ways. (p. 43)

One oft-noted property of play is that it is created within, and can be distinguished from non-play only within a social context (Lutfiyya, 1987). Goffman (1974) used the concept of "keying," which refers to a systematic transformation in meaning assigned to behavior or action. Keying cues participants who share a common cultural framework to interpret behavior differently. For example, a wink, a smile, or a certain tone of voice will key the listener that the speaker's words or actions are to be taken as sincere.

Similarly, Bateson (1972) noted that in situations where "this is play" is conveyed the literalness or seriousness of the message is transformed and is not meant as it might be ordinarily. Signalling the operation of the play context permits the exploration of behaviors that can then be engaged in without permanent consequences; after an interlude of play, the unaltered social world is then returned to. The play context, like private thought, is a domain for experiencing alternative realities.

DEVELOPMENTAL PERSPECTIVES OF PLAY

The research literature on play is overwhelmingly that of children's play. Within that vast field, numerous aspects of play have been investigated; one of specific relevance to RfG is the development of social pretend play.

The Development of Pretend Play

Children's play may be classified as to whether it is solitary or social, pretend or simulative. Howes (1988) defines social pretend play as "the integration of pretense into social interaction between partners within a turn-taking structure" (p. 1254). Cooperative social pretend play appears around age 25 to 36 months, peaking in the fourth and fifth years. As the Singers (1990) note, "In cooperative social pretend play, both players in effect follow a script, understand that their partner is playing a role, and use symbolic content in their play" (p. 72). On the basis of a series of observational studies, a number of researchers, most particularly Howes and her students, take the position that social pretend play is closely linked with the development of social competence, particularly competence in forming peer relationships.

Bretherton (1984) points out that social pretend play, even in its most rudimentary form, involves coordinating an internal world that produces "nonliteral transformations" with the external world of social relations. Howes (1992) brings out the connection of children's social pretend play to theater: "More complex social pretend play engages the child in counterfactual or would-be thinking as children manage multiple roles, invent novel plots and deliberately interweave pretense and reality" (p. 5). She identifies three functions of social pretend play: "Initially, the communication of meaning through social pretend forms, subsequently, expressing and exploring issues of control and compromise by negotiating social pretend play meanings and scripts, and finally, exploring issues of intimacy and trust within social pretend play" (p. 5). The first of these functions is most important in the toddler period and usually has the child's mother or an older sibling as the play partner and involves "the ability to understand that nonliteral meaning can be shared and collaboratively elaborated" (p. 5). The second function, prominent during the early preschool period, emerges in the context of peer play; a script in social pretend play is defined as "an organized, multievent play sequence in which the two children arrange pretend acts into a meaningful sequence" (p. 70). Within social pretend play, children balance their individual need to control the play with the necessity for compromise in order to play together at all. The third function, peaking in older childhood, occurs in the context of peer friendship, presumably because the risk of self-exposure is offset by the trust and intimacy of the relationship.

A Cognitive-Affective Theory of Play

Building upon the theoretical work of Silvan Tompkins, Singer and Singer (1990) point out that

> most forms of play involve situations of moderate challenge, novelty or incongruity. Playful interactions between self and others . . . usually result in a somewhat reduced level of novelty or incongruity that evokes joy. Such interactions may also produce the conscious or automatic realization that within the defined structures of play one can continue to experience moderate challenge along with a further reduction in incongruity. (p. 40)

Making sense of and gaining mastery in the physical world is a far more straightforward task than is the comprehension of the social world with its inconsistencies, arbitrariness, ambiguity, deceptions, and levels of meaning. Unfortunately, playful activity in the service of reducing incongruity may itself evoke adult sanctions in the world of some children (as noted below), further complicating their task of social mastery. Even in a social environment where adults are available and helpful in offering explanation and reassurance to the child, understanding of some new social phenomenon is built upon a foundation of meaning derived from earlier successes in achieving understanding. Thus in order for play to serve the function of reducing incongruity, both adult support for pretend play and the prior acquisition of a set of rich and complex schemas are needed.

Adult caregivers may help children develop better schemas (thereby reducing their fear or confusion) by explaining, labelling, and storytelling. Within the narrative mode of thinking, the "truth" of such a story or explanation is secondary to its effectiveness in providing a sense of understanding.

> For the child it often makes little difference whether the schemas are mirrors of "reality" or whether they are legends, myths, or fairy tales. Indeed, one might as well point out that myths of an afterlife or of religious salvation provide us as adults with fairly effective schemas into which we can assimilate unanticipated bereavements, natural disasters, or sudden illnesses. (Singer & Singer, 1990, p. 204)

Additionally, the Singers point out parallels between the compensatory function of imaginary companions for children, cognitive-behavioral techniques of covert modelling (sometimes with inner guides or magical healers), and traditional religious belief systems (with their patron saints and guardian angels), or even the Greek muses.

Piaget's View of Play

The considerable influence of Jean Piaget's theories of human development also extends to his views of play, which he saw as a temporarily-employed means of learning and mastery utilized only in early childhood. According to Piaget (1962), symbolic, or pretend, play is a stepping-stone which permits the child to make sense of and master the complexity of adult reality (an "assimilation of the world to the ego"); once mastered, play serves no further purpose and is discarded. As a theorist Piaget thereby viewed play only within the structure of paradigmatic thought and placed no value on it as a source of social identity-formation, creativity, or social playfulness in later life.

Psychodynamic Views of Play

Most psychoanalytic, neo-Freudian, and even object relations theorists have not viewed play as intrinsically important to adults. Freud saw play and fantasy as motivated by both the projection of wishes and the need to master conflicts and fears through reenactment. Thus, play is a fusion of, or alternation between primary-process wish-fulfillment and secondary-process ego mastery.

A different view was taken by Winnicott (1951), who described an "intermediate area of experience" lying between the most personal, subjective sphere and the world of external reality. According to Lewis (1993),

> in this intermediate area of experience, the individual is able to draw from both internal and external reality in creating a unique and personally important world of an unchallengable nature that is shared only in intimate relationships. Children's play may be thought of as built upon and further elaborating this highly cathected personal world in which reality is both acknowledged and suspended. Thus, involvement in play enhances the child's knowledge and acceptance of both internal and external reality while providing a bridge between the two. (p. 7)

Similarly, the anthropologist Herzka (1986) proposes that, through play, children learn how testing fantasy teaches about the limits of material reality, while real experiences stimulate imaginative consciousness. In this way, imagination is prevented from being severed from reality.

PLAY AS SELF-HEALING

Singer and Singer (1990), show that for children pretend play is frequently self-healing and constitutes an effective means of social and emotion adaptation to stress. Decisively refuting the stereotype of the unhappy, dreamy, withdrawn child and citing both their own and others' research, these authors show that joy and liveliness are associated with imaginative play; that pretend play is uncommon among angry, anxious, conflicted, or hyperactive children; that children who use imaginative play have superior impulse-control and are more popular with peers and teachers than those who do not. Moreover, children who had imaginary companions were better adjusted in day-care, had more friends and were more adept at talking with adults; these boys were less aggressive while the girls were less prone to anger and fearfulness. In sum, children use pretend play for self-healing and growth as a part of normal development.

In a series of case studies comparing two groups of children, Fineman (1962) showed that the group displaying a high degree of spontaneous pretend play (the "high group") were able to use play to cope adaptively with interpersonal conflicts and stressful events, while the "low group" remained on a more infantile level in seeking maternal attention and material gratification. Fineman also observed that the high group children were capable of relinquishing pretend play upon request, were less likely to regress in order to maintain fantasy, and could "begin to be able to define the boundaries between imaginary play and the often contradictory elements of external reality" (p. 180).

PLAY AS THERAPEUTIC

According to Winnicott (1971), the aim of psychological healing is

> [to bring] the patient from a state of not being able to play into a state of being able to play. . . . It is in playing and only in playing that the individual child or adult is able to be creative and to use the whole personality, and it is only in being creative that the individual discovers the self.

Winnicott also suggests that, in both child and adult therapy, therapists attach too much importance to the healing power of therapeutic talk to undo defenses, rather than allow the unfolding of the transitional play process to accomplish this.

Play Therapy

The direct interpretation of children's play, characteristic of early psychoanalytic play therapy, has given way to a more client centered approach in which the playing unfolds with minimal adult intrusion, while interpretation is kept closer to observable behavior and the child's own themes and language. A further trend is for the therapist to participate more in the child's play-world, thus becoming a participant-observer. Play in therapy has thus become used less for its revelation of intrapsychic conflicts as interpreted within the adult therapist's theoretical model, and more for its ethnographic insight into the child's world-view, and even as a growthful and healing experience in itself. In other words, contemporary play therapists not only create a space in which imaginative play may occur, they display acceptance toward play activity and may even model how to play. As the Singers observe,

> the major role of the adult is to serve as a "new object," that is, a new kind of adult model who accepts feelings, tolerates and encourages pretend play, and allows the child to explore and experience new schemas and scripts. . . . If the adult's own willingness to listen and to share thoughts and play possibilities is conveyed to the child in a spirit of liveliness and humor, the therapist can open the child to the joys of introspection and controlled fantasy. The therapist's enthusiasm may help the fearful, despairing, or angry child trapped in a limited world into one who can savor the excitement of reshaping the seemingly "given" world into a new one that is full of possibilities. (1990, p. 229)

Their review of the research literature point up two major findings: play therapy has a comparable effectiveness to adult therapy, and children who have some facility at imaginative play do better when offered play therapy.

ADULT PLAY

The human capacity for private speech and fantasy, once developed, is active throughout the life span. Research cited by the Singers (1990) shows that most of waking conscious time is spent in task-unrelated thought and imagery. They hypothesize that adult daydreaming serves a comparable function to children's pretend play.

Adult play is readily recognized in organized, competitive games and sports competitions. The performing arts, as well as pageants, festivals, and societies that exist to recreate historical periods and events also serve to provide a contrast to the conventions and purposive striving of everyday existence. The historian Johan Huizinga (1949), using a phylogenetic model, saw much adult social behavior as an outgrowth of both the individual past in the form of child's play, and of the cultural past in the form of rituals and myths of earlier civilizations. For Huizinga, human society has a playful, competitive element that adds drama and focusses purpose to our lives.

Even though play is extolled here and elsewhere as desirable in a variety of ways, it should also be noted that being playful can be experienced as stressful or unsafe for oneself and threatening to others on occasion. Particularly for the sizeable proportion of adults whose upbringing was characterized by the menace of emotional unpredictability from their caretakers, spontaneity and unselfconscious playfulness do not come easily. Such adults presumably are less effective as play-encouraging role models to their own children. Even when accessing playfulness is not problematic, we all have thresholds of discomfort that can be crossed when play becomes too involving and we lose the security of (a) ourselves knowing the boundaries between play and reality, and (b) being confident that others will know and respect these boundaries.

Blatner and Blatner (1988) enumerate some of the overlapping major factors that inhibit adult playfulness: repression of the inner child; social attitudes of disapproval toward childishness, naughtiness, fantasy, and phoniness that are rooted in envy of, or hostility toward, children; and corruptions of play such as competitiveness, hostility disguised as playfulness, and judgmentalness. For adults to overcome the inhibiting effects of such factors so that playfulness may manifest and enactment be attempted often requires addressing these issues first in verbal psychotherapy and then relearning to play supported by an accepting adult model.

The Dark Side of Play

After infancy people of all ages engage competitively in sports, contests, and games, relishing the meta-rules which permit ruthless, deceptive, and aggressive conduct within the play-context, but at times losing any awareness of the boundaries between pretense and reality. It should be remembered that not all play is socially adaptive, safe, or fun for all concerned. Younger children play-fight, name-call, and tease; older children and adolescents may become involved in enacted fantasies, pranks, adventures, and games featuring violent, physically or sexually risky, sordid, and antisocial themes with real-life consequences. It is such behavior that gives acting out a bad name among many mental health professionals.

There appears to exist a powerful fascination, especially during adolescence, with exploring the experience, limits, and consequences of being in danger; of being "bad" by breaking rules; and of adopting a persona that is disapproved of by conventional society. Through exploration of pretense some people (typically, those who are alienated, bored, and lacking enduring positive experiences with trustworthy social others) discover an attraction to the power of cruelty or the allure of rituals of evil (Satanism, in particular). For such persons, the element of pretense or playfulness that led to their discovery may disappear as they become inducted into that world; often, the persona they offer others in the world of conventional social reality itself becomes a pretense to conceal the persona developed in the darker world.

It may therefore be objected that play and improv enactments that encourage the exploration of such "negative" sides of oneself run the risk of stimulating unhealthful and antisocial tendencies. I will state that it is important for a therapist to be selective in offering improv scenes that feature "darker" themes and that the boundaries between play and reality must be clear at all times. However, I reject the notion that the use of imagination and enactment of pretense in therapy brings about dyssocial conduct in everyday life, any more than saloons bring about drunkenness, or churches create piety.

THE PERFORMANCE OF PLAY: AN INTERVIEW WITH DAVID SHINER*

David Shiner is internationally acknowledged as a leading performance artist and clown. He honed his craft as a street performer in Europe for 11 years and has starred in national circuses throughout the world. As the star of Broadway's *Fool Moon*, he earned rave reviews and won a Golden Globe award. His work is characterized by the angry, intense persona of his clown and by the breathtaking confrontations he orchestrates with unknown members of the audience at each performance.

David Shiner is a master of a form of improvisation that operates at the boundary between public social behavior and our expectations from theatrical entertainment. Working entirely in mime and taking his cues for action entirely from specific body language, Shiner brings audience members on stage to play recognizable roles in everyday scenarios. As he says, the point of such improvising is not to succeed but to go beyond your self-imposed limits. In Shiner's performances, as in RfG groups and workshops, the delighted involvement of the audience demonstrates the healthy stimulation afforded by witnessing spontaneity.

DAN Can you tell me something about the distinctive way in which you work as a stage performer, and also maybe bring in a little about your work as a street performer?

DAVID Well, I guess the most distinctive aspect is that most of my fellow actors are people from the audience. This creates a wonderful opportunity for spontaneous play and theater and also the down side, the risk of it failing, which creates this wonderful tension that makes it really work.

DAN So you're on the edge somewhat as you perform?

DAVID Oh, I'm on the edge all the time, and that's why it's also so tiring and fatiguing, because it takes an immense amount of concentration to be aware of what's going on in every single person on stage who is working with me, whether it's on the street, in the circus, in the theater, it's always the same. I am able to be aware of each individual personality type and to know beforehand what they're going to do. After many years of doing this I can pretty much tell, I can categorize just about everybody immediately and know pretty much what direction they're going to go in.

*This interview took place in New York City on May 3, 1993.

DAN Can you say what these categories, these types, are?

DAVID Well, there are the people who want to have absolutely no fear of getting on stage . . . they sort of want to take over, to be in control. Then there are those that are completely and utterly insecure and afraid—they freeze on the stage—it's very difficult for them to break out of their shell. There is the type that is actually already an actor and so what they do is no surprise, it's not spontaneous, because it's controlled and done with awareness. What makes this work so much fun for the audience is watching normal people going beyond themselves, having to go beyond their capabilities, having them do something which seems impossible for them to do. The audience wants to see them *attempt* to succeed, so they are forced to step outside of their own limitations, one way or another.

DAN Are the players very aware of the audience or are they mostly focused on you and the immediate situation?

DAVID No, they're not aware of the audience. I can tell you right now, the only thing they are aware of is the voices in their heads: "What am I going to do? What is he going to ask me to do? Will I be able to do it? Am I going to look good? Am I going to succeed? Am I going to fail? Are they going to see who I am? Who I really am?" That's the real fear: Are they gonna see who I am? And *that's* of course what I want everybody to be able to see.

DAN This fits in so beautifully with the improv work that I do because when people allow themselves to go to places they don't normally go it allows them to experience another side of who they are. And yet people fight it on a lot of levels and in a lot of ways.

Anything else about other types? So far, you've got the insecure people, the people trying to control, the professional actors, and the rare but desirable innocents.

DAVID You also have the egomaniacs. These are usually men that are extremely competitive. They're just concerned with winning—that one little thing—and so they miss out on the whole, they don't see the whole process.

DAN How do you size people up initially? What cues you as to which type of person is in front of you?

DAVID It can be many different things. It can be just the way they're looking at me, the way they're dressed, how they're sitting, the way their head moves, . . . this is difficult to describe because I can tell different types just by the body build—you can tell quite a bit about people just by the way they look physically. You can tell a lot about what their intentions might be, in what direction they tend to go, yet it's always a 50–50 thing, that's the interesting thing about it. Sometimes I can hit it right on the head and they do exactly what I thought they'd do—and sometimes they do the complete opposite! So there is always a certain risk, a grey area where you have absolutely no idea what the person is going to do or what they are going to be like; even though you've typecast them physically they still don't meet your expectations at all. So it's a chancy thing. Some nights I don't even have time because the audience will get into the theater only five minutes before curtain and I don't have time to find anyone, so I have to just pick them out of the audience randomly.

DAN Does that bring up any surge of adrenaline for you, if you're dealing with people who you haven't picked in advance?

DAVID It just creates more stress because anything is liable to happen and I have to be ready for it. Because again, it's a situation where the act can succeed greatly or it can fail miserably, and sometimes it does. That's the risk. I'm dealing with four different personality types and I have to change immediately for each and every one to pull out the most I can from that particular type of person. I know immediately where their fears are, what their limitations are, what they are apt to do and what they are apt not to do. My act depends on knowing as much of that as I can as soon as possible. For example, I can tell a lot about a person just when I grab his hand and bring him up on stage. How he shakes my hand, how he looks into my eyes, when I feel his body, how his bones are moving. I can tell right away what he is going to do. Obviously a person who's stiff, who's not moving or is resisting, is not going to do a lot. Someone who's allowing me to push them, who's flowing easily, whose bones are moving and muscles are relaxed, who has no tension in the eyes—that person is going to do exactly what he's been asked to do and there'll be no problem. I can feel energy emanating from him; it's hard to describe, but I can just feel what the Germans call *ausstradl*—

DAN What the person's sending out.

DAVID —what the person's sending out. I know immediately where he's at. What I work with mostly is just intuition. I know intuitively, just by the energy, what the limitations are.

DAN Have you an intention for each person that you play off of, who you bring into your world? Is there a value, some experience or adventure, that you aim to give?

DAVID Well, to bring them all together. To bring them closer together. That's the beauty of clown acts in the circus. Here is [my] character, aggressive, even abusive, but for some reason you like him anyway. He has a charm about him, the way that he does things. It brings everybody together. It creates a shared experience where they are caring—they want that person on stage to succeed because they put themselves in his shoes.

And when I take someone up on stage and he doesn't do the routine right, I love to really make fun of him. "Are you taking yourself that seriously? Are you taking this whole thing — having to succeed or fail — are you taking that seriously? The point is not to succeed here. The point is to open up and go beyond your limits, that's all — just to break out of your shell. Stop pretending to be what you're not and allow yourself for a moment to act like an idiot, to be a fool in front of everybody and still be loved!"

DAN The way that I've been looking at improvisation in this book is linked to a position called *social constructivism*, which is that we create, or cocreate, a reality with other people. That it's not as though things *are* a certain way and that we more or less know it or adhere to it, but rather that we're always in the act of creating what goes. In that way, David, I see you're creating something that is very absorbing for the onlooker, the audience, as well as for the person you're working with. Your magic is that you take things beyond the conventional rules and usual niceties that people expect and into the spontaneity and immediacy of two people who are now dealing with this unusual situation.

DAVID Well, I was thinking of this one instance that I brought up this very, very angry guy — you could see it. And he didn't like the fact that I was making fun of him; he didn't see the whole point of it. The most basic thing that my character is trying to say most of the time is: "Stop hiding, stop running away; the farther you run, the more pain you'll be in. Accept where you are, accept the facts and realities of who and what you are right now. Acknowledge the fact that you're freaked out, you're neurotic, you're scared. So, show it — show us — I can deal with it, I'm okay with it. Show me that you're upset. Show me that you're afraid. I'm not going to judge you for that."

DAN One apparent difference in my work is that I'm saying, "Go into the pretense, go further with it. Find yourself in pretending." In other words, by knowingly deepening or intensifying the pretense I get people to achieve that same recognition.

DAVID Well, while I'm performing, I'm tricking them. I'm setting a stage. I'm a clown and it's a theater, so I can do this and it's okay. But the fact is that many people actually change, they actually write letters saying, "I've never done anything like that in my life! It felt so fantastic to hear people laugh at me, to feel that I succeeded." They do experience something more than just going up and acting like an idiot.

DAN A couple of different questions here. Do you see yourself as improvising? Do you see what you do as improvisation?

DAVID Absolutely. It's creating a rough structure that I can always fall back on. I mean, actually, a very specific structure that I know I'm in, but within that structure I can allow myself to play as much as I want to. And that's the trick. You don't just go out and improvise without a structure because you need those four walls to bounce within.

DAN So, do you really care whether, for example, the scenario turns out the way that it has before? That's really irrelevant?

DAVID It's irrelevant.

DAN So, you really are exploring the moment, even though you have a structure in the back of your mind.

DAVID Yeah, certainly.

DAN A concept that I make a lot of use of is status.* I see people trying desperately to keep their own status from being lowered by others. That doesn't mean that they're always trying to play high status — they may play low — but they want to be in control of whether they go low or not. I see how your clown *plays* high status by his overbearing demeanor, but *is* not high status, as signalled by his dressing in ridiculous clothes, being suprised and making faces; these undermine his high-status message. If you were a tyrant, as opposed to playing at being tyrannical, you wouldn't be lovable or funny. As it is, the audience is led to see through your status pretense, which allows them to feel bemused and superior.

DAVID Right, right. Well, that's the clown.

DAN I look upon improvising as getting adults to re-experience the play of childhood.

DAVID Really? As a child?

DAN Yeah, because there are a number of contaminations or corruptions of play that adults buy into. As a result they lose some of that magical connection to the world that they had when they were children.

DAVID And I think it's completely possible to have that connection again: to see through the eyes of a child and have it be okay. I mean, who'd even question it? It's just . . . it's there: that sense of wonder and joy and sweetness.

DAN Partly, it's the unself-consciousness of immersing yourself fully in what's going on rather than having to say, "Well, how do I look doing this?"

DAVID Right, right. "Am I going to be judged?" All of it can also come from a tremendous amount of caring for other people. That's really the essence of it.

DAN When you were describing the different player types at the beginning of this interview, it occurred to me that they have — and you have with them — different problems or conditions to meet because of the status inclinations that they bring to play. The egomaniac is going to hold onto high status at all costs. And the naive, innocent will be much more receptive to having status conferred on her.

DAVID Yes, that was an incredible lesson for me. Even as the performer, when I observe people, the ones that are sweet and naive are the ones

*Status is discussed in detail in Chapter 7.

that flourish. They're the ones that are loved most dearly by the audience. The audience doesn't want to see anything that's false.

DAN The paradox is that people come to the theater, which is a kind of room in which illusion is supposed to be created, in order to see the truth — or to get to the truth. . . . Do you ever worry about picking somebody who's emotionally fragile and won't be able to take it?

DAVID No, because there's always a lot of support. I give a lot of support — whether people see it or not — the fact that I care so much, I never worry about that.

DAN It's real remarkable to me how completely attentive you are to the person with whom you're working. Even when you're playing an aside for the audience you really don't take focus from the person you've brought on stage.

DAVID It's funny that you asked that question because I never, ever question that. And I've had some cases like that. But anyone who's that far gone would refuse to come on stage. Although, recently, I did have someone like that — he troubled me, this person. A few weeks ago I had a guy on stage — nothing emanated from him, absolutely nothing. He was cold as ice. And for the first time in my life, I was concerned because, I thought, this person has a serious problem. You know, he almost could have been psychotic. It was scary. Usually something's always there; whether it's fear, insecurity, overconfidence, joy, whatever, there's always something. But this guy, nothing — absolutely nothing.

DAN How did you handle it?

DAVID I just went through the motions. It really threw me off because I couldn't do anything with him. At one point I said to him, "Get real with me, stop this!" but nothing came out.

DAN You talk to people you bring on stage in a way the audience doesn't realize that you're actually directing?

DAVID Sometimes, yeah. When I know that they need to be given some security or some indication.

DAN I would imagine some people really are not good at picking up on things that are not reinforced or accompanied by some words.

DAVID Yeah, it helps. When I take them up I always say something. The moment I put the hat on I say, "Just relax, be yourself, this is very easy, just have a lot of fun." And it usually breaks the ice.

DAN You do one bit with having a kid come up on stage — what do you find different about working with kids than with grown-ups?

DAVID They don't lie. They respond very honestly and immediately, which can be very, very funny. And they're not hiding yet, they haven't built up this whole incredible huge structure in order to pretend to be someone they're not or in order to protect themselves from whatever they're dealing with. They don't come on stage with all this baggage. That's why

we can laugh so easily with them, because what they do is so spontaneous. It's like a little puppy. A puppy doesn't think, it just reacts immediately.

That reminds me, so often I get actresses on stage and I see them
acting from the moment they get on stage. And I'll say, "Stop acting,
they'll hate you." Then they'll just freeze. They don't realize that what
they have to do now is the greatest challenge an actress can have, to act
like a woman who's never been on stage before.

DAN Not only does it make for immediacy of theater to watch people being
themselves, removing the social mask, but also when they surrender to
the moment the scene becomes instantly recognizable. You then know
what people are going to do, in the sense that you know what the
reaction is about, which allows for surprises and for spontaneity. So it
means that the experience of watching it is also part of the adventure.
The audience is also in a position to adventure with the people on stage
because they're seeing something that is really being created in that
moment.

DAVID Right. For me, that's the height of theater. It's walking that fine
line, it's not rehearsed, it's not all planned out. We're two human beings
and what's going to happen between us? That's what gets the audience
sitting on the edge of its seat, fully engaged. Because anything that
happens unexpectedly is a wonderful surprise. That's the essence of
theater: to take a little journey—oh, where is the next surprise? To keep
building those surprises, to keep the audience engaged.

And diff'ring judgments serve but to declare,
That truth lies somewhere, if we knew but where.

—William Cowper (cited in Partington, 1992, p. 222)

CHAPTER 3

Comparing Rehearsals for Growth with Other Psychotherapeutic Techniques

THE SOCIAL CONSTRUCTIVIST PERSPECTIVE

ROOTED IN KANTIAN PHILOSOPHY, social constructivism or constructionism is a theoretical stance, a way of thinking about personality and therapy that has achieved prominence in recent years, particularly among family therapists. Social constructivism is a departure from a belief (termed objectivist) in an objective reality that is discovered; instead, described reality is constructed or invented (Efran, Lukens, & Lukens, 1988; see also Lankton, Lankton, & Mathews, 1991, p. 242). From the social constructivist perspective, our self-identity is an intersubjective phenomenon. In particular, "we live and understand our lives through socially constructed narrative realities that give meaning and organization to our experiences, to our self-identities. Our self-identities, who we are, is a function of the socially constructed stories we are always narrating to ourselves and others" (Anderson, 1992, p. 19). Social constructivism-informed therapists typically regard the construct of self as a "relational self" (Gergen, 1991), meaning a self that is defined impermanently as a consequence of current social interaction, as opposed to an enduring, unitary, objective self. The experience of a sense of self results from the internalization of interpersonal conversations; these conversations are organized by narrative-mode thinking into stories; and these stories are used to understand experience.

As mentioned in the Introduction, RfG arose out of my involvement with theater improvisation; practice preceded theory. In my attempts to rethink earlier held notions of change and healing in psychotherapy, I have come to recognize a close correspondence between my observations and discoveries and the thoughts of some social constructivists. Although I do not posess a scholarly depth of understanding regarding its philosophy, there are three widely held notions concerning social constructivism and its application to psychotherapy that I regard as mistaken or impractical. In an excellent chapter, Efran and Clarfield (1992) take issue with several such notions; I shall first state the notion, then quote from their comments, and, finally, add my own viewpoint regarding RfG.

Notion #1: Social constructivism is equivalent to a relativism in which any reality is as valid or accessible as any other.

> We consider this "one is as good as the next" interpretation of Constructionism fundamentally wrong-headed. (p. 201)
> We believe what we do and do what we believe. We might wish that . . . a malignant cancer were a harmless wart, but wishing doesn't make it so. We have deep structural obligations that require us to play by the rules we have devised. Constructionism is therefore *not* a license to engage in pretense or encourage people to rely inordinately on wishful thinking. In fact, most individuals whom therapists see are already too heavily involved in fantasy and fabrication. (p. 213)

My position is in agreement with Efran and Clarfield in rejecting relativism (or radical constructivism). My own point of view is agnostic as to whether objective reality is knowable; at the level of ordinary waking consciousness it seems to me that our experienced world imposes constraints that limit human choices in many domains. Relationship, however, is not one of these domains; it may be cocreated apart from external constraint. This is not to overlook that objective-seeming existing conditions can, and often do, provide an influential frame of reference that shapes relationships as well. Two boys, one the son of a business owner and the other the son of that owner's employee, may cocreate a friendship independent of their fathers' status, yet at some point it is likely that their friendship will be influenced by the larger social context. Still, they may remain friends and construe their relationship as that between social equals. As Duncan (1962) notes, "the purest form of relationship exists in social play" (p. 328). Relationship patterns that we observe and experience are the product of habitual choices that can be altered simply by making other choices. "Simply," it should be emphasized, does not imply "easily."

Efran and Clarfield state that "Constructionism is *not* a license to engage in pretense or encourage people to rely inordinately on wishful thinking." Of course, RfG does encourage pretense and freeing the creative imagination—but with the crucial proviso that the context of play and fantasy is clearly demarcated as a special area within the therapeutic experience and is not to be confused with the social reality of the entire therapeutic enterprise (which is itself distinct from yet congruent with the larger social context). By maintaining a clear boundary around the play/pretense area of therapy, RfG works within the "deep structural obligations" referred to by Efran and Clarfield above. This can be clarified with a theatrical analogy: What takes place on stage during a theatrical performance is a representation of an altered reality that contrasts with the concurrent social reality of a theater-goer in his role-relationship with other audience members, the theater management and staff, and the performers on stage. And, of course, the "alternate realities" cocreated in the course of RfG carry no structural obligations outside of the enactment.

Notion #2: Social constructivist therapists ought to be non-interventive and non-hierarchical.

> After all, how is an "invented reality" to get itself invented, if we all sit on the sidelines, feigning neutrality and waiting for something to crop up? (p. 205)
>
> The very idea that hierarchy can be eliminated in therapy strikes us as absurd and counterproductive. The client has a problem and is seeking help from someone who presumably knows something about how to improve matters. . . . Moreover, therapeutic encounters usually take place on the therapist's turf and involve remuneration. In a society like ours these factors alone are sufficient to fix and communicate the shape of the hierarchy. (p. 207)

Some social constructivist therapists make the claim that their methods embody a greater respect for the phenomenology of the client than objectivist-based, intervention-oriented therapies, in that the therapist is not an expert on the changes that the client need make in their lives or their stories. This claim is reminiscent of the stance adopted in the 1940s and 1950s by client-centered therapists to distinguish their approach from those of both psychodynamic and behaviorist clinicians. In using RfG I take a stance that is neither "I'm the expert and I know what you should change in your (faulty) life," nor "I respect you so much that I will do nothing that might interfere with your life and will only perhaps suggest alternative ways of looking at things." Instead, I say: "Let us go on an adventure together so

that we might discover unexpected resources and open us to the possibility
of change when we tell and enact new stories." In saying this I am holding
myself out as an expert in guiding clients to make their own discoveries
rather than conduct a guided tour toward what I expect to find.

Notion #3: Constructivist therapy is limited to interpretation and is
ineffective in ameliorating "real problems."

> "Real problems" *are* interpretations — they are never simply collections of facts.
> Moreover, interpretations are consequential — not simply epiphenomenal.
> (p. 213)

This notion is sometimes directed toward the entire field of psychotherapy. In addition to agreeing that "problems" are interpretations, RfG is a
constructivist therapy that is not limited to verbal conversations in its methods. RfG enactments create novel experiences that challenge conventional
assumptions and open up unexplored possibilities, not only for reinterpret-
ing client's views of their problems but also for their resolution in action. I
also like the definition "A problem is a person's wish for change that he or
she does not know how to achieve" (Salamon, Grevelius, & Andersson,
1993) in that contracting with clients to work for their desired changes
carries no implication of their fault or failure and defines the therapist's
social role as a consultant/expert rather than paragon or authority.

A useful distinction can be made between what is *attended to* that is
factual and what is *chosen* that is construed. For example, one may attend
to illness (the factual condition of health) and make choices regarding sick-
ness (the attitude and social role of how to regard inwardly, and display
outwardly, such health facts). The rub is, as with the Serenity Prayer (attributed to St. Francis of Asissi and utilized in Alcoholics Anonymous),
how do we acquire (or trust that we have already acquired) "the Wisdom to
know the difference" between the factual and the construed?

In epistemology, truth can be defined phenomenologically (as it appears
in direct experience), by consensual validation (as in agreement with the
perceptions expressed by others), by correspondence (as agreeing with
objective evidence), and by coherence (by definition or logical consistency).
The truths explored in various psychotherapies differ in their emphasis
upon these different definitions. Gestalt therapy, client-centered therapy,
and psychodrama are primarily concerned with phenomenological truth;
reality therapy (Glasser), confrontation problem-solving (Garner) and direct decision therapy (Greenwald) focus on truth by correspondence; psychodynamic therapies explore the truth as known by coherence. Along with
other social constructivist approaches, RfG attends to truths derived from
consensual validation.

All psychotherapies, if only to justify their usefulness, presuppose that
the changing of our lives is possible. In contrast to RfG, a majority of
therapeutic approaches regard the uncovering and reexperiencing of the

historical past as necessary for constructive change. Whether this takes the form of cathartic reliving, taking inventory, acquiring explanatory metaphors rooted in past experience, or conducting family-of-origin research, the common underlying belief is that we are bound to some historical "truth" that we cannot ignore if we are to improve. Cognitive and behavioral therapies, as well as some systemic approaches, do not subscribe to the therapeutic necessity of attending to the past, yet hold a functionally similar viewpoint regarding the necessity of attending to the "factual" present.*

A Classification Scheme
for Therapeutic Methods

Below are a variety of psychotherapeutic approaches that have some useful correspondence with RfG regarding method, philosophy, and/or problem application. No attempt has been made to exhaustively catalog the hundreds of methods extant nor search for lesser known ones that might have other or greater similarities or differences. These approaches are categorized according to three properties that are distinctive of RfG:

1. A perspective in which alternative realities are Created or cocreated versus a belief in the indispensability of the historical or present Truth that therapy needs to unearth and attend to. Approaches are also classified under "truth" if they presuppose an underlying, unitary self. (C vs. T)
2. Significant use of Action methods versus exclusively Verbal technique. (A vs. V)
3. An interactional/Systemic paradigm versus an Individual one; approaches that address the group-as-a-whole are classified as systemic. (S vs. I)

RfG is classified as CAS; the classification of other approaches is included below.

Approaches Where the Client is In-Role

From a sociological viewpoint, we all are always (passively) "in" or (actively) "playing" some role. The criterion here for being in-role is whether the client *intentionally* suspends or distances from a this-is-who-I-am state of ownership and identification with a social role, replacing it

---

*Approaches that are founded upon a belief in some historical "truth" may, of course, be reinterpreted (deconstructed) from a social constructivist perspective. Spence (1987), for example, presents psychoanalysis as an unwitting collusion between analyst and patient in the cocreation of an elaborate story about not only the patient's life and relationships, but also the therapeutic relationship itself.

with a this-is-who-I-pretend-to-be dramatic role. Notice that disassociative or trance states are not part of being in-role by this criterion. In RfG games players are always in-role, although in some exercises they are not.

TAI Psychodrama and TAS Sociodrama

Central to psychodrama is the spontaneous enactment of scenes that are both created by a client (the protagonist) and feature the protagonist as the central character. The subjective reality of psychodramatic enactment is a sort of waking dream, a trance state. Enactment is therapeutic work, not a way of accessing playfulness; it is the (re)playing of original, spontaneous feelings and perceptions, reflecting the experienced truth (phenomenal reality) of the protagonist (Seeman & Wiener, 1985). Other players in-role as auxilliary egos are allowed to improvise their roles only to a slight extent, since they serve merely to play extensions or projections of the protagonist rather than characters of their own devising. Psychodrama aims to induce an intense cathartic experience primarily for the individual protagonist (who is both author and central character of the drama) yet also for the auxilliary actors and for the group audience.

Whether scenes created and enacted in psychodrama are based upon actual, projected, or hypothetical realities, the clinical emphasis remains on the spontaneous, here-and-now experience of the protagonist—experience that is typically emotionally intense. In RfG enactments, by contrast, players are not very likely to become so emotionally affected, since (a) the role has not been warmed-up to, having been defined largely on the spot; (b) other players, the therapist/director and/or audience members make offers that significantly shape the role's definition; (c) meeting the objectives and adhering to the form of the improv necessitates the use of cognitive skills that detract from intense emotive experiencing; and (d) adhering to the principles of improv requires that players attend closely to one another's behavior, which is incompatible with full absorption in one's own subjectivity.

Despite the above-mentioned differences, psychodrama has greatly influenced the format I use in improvisational group therapy, particularly as to the role of therapist/director and the cycle of warm-up–enactment–sharing (see Chapter 10).

One psychodramatic technique is the *Magic Shop*, a scene in which a player in role as himself encounters the proprieter of a Magic Shop, wishing to obtain abstract qualities such as courage, contentment, or security. The proprieter asks the player what he is willing to pay or barter for this quality, such as "willingness to risk being thought a failure by others" or "pleasing my mother." This scene uses the familiar premise of a commercial exchange to highlight and externalize the ambivalence clients experience around psychological growth and change.

Another approach that utilizes psychodramatic enactment is one developed at the Family Institute of Cambridge (Chasin, Roth, & Bograd, 1989) in which family members dramatize their hopes and fears of the past or future as a means for therapist and family members to acquire a more coherent sense of the protagonist's meanings and wishes. These authors regard the value of such enactments as moving the therapeutic process away from talking about present difficulties and toward taking action to modify past patterning and attaining future goals.

Sociodrama was developed by Moreno (1934) as a way to address larger social problems, particularly intergroup conflict. Similar in form to psychodrama, it differs in that (a) the scenarios deal with general, rather than personal issues; (b) the audience is more actively involved as cast members—the players represent types or classes (e.g., Moslems or fathers or police officers) instead of individual roles; (c) there is more scope for improvisation during enactment; and (d) the focus of change is on the group rather than the individual.

While psychodrama is rooted in historical truth, Playback Theater (developed by Johnathan Fox) is a form of sociodrama that does allow people to explore alternative realities and gives the players some scope for improvisation (Salas, 1993). In this form, audience or group members narrate personal stories that are acted out on the spot by either trained actors or other group members. The therapist/director (called a conductor) elicits the story, supports the teller, and may invite him to participate in the enactment to decrease his emotional distance; improvised music and props are employed to heighten the intensity of the drama. These scenes, which are improvised within the general structure of the narrative, can be reenacted (transformed) in a variety of ways, drawing on the heightened involvement of audience, players, and narrator/author. The therapeutic value of Playback Theater lies in the public telling of one's story to a receptive audience. Johnstone's almost identical *Life Game* (see p. 20) grew out of a desire to involve and connect the audience by dramatizing real-life stories, although no therapeutic application was intended. Although outside the scope of this book, the theatrical forms of some street theater, particularly Forum Theater developed by Boal (1992), also draw upon the power of drama to mobilize people toward raising consciousness, group problem-solving, and social action.

CAI Drama Therapy

The aim of drama, whether or not in therapy, is seen as experiencing a reality from everyday life altered by imagination—thereby being transformed. In its broadest sense, drama therapy is that application of the direct experience of theater art (as opposed to passive spectating) for the purpose of bringing about change in individuals and groups. Unlike psychodrama, which developed clinically into a detailed and highly structured technique, drama therapy has evolved without a central core with the result that there exist no standardized methods. Johnson (1992) identifies five general goals of the drama therapist: "(1) tell a story or solve a problem; (2) achieve a catharsis of emotion; (3) deepen inner experience; (4) understand the meaning of images and actions; and (5) strengthen the observing ego (p. 120)."

Drama therapy has evolved from a reliance on scripted roles (utilized in order to expand role repertoire and evoke reactions that pointed to further role choices) into using improvisations that reveal the role types invoked by the client. In one representative drama therapy approach, the therapist, working in a group setting, first facilitates the invocation of role by setting the stage and next helps the client externalize and separate one role from the many available internalized ones. Then the therapist has the client name and develop the role through enactment, accepting the client's caricature of the role's quality as a transitional need for safe play before proceeding to a more personally meaningful depiction. Finally, after the completion of the enactment, the therapist and client attempt to make sense of the role choice and the qualities of its enactment. As with psychodrama, the emphasis is on the individual's experience and the other players' contributions to the enactment are not closely attended to, except as either a joining in the depiction of a universal role-type or as a prelude to their taking up their own enacted roles.

In recent years some leading practitioners of drama therapy have expanded considerably the active use of the self of the therapist to improvise in-role along with the client. In this respect such drama therapists are different from psychodramatists, who do not take up a dramatic role. Johnson (1992) has developed an autonomous form of drama therapy called *transformations* in which roles and scenes are constantly transformed and reshaped according to the client's ongoing stream of consciousness and internal imagery. It is based upon Viola Spolin's (1963) improvisational technique in which two actors begin any scene; during the enactment either actor, using any external cue, associates to a different character, situation, or mode of playing the scene. At this point, that actor *initiates a transformation* by beginning to act as another character, in a new situation or via a diferent mode. The other actor then picks up on the change, either accepting the new role assigned him by the first actor, or selecting a role to fit the first actor's alteration. The scene may be changed at any time by either actor initiating a transformation. The only rule is that each actor accept all transformations; the optimal result is that the actors cocreate a seamless, free-association–like flow.

In Johnson's transformations technique the therapist and client play a scene in which the therapist guides the client "to increase . . . access to and tolerance of internal states that have been cast aside, labeled as unacceptable, or are seen as threatening" (Johnson, 1992, p. 128). The therapist accomplishes this by making purposeful interventions and initiating transformations during the scene that alter the stage reality and redirect the client's focus (Johnson identifies eleven specific interventions, four of which are specific to the transformations technique). These four shift the context of the scene so that the client changes his position between involvement and observation. In addition to demanding of the drama therapist a high degree of empathy and skill at improvisation, this technique evidently requires a client who has had considerable prior experience with drama therapy enactments.

In RfG, as in Johnson's use of transformations, clients are directed into roles in order to thrust them into an intense, immediate, yet safe and supportive experience of functioning as someone else. However, my selection of improv enactments is more focused and goal-directed; I offer improv to teach principles of good relationship functioning and as an intervention to test or expand the client's or relationship system's functioning. In improvising, the client obtains both a general experience of difference from one's habitual use of self and the specific challenge of making a goal-directed change in use of self. Thus, in the course of "solving the problem" posed by the instructions, new possibilities in behavior, attitude, and emotion may emerge. Even failures in RfG improvising are useful, since they permit therapists, clients, and their observing or interacting partners to experience and witness directly certain personal and interpersonal limitations.

CAS Pretend Technique

Cloe Madanes (1981) has developed a family therapy technique of prescribing the pretending of a symptom. In the strategic family therapy framework, symptomatic family members are seen as getting the benefit of love, concern, attention, or exemption from duty for their symptomatic behavior from other family members. In the pretend technique, the therapist arranges to have the symptomatic member pretend to have the symptom and for the other family member(s) confer the same benefit as if the symptom were real. This is then used to undermine the family belief that the "real" symptom is necessary any longer. Minuchin, writing of this technique (cited in Madanes, 1981), states:

> Let's pretend the world is different. [Madanes] creates a therapy of "as if" where dragons are mere butterflies observed with a magnifying glass. In this therapy . . . the symptom's communicative power to the other . . . loses meaning . . . In the imaginary field of rearranging realities, family members, in effect, break loose from an "only" way of being. (p. xviii)

What is significant about the pretend technique within the RfG framework is that the enactment of the display-pretended-symptom/confer-benefit transaction creates a distinction between real life and performance such that the performance context, operating under the voluntary control of the players, is seen as operating in the same way as the presumably involuntary symptomatic pattern. As a consequence, the players are more suggestible to the notion that the original symptomatic pattern is a social construction that can be intentionally altered. In RfG, pretense is used primarily to teach and practice the expanded possibilities and choices available to all of us, including the possibility of setting aside belief in self-defining and self-reinforcing limitations.

TVS Symbolic-Experiential Family Therapy

There is much in spirit that is similar between symbolic-experiential family therapy and RfG. This approach, pioneered by Carl Whitaker (Whitaker & Keith, 1981), emphasizes the centrality of emotional experience in shaping meaning and places the therapist (often working with a cotherapist) in the role of an active coach and in the frequent position of gadfly/catalyst.

Whitaker is an exemplar of the spontaneous and creative therapist. Minuchin referred to him as "a destroyer of crystallized forms" (Neill & Kniskern, 1982, p. ix) since he is likely to present himself to the clinical family as a provocative and unpredictable figure, questioning and commenting so as to achieve a destabilizing effect. Except perhaps at the very beginning of therapy, the symbolic-experiential therapist participates out of his aliveness and creative use of self rather than from a preplanned or intellectual position. Moreover, the therapist's sense of the absurd and access to his own craziness (which, Whitaker says, "can be colored pink by calling it creativity" [Whitaker & Keith, 1981, p. 194]) both models a desired stance for clinical family members and serves as a tool for intervening with dysfunctional family patterns. This leads to a psychotherapy of the absurd in which the therapist augments the unreasonable quality of a client's response to the point of absurdity, using teasing and sarcasm to signal and invite an overdistanced response, even at the risk of the client feeling made fun of. Roberto (1991) writes that the intention of symbolic-experiential therapists is

> to create maximum disorganization as quickly as possible in clinical families. Our commentary is likely to be dramatic, metaphorical, humorous, and stepped up in intensity from the information given to us. This escalation is a deliberate attempt to increase complexity, challenge fixed perceptions, and create a therapeutic context that includes the elements of curiosity and surprise. (p. 453)

Similarly, Whitaker and Keith (1981) state:

> [Our] basic objective is to induce regression by way of confusion . . . which may be brought about by nonrational participation or even by quite irrational presentations, such as teasing, play, or jokes. We feel no obligation to make sense and enjoy our inconsistencies. (p. 213)

According to Roberto (1991), the above-mentioned disorganization and regression induced by the symbolic-experiential family therapist are "mediating goals" that both create an altered affective experience among family members and disrupt their rigid repetitive cycling of interaction. Thus, symbolic-experiential therapists frequently "[encourage] family members to experiment with different roles within the group, with an attitude of play or openness to discovery" (Whitaker & Keith, 1981). As Whitaker and Keith go on to elaborate,

> *the family must learn how to play.* This goal sounds simple, but family groups oftentimes have great difficulty with it. To be more specific, families need to differentiate between playful sadism and real murder. They need to differentiate between sexual intercourse and flirting. Play is universal, It must be present to maintain health and facilitate growth (Winnicott, 1971). One manifestation of playfulness is the role availability in the family. All roles should be available to each person depending upon the situation and with the family's agreement. (1981, p. 200)

And,

> a basic characteristic of all healthy families is the availability of [the] "as if" structure. Play characterizes all metacommunication . . . [which] is considered to be an experimental process, an offer of participation that implies the clear freedom to return to an established role security rather than be caught in the "as if" tongue-in-cheek microtheater; . . . whimsy and creativity of the family can even be exaggerated to where family subgroups or individuals are free to be nonrational or crazy. (ibid., p. 190)

Whitaker takes a constructivist conceptual position when he states that "the symptom pattern in psychological illness is largely the result of the acceptance of a role" (cited in Neill & Kniskern, 1982, p. 289). The role is created and offered by the client's family, which leads Whitaker to declare: "The psychological treatment of an individual can be redefined as the treatment of the family scapegoat." (ibid., p. 289). On the other hand, the therapist takes a declared position on the functionality or disfunctionality of family behavior and clearly models support or challenge to these behaviors in sessions.

Symbolic-experiential family therapists model, provoke, and evoke dramatic roles for clients, yet they rarely instruct clients or directly invite them to assume or enact dramatic roles. They may assign tasks to their clients, but the intention is to treat these as occasions for play, rather than as therapeutically necessary.

> We may have them practice family rituals just for fun instead of being controlled by them. We propose tasks, but they do them only if they are curious enough . . . It is not important to us if they do the task. If they have not done it or if it has not worked well, we might say, "It's probably smart that you didn't try to change things too much. I forgot to warn you that thing could get worse." (Whitaker & Keith, 1981, p. 199)

Another major distinction between the methods of symbolic-experiential family therapy and those of RfG is that in the latter, theater is used as a defined and marked-off part of therapy; in the former, therapy is theater in which the clients cannot be sure whether the therapist is serious or playful, absurd or practical, metaphorical or literal at any given moment. A consequence of this difference is that, in RfG, the therapist is not always "on stage" with the client(s) but functions most of the time as a guide and director of the client's exploration of pretense and play. In this way the clients' awareness of the therapist/director in the capacity of observer functions to bracket the play experience so that they may have the safety to explore the "as if" within the limits of their own present risk tolerance. Yet because the therapist/director sometimes enters the play-world, she or he both reduces the social distance between them, thus lessening the perception of functioning as a judgmental observer, and models how to move freely between the worlds of pretense and reality.

CVS Narrative Family Therapy

White (1992; White & Epston, 1990) has developed an approach of "deconstructing" the dominant, taken-for-granted modes of thought and life that the client/family presents, thereby empowering alternate choices. By engaging in "externalizing conversations" the therapist encourages the client to separate her or his sense of identity from the the problem description and to view the self as "having problems with the problem" instead of problems with (i.e., within) the self. An interesting result of this method is that the externalized problem entity becomes a character in the world created between therapist and client. White uses primarily verbal questioning to reauthor the client's story (a) by "landscapes of action," in which "unique outcomes" (exceptions to the dominant story) are elicited across the client's past, present, and hypothetical future; and (b) by "landscapes of consciousness," in which the therapist invites clients to consider how adopting alternative stories can result in changing interpretations and meanings of actional changes.

White and Epston's methods are largely verbal questioning and therapist letter-writing; however, White occasionally evokes and himself enters into the playspace during sessions. Barragar-Dunne (1993), a drama therapist working with White's narrative therapy model, has utilized a variety of action techniques (drama, psychodramatic enactment, movement, masks, puppets, and drawings) to facilitate the externalization and re-storying of the problem.

TAS Virginia Satir's Approach

For Satir, the past shapes us but does not prevent us from relearning how to view ourselves and how to reinterpret our experiences, particularly those of our families of origin. Family reconstruction, her most comprehensive method, uses a combination of Gestalt, psychodramatic, sculpting, hypnotic, letter-writing, and movement techniques within a dramatic form to "go back to old situations with new eyes" (Nerin, 1986). In addition, Satir developed an experiential style of family therapy that used action techniques, pretense, and simulation to alter perceptions of self and others. Unlike their use in RfG, however, these techniques were employed within a framework of helping individuals and families to achieve the culturally-defined positive potential of authentic selfhood rather than the exploration, discovery, and choice of other possibilities. This issue is discussed in further detail in Self Therapies and RfG below.

APPROACHES WHERE THE CLIENT IS NOT IN-ROLE

TVI Cognitive Therapy

According to cognitive therapists we construe reality according to our beliefs and we experience that constructed reality as real. However, unlike the stance of social constructivist therapists, the underlying point of view of cognitive therapists is that the client's difficulties stem from having the wrong (i.e., irrational) beliefs which the therapist is expert in diagnosing and correcting; this implies the therapist's belief in objective truth, or at least the possibility of attaining a closer approximation to such truth. Although its distinctive methods are largely verbal (e.g., disputing and instructing) some cognitive therapies, notably rational-emotive therapy, make use of self-experimentation and role-play to test behaviors and beliefs in real-life and enacted scenarios.

TVI Transactional Analysis (TA)

Transactions are chains of social stimulus-response events between the ego states of two persons, both striving to satisfy their need for "strokes" (recognition), structure, and stimulation. Games are ongoing series of ulterior (partially concealed) transactions progressing to a psychological pay-off, usually with a dramatic outcome; they are thought of as inauthentic and manipulative ways that people seek to obtain payoffs and to maintain their life positions (Berne, 1964).

TA theory views interaction from a nonsystemic perspective; although a game is the product of both players' "moves," the clinical focus is intrapersonal. Consistent with TA's roots in psychodynamic theory, clients are thought of as unconsciously seeking others with whom to play out their life scripts and to repeat their games habitually. Therapy methods, usually applied in groups, are verbal and confrontational, consisting of unmasking the "phoniness" of gameplaying and its replacement by intimacy. Thus TA "games" are not actually playful, while "players" are psychologically but not dramatically in-role. Following Berne, Harris (1969) uses a dramatic metaphor in broadening their theory to include "script analysis" (analyzing lifestyle patterns) yet opts for interpretation over enactment as the preferred means of change.

TAS Structural Family Therapy

While I (hesitantly) classify Minuchin's and his colleagues' approach to family treatment as truth-based (since there exists a belief in underlying organizational constructs such as boundary, alignment, and subsystem), there is also a clear recognition and influence, especially in his later writings, of a social constructivist perspective. This takes several forms: (a) an awareness of these spatial and organizational constructs as metaphors, not actual entities; (b) a viewpoint that families live by and within constructed realities; and (c) interventions that are designed to influence metaphorically the family's perceptions as well as their functioning. On the other hand, it is clear that the therapist's (a) monopoly on the reframing of the problem; (b) challenges in-role as expert to family member's views concerning problems and solutions; and (c) hierarchical emphasis on the therapist as the agent of change all set the Structural model apart from the practices of most social constructivist therapists.

The roles assumed by the structural family therapist have been explicitly derived from a theatrical metaphor: producer (production of the conditions that will make the therapy possible); stage director (creation of conditions that challenge the existing structure and stress it toward improved functioning); protagonist (intervention as an active participant in family transactions, though not in the form of personal self-disclosure); and narrator (development of new meanings through the coauthoring of a revised "script" for family transactions; Colapinto, 1991). In general, the therapist makes active use of self to fulfill all of the above-mentioned roles.

The use of theatrical forms is further evident in the use of action techniques, particularly enactment (used in the sense of replaying family patterns in the presence of the therapist, but without the awareness of being in-role that defines enactment as used in RfG), crisis induction, and unbalancing (which are de facto *status transactions*, as described in Chapter 7). The therapist may, in restructuring operations, create the role of audience-as-spectator by excluding certain members from participating in some transaction, or even more dramatically by moving a family member away from the area of the session to isolate and place that member in an observer position.

While the structural therapist's interventions frequently take the form of metaphorical description (e.g., "Your daughter is the grandmother in this family") and directives for changing habitual role behavior, such interventions are not aimed at creating dramatic roles; that is, clients are not invited to enter the playspace, to try *being someone else* — only to function differently as themselves. For this reason the structural approach is classified among the not–in–role approaches.

Since the structural model emphasizes assessment and intervention based upon behavior that occurs in the immediacy of the therapy session (rather than reliance on descriptions of behaviors), presence and a commitment to action in the moment are required of the therapist. Due to these requirements for immediate, flexible and active use of self, improv training is particularly valuable for the development of the structural family therapist.

CVI Storytelling and Therapeutic Narrative

Goolishian and Anderson have developed a social constructivist therapy that is advanced through a process of conversation that focuses on the meaning of the client's narratives. "The job of therapy is to help people reach for, restore, access and create self-identities that are freeing, self-identities that allow them to to develop an understanding of their lives and its events — that permit self-agency, or simply a sense of self-agency" (Anderson, 1992, p. 20). The therapist, working alongside the client(s), cocreates new meanings out of their stories.

When a social constructivist viewpoint is implemented within a tradition of exclusively verbal psychotherapy, the result is inevitably a technique of therapeutic conversations in which change is seen as the outcome of verbal restorying. Most narrative approaches, although developed by clinicians trained in systemic therapies, direct their interventions toward shifting the stories of individuals.

By contrast, RfG broadens the armamentarium of therapeutic techniques to include action and drama so that beneficial changes in meaning, cognition, affect, and behavior may also be facilitated by verbally unmediated experience of enactment. Because the story in an improv draws on the combined contribution of all the players, it is feasible to construct and alter narratives of a *relationship system*, rather than being limited to working with those of individual clients.

TVI Gestalt Therapy

Gestalt stresses the immediacy of awareness as the focus of therapy, as opposed to the exploration of the past or constructing explanations. Perls, the founder of Gestalt therapy, considered the fundamental error of psychoanalysis to be the assumption that we are bound to our past, that memory corresponds to reality. While not considered a social constructivist, his position was that claiming infantile traumata, as the root of neurosis, was a falsification in which the patient indulged in order to avoid responsibility for growth. On the other hand, his model posits a "true self" at the core of illusory layers: Beneath the surface "phoniness" of social roles lies the layer of emptiness; beyond emptiness lies the layer of real life, of true feelings, and of strivings.

The role of the Gestalt therapist is a confrontational one, designed to challenge the client's superficial adaptation and to guide the client through the completion of the "unfinished business" of the past so that she or he may live with awareness in the present (to establish the "continuum of awareness"). Enactment in Gestalt therapy largely consists of dramatizing the struggle between parts of self by verbal means. As Naranjo (1968) says, "As awareness leads to some action, so does deliberate acting lead to expanded awareness" (p. 133). Gestalt technique also makes use of "playing the projection," particularly with dreams; the dreamer is guided to verbally reenact the dream and supply dialogue for its elements. Both of these techniques can be extended into full action with movement through improv, although RfG is better utilized to deal with displacement material than enacting actual, present feelings. RfG also can be valuable in advancing the Gestalt goals of heightening awareness in the present and of experiencing the risk of acting without what Perls termed "rehearsing" (knowing and anticipating).

CAS Therapeutic Rituals

While rituals undeniably are staged events and frequently induce a trance state in participants, it appears that persons engaged in ritual (whether therapeutic or cultural) are not in-role by my definition, in that they are not necessarily aware of taking a dramatic role (i.e., of becoming someone else) at the time. Gilligan (1993) points out that (traditional cultural) rituals "involve a *predetermined behavioral sequence*, such that little cognitive decision-making is needed during its enactment" (p. 239). Therapeutic rituals, however, can be devised to fit each case and may be designed to include "open" aspects, which permit improvisation and spontaneity, as well as specified, "closed" ones (Whiting, 1988). This combination of order and spontaneity is also characteristic of RfG games and exercises.

The pretense implicit in therapeutic rituals lies in the symbolic use of communication, objects, and action. Symbols carry multiple meanings and are processed as metaphors that link simultaneously the sensory and cognitive poles of meaning. A ritual such as the burial of a brick from a house that was lived in during an unhappy life-period combines the metaphorical/symbolic action of burying (putting out of sight, saying goodbye to, moving on from, etc.) with the symbolic association of the brick with the house and the house with the unhappy life-period. Myerhoff (cited in Roberts, 1988) points to a contradiction inherent in ritual which corresponds to the contradictions across levels of stage and non-stage reality. That is, the reality in ritual is that of "sacred" time and space yet purports to define mundane reality. As Roberts points out, "Therapy works with this same contradiction, in that it is seen as a process to rework day-to-day interactions yet happens in a special time and space that is outside of the usual boundaries of daily interaction" (1988, p. 7). In order to maintain the illusion that ritual is not pretense, the ritual process must be entered with a suspension of disbelief: "Critical, analytic thought, the attitude which would pierce the illusion of reality is anathema to ritual. The fiction underlying ritual is twofold: first, that rituals are not made-up productions, and second, that the contradictions embraced by their symbols have been erased" (Myerhoff, 1977, pp. 199–200). Also: "*No meta-commentary* (such as self-talk or evaluations) is permitted, such that no part of the system is split off in an 'outside observer' role" (Gilligan, 1993, p. 239).

When prepared for, enacted, and followed through properly, the "as-if" linking of symbolic/associative meanings in the ritual occurs and results in the culturally or therapeutically-intended effects. To effect this linking, it appears necessary to be inducted into out-of-the-ordinary awareness. Van der Hart (cited in Roberts, 1988) points out that a necessary element of all successful rituals is a high degree of performance involvement on the part of the ritual-doers. Rappaport (cited in Roberts, 1988) lists six key aspects of ritual, one of which is "evocative presentational style—where through staging and focus an 'attentive state of mind' is created" (p. 7). There appears to be no clear consensus among ritual-using therapists whether there is an optimal degree of involvement with the ritual such that a balance between involvement-with and distance-from the effect (e.g., "leaving unhappiness behind," as in the above-mentioned example) is sought, directly comparable to the esthetic distance deemed optimal for emotional catharsis (see Chapter 1).

One form of therapeutic ritual of particular relevance to RfG, due to its social constructivist rationale, has been described by Gilligan (1993). Combining White's construct of externalization with an Ericksonian hypnotherapeutic approach, he has developed a four- to six-week method of therapeutic ritual for working with traumatized individuals, couples, families, and groups. The client's presenting problem is seen as a manifestation of trauma-as-dysfunctual-rituals which have led to "a disidentification with the rest of the world and a misidentification of the self as 'being' the traumatic event" (p. 240), resulting in a negative self-identity. Since ordinary conversations regarding shifting identity serve only "to conserve [the client's] existing frame of reference" (p. 241), while the therapist's standard use of hypnotic methods to recall and reexperience traumatic events may perpetuate the client's story of trauma and deepen the distress, Gilligan uses ritual to move clients out of old and into new identities.

To accomplish this, problematic patterns are first identified and then framed positively as incomplete healing or change attempts. Therapeutic or healing rituals are then described as actions leading to externalizing the trauma so that the client may assume an identity apart from it. Once the client has committed to a healing ritual, the therapist, guided by hypnotic questioning, collaborates in planning the ritual. This consists of (a) creating symbols (by writing letters, painting, and drawing), (b) gathering physical symbols of old and new identities, (c) identifying the details of the ritual act, and (d) preparing inwardly beforehand (prayer, fasting, or meditation). The ritual is then performed in which the old identity is replaced with the new; in a postritual process, the new identity is further solidified and attached to the community by having the changed identity witnessed by an audience.

SELF THERAPIES AND RfG

Therapists as diverse in orientation as Rogers, Perls, Satir, and Bowen, all of whom believed in the existence of some sort of authentic self, claimed that tragic interpersonal outcomes, dysphoria, and dysfunctional behaviors stem from incongruity between the authentic self and the social self that is taught to or forced upon us, predominantly during our impressionable, formative years. They believed that the task of therapy is to lead us back to the authentic self and viewed the therapist as a model of authentic selfhood in whose presence the client's innate moral goodness, strength of character, autonomy, and positive self-esteem will emerge as authentic self-qualities. In the presence of a therapist who lives in complete congruence with these values, this modelling will most often take root and inspire the client to shape her life in this direction; with a therapist whose life is less than fully congruent with such values, the client may come to experience these values as prescriptive, even coercively thrust upon them. This shows up most visibly in encounter groups where tolerance and acceptance is selectively offered to those members manifesting a "loving self" while considerable social pressure is brought to bear on those who do not.

From the social constructivist standpoint, the behaviors, cognitions, and emotions that are encouraged in the context of any therapy are con- structions-as-instructions that are believed to be effective in promoting ben- eficial outcomes. In effect, the client is being invited to play the role of a more successful or desirable person. Like therapists offering support to clients, we *endow*, or *give character to* our clients by attributing to them socially valued qualities that they might otherwise be unfamiliar with or consider as "not-me." Dramatic techniques, such as RfG, are different from most other therapeutic methods in that they add a well-defined context- marker that establishes play and experimentation-within-play as permission to be "not-myself," not only in the playspace and during therapy but also throughout life. Approval for such play amounts to a positive valuing of the flexibility to redefine self at will and frees the client from the onus of always having to find and portray "one's true self." A major role for RfG in therapy, then, becomes the encouragement of playful exploration as a mental health resource. And, while I certainly attempt to influence my clients to manifest improved functioning, thinking, and feeling, working to coestablish and meet specific goals beyond increased playfulness, I continually remind myself of my belief that *improving the capacity to change one's self-definition is of greater and more lasting value than effecting any specific change.*

PART II

Principles and Techniques of Improvisation

Ah! Don't say you agree with me. When people agree with me I
always feel I must be wrong.

—Oscar F. Wilde (cited in Daintith et al., 1989, p. 12)

CHAPTER 4

Accepting and Blocking Offers

T HE BLOCKING/ACCEPTING DISTINCTION is fundamental to all of improvisation. This chapter includes a sampling of games and exercises that
require or demonstrate the results of the intentional acceptance or nonac-
ceptance (blocking) of offers. An offer is any communication that signifies,
indicates, or assures some aspect of social, historical, psychological, or
physical reality. Defined in this way, it is virtually impossible NOT to make
offers on any occasion in which there is awareness on either the sender's or
receiver's part. As Gregory Bateson (1972) stated, "It is impossible to NOT
communicate."

Offers are often made unintentionally to others, yet there are dimensions to even a deliberate offer that are unintended or outside of the offerer's awareness. These include offers made to oneself, such as an improv
exercise when a person's spontaneous movement leads to a repeated phrase,
or where the words of a song that one is humming to oneself registers on
that person's consciousness to indicate some previously unaware-of mean-

59

ing. Autogenic techniques (Luthe, 1976) and self-speech (Vygotsky, 1978) are further examples where the self-offer has the purpose of indicating a desired change in affect, cognition, or behavior.

The offers of greatest interest, however, are ones that are made interpersonally. To initiate and progress through a scenario with an intelligible and esthetically satisfying outcome requires some agreement and alignment among the players regarding place, time, character, intent, and relationship; in other words, a largely consensual social reality needs to be created and maintained. Notice, however, that dramatic tension results from *imperfect* alignment; misunderstanding, conflict, incompletely shared information and manipulation add realism, depth, and "spice" to the result.

LEVELS OF BLOCKING

Total blocking is rare in real life; usually, there exists some awareness of the other person that governs the personal space of the players, their taking turns to speak, and their acknowledgment of the presence or impact of one another. Treating another person as though she or he doesn't exist is such a grave violation of ordinary social convention that it is deliberately employed only as a way of destroying another's identity (or, in some tribal societies, as a way of condemning a person to death).

Conventionally, a profound block might be represented by the following dialogue (which is really a sequential monologue — each person speaking without regard to what the other is saying):

A I've just bought a new blue station wagon.
B There are no more pickles in this jar.
A Only mother knows who your father is.
B November was colder than normal.

Assuming that A and B are not making eye contact or matching inflection (so as to suggest perhaps, that they are spies communicating in code), each is ignoring the offers implied by the other's statements.

At another level, consider this dialogue:

A I've just bought a new blue station wagon!
B Well, It's really more of a green van.

Here, the topic and existence of a vehicle are agreed upon. This dialogue is realistic to the extent that it features a common status maneuver whereby B raises self and lowers A by disqualifying part of the content of the statement. If B adds, "You've got to get new sunglasses," he would, at least, be making an offer upon which a scene could be developed. If he leaves matters where he only disqualifies A's offer, the strong likelihood is that nothing will develop.

Blocking can also occur at the affective level. Consider this example:

A (enthusiastically) I've just bought a new blue station wagon!!
B (bored) How very nice for you.

Not only is B refusing A's emotional offer (enthusiasm) but he is also not advancing the action, or contributing anything in return. As a further experiment, try this: Arrange for someone to listen to you speak on a topic that holds great interest for you. Begin speaking while she or he remains emotionally neutral, merely nodding and saying "yes" occasionally. Unless you are only looking for a passive audience for your monologue, I predict that you will experience a sense of burden that increases while it dawns on you that you are carrying a conversational ball that grows increasingly heavier.

Verbal blocking also can occur when one player has an agenda other than playing the scene for its own sake, in a playful spirit. This can take the form of "pointless originality," such as might occur in the game *One Word at a Time* (in which two players alternate saying a word that contributes to telling a mutual story; this game is described more fully below). Suppose the following story: "Robert—proffered—me—hydrocortisone—to—scintillate—with—tumultuous—." It appears that the second player is going out of his way to add a highly unusual word on his every turn. Especially when accompanied by a telling delivery (for instance, sending knowing looks to the audience, a tone of condescension in his voice, glaring at his partner), some kind of superior, competitive, or rebellious message is being conveyed.

Blocking can also occur when one player disqualifies another by body or facial gesture, or by vocal inflection (such as a sarcastic tone). Nonverbal blocking often takes the form of ignoring or being oblivious to the body offers of other players, violating the stage reality of mimed props (such as walking through previously established furniture), or even stopping further physical action and becoming a "talking head." Frequently, the blocker is overly focused on her or his own performance and has tuned out these other features in order to save herself or himself from embarrassment or to exert overcontrol.

"Waffling" and "wimping" are the names stage improvisers give to two similar kinds of reponses that fail to advance the action of the scene. Waffling (Belt & Stockley, 1989) is acceptance of an offer with resistance:

A I've just bought a new blue station wagon!
B Oh, was it new when you bought it?

Asking questions instead of making statements or canceling out a previous action (such as getting a wrong number when making a phone call), are examples of waffling.

Wimping is the resistance to an offer without overt negation:

A I've just bought a new blue station wagon!
B What station wagon?

Appearing inattentive, implying "I don't know," or repeating what has already been done or said are examples of wimping. In the absence of overt blocking, waffling or wimping are likely sources of blocking whenever the energy and forward momentum of a scene has been diverted or weakened.

Blocking can occur even when there is full verbal and gestural assent to an offer. This happens when the *premise* of a scene is violated by such assent:

A (menacingly) Well, are you going to clean up your room?
B (cheerfully) Oh, yes, right away!

A's offer entails a conflictual premise which B's compliance blocks.

Blocking can also involve making character choices that avoid the "danger" of advancing the action. Note the following example from Johnstone (1992):

> Ann is sitting in her "car" talking to Brian when her "Husband" arrives and starts haranguing her. Brian immediately ages 40 years, and establishes that he's just a hitchhiker. He claims that he's "trying to be original" but I see him as refusing the role of "lover," i.e., as blocking the "Husband's" attempt to get him into trouble. (p. 10)

Finally, acceptance of a tangential aspect of an offer may function as a block, akin to getting lost in details or a side-plot during the narration of a story. For instance, imagine a scene about a funeral in which character A mentions a Cadillac hearse. If B builds on this detail by bringing up how he delivered pizza in a Cadillac hearse while in college he is diverting attention and energy from the theme (the funeral).

ACCEPTING OFFERS

Accepting the other's offer entails a willingness to give up what is often experienced as one's prerogative to define self as distinct from others—a partial surrender of freedom of choice. That such freedom is seen as largely illusory from other perspectives hardly matters; Western (and particularly American) culture places such a high value on expressing individuality that anyone electing to forgo this is suspect. Being a yes-man has only negative connotations. Thus, to accept the assertions of another in an unqualified manner invites the original offerer to suspect that he is being mocked, lulled into a too-trusting stance, or in various other ways being duped. Con-men, knowing this, employ a technique called "qualifying the mark" whereby they appear initially suspicious or reluctant to accept the mark (i.e., the sucker/victim's offer of funds) and have to be "persuaded" to accept the money.

On the other hand, there is an increase in positive emotional energy in having one's offer fully accepted by another, especially when the other player advances the action by building a further offer upon the initial offer. This can lead to a euphoric experience for both players, as in the following (*Yes, And*) exchange:

A I've just bought a new blue station wagon!!
B Great! Let's go for a drive to see Aunt Harriet!
A Yes, and we'll have plenty of room to take her all the apples we picked!
B Of course! And then she'll bake us some of those fabulous apple pies, too!
[etc.]

Since improv suspends the constraints placed on imagination by realism, it is common for clients to object to playing *Yes, And* because it "isn't realistic" (i.e., that unqualified and uncritical acceptance in the "real world" will lead to delusion, folly, or exploitation). This criticism has a valid point (you'd be crazy to uncritically accept all real-life offers!), yet I'm not advocating this, only encouraging players to take the opportunity to *safely* explore (since it's enacted in a play context) the resultant freeing of emotions and imagination.

As noted above, the fear of being changed underlies blocking, which is a way of retaining control. Even when the habit of blocking is largely eliminated, improvisers resort to negativity (making offers in a critical or hostile tone) as a way of retaining the feeling of controlling. Improv teaches people to give up their tendencies to want to remain safe and to control the future.

GAMES AND EXERCISES TO TEACH ACCEPTING OFFERS

As noted above, a problem in getting adults to play is their overconcern with rules and results. RfG aims to get people to play without anticipation or judgment and then see what happens. Owning all results and playing without fear of imperfection is freeing—the meta-rule is "follow the instructions and you can't do it wrong." In improv this means "doing the form," to activate oneself and accept the offer. Honoring the instructions for improv differs from obedience to the rules of society in that no disapproval or sanction accompanies refusal, except where such refusal obstructs the freedom of others to play. Naturally, this problem will arise for some individuals who are currently exploring their power to say "no," yet by my genuinely respecting their right to refuse to participate I find they will frequently join in later, particularly if offered games in which social convention is flouted. Over time, I become more concerned with participants who never rebel than with those who do so from the outset (this issue is dealt with in Chapter 9 in greater detail).

Since, as noted before, accepting offers is fundamental to improv, all games and exercises, done in the proper spirit, will embody and teach this principle. The games that follow in this section are more basic and can be readily introduced to players without prior improv experience.

Verbal Blocking and Accepting of Offers

BLOCKING AND ACCEPTING OFFERS

This series of quick exercises and games is used to teach the variety of blocking levels described above, ending with full acceptance of verbal offers. When time permits, the entire series may be presented; otherwise, *Total Blocking*, *Yes, But*, and *Yes, And* will suffice.

Two players are asked by the therapist/director to come to the front of the group to demonstrate. They are told that this is a rehearsal and doesn't count, that the group will learn to do the exercise through their efforts. Then one player is asked to make a simple statement, for example, "The moon is blue," which the second player totally ignores, or blocks (e.g.,"I've never been to Detroit"), negating totally the reality of the partner's offer. The second player then offers a simple statement, which is blocked by the first, demonstrating the impossibility of creating a working relationship or a scene in this way. Each is isolated from the other and both look unhappy and bored. This is called *Total Blocking* and is an example of what NOT to do when improvising. Then, in pairs, the other players briefly practice *Total Blocking*.

In similar format, the group is taken through *Negating/Disputing* (each player directly contradicts the other's offer); *Yes, But* (each statement after the first offer begins with the words, "Yes, but . . . "); *Accept Verbally/ Block Physically* (the players agree verbally while disqualifying one another nonverbally, such as by shaking their heads, looking away, making facial grimaces, walking away while the other person is still speaking, etc.); *Accept Physically/Block Verbally* (players behave attentively, nodding, maintaining eye contact, etc., while at the same time negating/disputing or responding with "Yes, but . . . "); *Merely Yes* (the second player responds to the first's offer by agreement, but without adding anything else).

Accepting offers consists of the players accepting what the other does and says positively, then advancing the action through a counteroffer. The players notice and receive each offer, thereby validating, and making each other look good. This is achieved through *Yes, And* (each statement after the first offer begins with the words, "Yes, and . . . "). *Yes, And* may also be played as a group exercise, where the offers are made either randomly or in turn. When the group is endowed with the premise of solving a task, the exercise becomes a simulation of a brainstorming session.

After each exercise players are invited to report on their experiences; the therapist/director may elicit comparative responses, including reports of the energy or enthusiasm players are left with at the conclusion of each level. It can be useful to emphasize the vast difference between *Yes, But* and *Yes, And*; all due to one little word!

OVERACCEPTING

This is an exercise that explores overaccepting an offer. It gets to be outrageous and often breaks down any inhibiting self-consciousness remaining in the group. The receiving player repeats and then overaccepts the purposely-mundane, emotionally bland offer by escalating the emotional intensity, leading, after a couple of exchanges, to the fullest extreme possible. In effect, the receiving player is doing a monologue in which he explores going in the emotional direction of the initial offer as far as he can. Once he has reached his limit he makes a bland offer to the first player, who then practices overaccepting it. When physically enacted, *Overaccepting* becomes the exercise *It's Tuesday*, described with an example on page 133.

OVERACCEPTING TOGETHER

The difference between this exercise and the previous one is that a dialogue is developed in which the emotional energy increases on each turn. For example, the first player offers, "Sodas cost 75 cents in this machine" in a controlled, but slightly annoyed tone. The second player responds, with greater intensity, "Yeah, they're robbing us students blind!" The first player now "gets into it," saying loudly, "You're damned right! I'm gonna get even with this vending machine!" (mimes using a crowbar). The second player jumps alongside the first, fairly screaming, "Right!! Let's rip the damn thing wide open!!" etc.

The purpose is to give in entirely and make the other person look as wonderful, powerful, and imaginative as possible. This game creates a great deal of good will when played fully; with a little coaching, imaginations open up, causing the players to begin advancing the action physically and leading into playing full scenes.

ONE WORD AT A TIME

Two players, standing sideways with arms around each other's shoulders and looking frequently into each other's eyes, narrate an improvised story, alternating words with each other. This is a clear demonstration of co-control, where the dyad cannot function successfully without each player giving and receiving support. It is necessary to give up preconceived associations and storylines as the other player will usually give the "wrong" word; if this is accepted and built on, surprising stories spring forth, to everyone's delight.

In a sense, this game places the players in the interesting position of choosing to block their own associative patterning in order to accept their partner's offer. Every time a player gives a word she or he is anticipating a specific direction for the sentence to go toward. Players can, with a modest amount of practice, become fluent in this game. The challenge at that point is to go faster, outstripping the mind's anticipation of where the story is going.

Even experienced players can develop mind-sets that result in occasional blocking. For instance, if player A starts by giving "FOR" (thinking: "For days, Joe worried about his job"), player B might add "GIRLS" (hearing: "Four" and thinking: "Four girls went to a party"). Player A now has to give up his original idea; he offers "DRESSING" (thinking: "For girls, dressing up is fun"). Player B now has to give up *her* idea and offers "THEIR," (thinking: "Four girls dressing their dolls were surprised when Mom came home"). Player A offers "DOLLS" (thinking: "For girls dressing their dolls, boys don't yet matter"). At this point, player B, who got the next word he anticipated, quickly adds "WERE"; player A is now stumped and the game breaks down. For him, the sentence "For girls, dressing their dolls WERE . . . " appears ungrammatical, so he asks B what she had in mind. When player B explains her sentence it becomes clear that she had understood the first word as "Four" while A was operating with "For."

This game can be used as a condition in other games, or exercises, and has a number of useful additional variations. In a more advanced version the players become a single person, enacting as well as telling a first-person, present-tense narrative; the players are instructed to go on an adventure to encounter and triumph over some danger or obstacle. In another version, one player can act out the story while the alternative words are supplied by an off-stage player or audience. More than two players can tell the story and more than one word could be uttered on a player's turn. If done outdoors with eyes shut and others to serve as guides, players can experience the story as a particularly vivid coadventure. Four players in two pairs can create a scene by alternating second-person, past-tense sentences while acting these out (e.g., Pair A: "WE — were — SITTING — at — THE — lunch — COUNTER — when — RALPH — came — IN." Pair B: "WENDY — looked — SCARED — after — WE — locked — THE — front — DOOR"). The result is two intersecting narratives that promote a sense of teamwork within each pair.

Accepting Physical Offers

SOUND AND MOVEMENT

A group of players, facing inward, make a large circle around one player, who moves and makes sound randomly. At some point this player spontaneously develops a short, repetitive pattern of sound and movement and makes eye contact with one of the encircling players. The contacted player imitates the sound and movement in full detail, moving as a mirror image, and vocalizing simultaneously; gradually, while both continue the sound and movement, they exchange places. Without any break in the action, the player in the center gradually changes the sound and movement, developing her own pattern. She makes eye contact with another player on the periphery and the exercise continues until each player has been in the center at least once.

A preferred variation of this exercise is to have everyone around the circle always imitating the central player; this heightens concentration and group involvement. A more advanced variation has the moving central player begin with nonverbal sound and then develop a phrase with an accent, giving character to himself. The player replacing him in the center drops the phrase and vocalizes nonverbally until she develops her own phrase with an accent.

The therapist/director should coach players to imitate the central player in full detail and to allow offers to develop spontaneously rather than be thought-up (thought-up offers are frequently accompanied by a discontinuity of motion or sound). This exercise frees up right-brain functioning and helps players experience group support and acceptance of their offers.

TAKE ONE, GIVE TWO

A group of players forms two lines facing one another. Player A, at one end, makes eye contact with B, the player opposite him, and makes a large gesture involving his entire body with an accompanying vocal sound. A immediately repeats identically the sound and gesture (A "gives" the offer twice). B observes A the first time, remaining motionless; on A's repeat, B fully matches A's action, moving as A's mirror (B "takes" this offer). Now B makes eye contact with C, the player next to A, and gives an entirely different offer twice. C observes the first offer and takes the second. Changing the offer, C gives her offer to D, the player next to B, and so the offers zig-zag down the lines, ending with the player at the other end. Then the offers zig-zag back up the lines to the beginning player, A.

This exercise, though difficult to teach and demanding to do correctly, produces high-energy fun for everyone, especially when done as fast as possible. Although a player can see his turn coming, he has no time to think up an offer that will be useful since his full attention is given to accepting someone else's offer. Also, his part of the action is over so fast that no one will remember it to analyze it, which frees him to let go of self-evaluation.

BODY OFFERS

Body Offers are examples of exercises that Keith Johnstone (1981) calls *Blind Offers*. Two players stand face-to-face; one places his body mindlessly in an extreme position and holds it there while the other player looks at this physical offer and enacts one of three options: (1) she completes the picture in her imagination that is suggested by the body offer given by placing her own body in some corresponding pose; (2) she puts her partner's body back to neutral (gently moving him to standing upright, hands at sides) if no thought or picture comes immediately to mind; or (3) she merely copies (mirrors) the position of his physical offer. It is important to stress that the position of the player making the offer be mindless and that no one position is better than any other. It is equally important to emphasize that the responding player should not pressure her imagination to come up with a scene in order to use option (1); the other options are equally good. There is often a strong tendency to think up a "good" position, or to make a "good" scene; this kills spontaneity. The player who made the first body offer then says "thank you," ending that round, and then receives a body offer from the other player.

OBJECT RELATIONS

While physical props are not generally used in RfG, it can be useful to employ a few simple objects, such as a short stick, a piece of cloth, or a cushion, to facilitate the making and accepting of body offers among players who are more inhibited or concrete in their thinking. Player A, alone on stage, is given an object (e.g., a scarf) which she uses to begin a physical action (walk a dog, using the scarf as a leash). The action is frozen and player B enters, including himself in the scene (perhaps as the dog being walked). Once the idea is established the scene is ended.

BODY FREEZES

Players are asked to move their bodies about the room randomly at somewhat slower-than-normal speed; when the therapist/director calls "Freeze!" participants freeze in position as statues. In one version players state who, what, and where they are when called on by the therapist/director; in another version, players quietly murmur these aspects to themselves. In this way, players learn to accept offers from their own bodies.

In this exercise, it is important to coach the players that it is all right to be nobody, nowhere, and doing nothing. Moreover, neither the therapist/ director nor anyone else present should make evaluative reference or attempt to analyze any of the players' choices. By taking away evaluation and performance pressure, imagination and creative energy flow more freely.

"YES" GAME

Despite its common name as a "game," this is an energizing group warm-up exercise. One of a group of standing players spontaneously calls out: "Let's all be . . . " followed by any plural or collective noun (nuns, motorcycles, horses, the ocean, etc.) Everyone shouts "YES!" at once and proceeds to physicalize that offer. After a short while someone else shouts out "Let's all be (the next offer)!" and the group switches to enacting that thing.

I prefer this "being" version of the exercise to one where an *activity* is called out (i.e., "Let's all do . . . "), since this latter version may lead to objectionable offers (e.g., "Let's all masturbate!") or physically risky ones (e.g., "Let's all punch a hole in the wall with our heads!").

MIRRORS EXERCISE

Two players stand facing one another, remaining silent while looking into each other's eyes and focusing on breathing. The designated leader begins to move slowly and the follower mirrors the action until the therapist/director calls "Change!" and they switch roles. After calling a few alternating turns at leading and following, the therapist/director calls "Mutual!" and they give up leading or following to move simultaneously. Care should be taken by the leader to move slowly and in such a way that the follower can keep up and not be forced to break the mirror. This elementary theater exercise is profound in its simplicity. It creates a bond between the players for the following reasons: eye contact is held throughout, there is a greater awareness of the physical capacity and limitations of the other person, and players experience the constant need to give in, adjust, and trust their own internal impulses.

While players usually report a preference for leading or following, both positions are familiar. By contrast, mutuality is an elusive experience for most dyads; some players express doubt that it is even possible. It seems as though mutuality comes and goes, easily replaced by leading/following. Yet the more concentrated the players are on each other the greater the liklihood for achieving and sustaining mutuality. When attained, mutuality has a transcendent quality. As Nachmanovitch (1990) points out, "The beauty of playing together is meeting in the One" (p. 94).

VERBAL MIRRORS

Also called *Simultaneous Speech*, this exercise is the verbal equivalent of the previous physical one. Facing one another, the designated leader begins a story while the follower-partner simultaneously mimics her in facial expression, vocal inflection, and words. The therapist/director calls "Change!" from time to time, whereupon the leadership switches while the same story is continued. When the therapist/director calls "Mutual!" both players continue the story without either leading or following. If the players slow down slightly and fully concentrate on their partner, mutuality, along with a powerful sense of closeness, will occur.

ACCEPTING IN MIME

In this advanced game players enact a scene without any dialogue. This requires them to pay close attention to one another's physical actions and to use movement to indicate clearly what/where/how the story develops. A somewhat easier variation is *Accepting in Gibberish* (see p. 82) where both mime and vocal inflection convey meaning. In both games, after the scene enactment, it is instructive to ask the audience and then each player what took place. The discrepancies can be hilarious.

SIMULTANEOUS LEAVING

Also known as *Three Persons Leave the Stage for the Same Reason,* this exercise is done with three players seated in armless chairs or stools in a straight line facing the audience or group. Without any words the players are to pick up on their own and others' impulses and create a common understanding of their situation that results in them all leaving the stage at the same time and for the same reason. The players need to look at one another frequently (requiring the player seated in the middle to swivel his head frequently to stay in contact with both partners) and attune to their partners by imitating one another's slightest physical offers (a foot tapping, a frown, slumping posture, etc.). As with *Mirrors*, the end-goal is mutuality rather than leader/follower interaction. When done in accordance with these instructions, the audience will clearly know their reason for leaving.

This is a difficult exercise to do well, although the effort to improve it will be quite valuable to the entire group. The therapist/director will want to have the players start over whenever they are not attending to one another's offers or where one player blatantly leads; this is not a token of failure but part of the rehearsal process. The therapist/director should also engage the audience in discussing how a rehearsal went but, as with other improvs, should discourage evaluation or commentary on any relationship between personality and performance.

Accepting Combined Verbal and Physical Offers

FREEZE WITH A LINE

This performance game combines the elements of *Body Offers* and *Body Freezes*. One player mindlessly moves his body while his partner watches. At some point the partner calls "Freeze!" and the player becomes a statue in the position at the moment "freeze" was called. The partner places her own body in a position offered by her imagination and speaks a line of dialogue consistent with her offer. In the initial variation the exercise ends with the player saying "thank you"; the player and partner play another round with roles reversed. Another variation has the therapist/director, rather than the partner, call "Freeze!" A more advanced variation has the player begin to move after the partner's line of dialogue and respond both verbally and physically; in this way the two may start an improv scene.

FREEZE TAG

Also known as *Space Jump*, this is an exercise of intermediate difficulty for at least three players; it also works well for small groups. Two players begin a scene while the other players wait off-stage. The therapist/director calls "Freeze!" when the players are in physically interesting positions; the performing players become statues in their positions and one of the off-stage players promptly "tags" (taps the back or shoulder of) one of the performers, placing her body in the precise position of the tagged player, who moves off-stage. Then, using the physical offer of the still-static body positions, she speaks a line of dialogue that begins the action of an entirely different scene. This new scene continues until "Freeze!" is again called; another off-stage player comes in, tags the player who has been on stage longer, begins a new scene, and so forth. A variation in which a therapist/director is not needed has the off-stage players wait in line; the player at the front of the line calls the freeze and enters the scene by tagging one of the players, who then goes to the rear of the line.

As an example, suppose players A and B have been playing a scene in which A has proposed marriage on bended knee to a seated B. At this point "Freeze!" is called and C enters, tagging out A. C now says to B, "First I'll pull you loose, Miss Shepherd, then we'll find those kids who put Crazy Glue on your chair," which establishes a classroom scene.

Freeze Tag develops flexibility in letting go of a mind-set in order to create something new in the moment. This is equally true for both the tagging player (player C in the example above) and the remaining player (player B above), who must give up the previously established role from the prior scene and accept a role consistent with C's offer.

GAMES WITH A BLOCKING PREMISE

While accepting all offers is the fundamental premise of improvising, the following are examples of how blocking can be implicit at some level in the rules. In addition to variations on *Yes, But* these are among a number of games and exercises that explore the constructive side of blocking. Here, the main distinction is between blocking that creates a scene through challenge and contrast, and one that prevents a scene from advancing or developing. Even when some blocking is acceptable, the rule about accepting offers still applies to the fundamental agreement about playing and to every other aspect of the scene.

WHAT ARE YOU DOING?

Two players, A and B, stand alongside each other. A begins a repetitive motion and B asks, "What are you doing?" A immediately names some activity *un*related to the motion he is doing (thereby blocking his own body offer) and B begins to move in accordance with A's stated activity. Now A asks, "What are you doing?" and B must instantly answer with a verbal self-block of his movement. The game continues until one breaks the rule, usually by answering with the activity his body is currently carrying out or by being unable to answer at once.

BORIS/DORIS

This complex game can be thought of as a playing of the projection (or catastrophic fantasy) that others are forcing a person to cooperate or accept offers. The scene is that of an interrogation, with A as the interrogator and B as the suspect. B sits on a stool or armless chair while A paces around him asking questions like, "Are you known as Lefty LaRue?" B answers uncooperatively, or not at all; he looks at the ceiling, insolently tells the interrogator to go to hell, asks the interrogator *his* name, says, "What if I am?" etc. A now explains that he will be compelled to call on Boris (who is invisible only to the audience), a seven-foot enforcer who demonstrates he means business by roughing up B. (B's eyes widen with fright; he screams in terror and/or pain and acts as though he is being hauled to his feet and strangled, thrown across the stage, his arm twisted, etc.) Much shaken, B collapses on his chair and A, acting quite in control, resumes the interrogation. Whenever A isn't satisfied with B's answer he motions for Boris to come forward to compel B to cooperate. The scene is usually played to where B eventually confesses all, but it can also develop where Boris is the one beaten up, B never breaks despite fearsome torture, or Boris is bribed to turn on A. Another version of this game is *Doris*, where seduction takes the place of brutality in advancing the action. And, of course, all parts, including the imaginary ones, can be played by either gender.

This game is very rich in possible applications (for one thing, young children are fascinated by both roles and thoroughly enjoy interrogating parents). The scene can also be set as a spouse questioning a partner, a tax audit, etc. Regarding blocking, B is actually in charge of what Boris does to him, so he can explore the choices of compliance and defiance of A's questions. On another level there is agreement about the premise of the scene, the roles A and B enact and also the audience (both outside and within the players) to be entertained. If B chooses to resist heroically the effect often becomes tragic or ugly and also feels anticlimactic (due to the action being stuck, rather than advancing toward completion of the story (i.e., the confession).

Asymmetrical Blocking and Accepting

In the following games, one player blocks and the other accepts.

STOP AND GO

Here, player A accepts all of player B's offers, while B blocks all offers of A, yet adds offers of her or his own. For example:

A Hello, Mary!
B (stiffly) I'm not Mary, I'm her sister Janet.
A Oh, yes, Mary told me she was a twin. Glad to meet you.
B No you're not. You were hoping for a night of hot romance!
A Er, well, it's true. So Mary will be coming over soon, then?
B Of course not. She sent me to tell you it's over.
[etc.]

Notice that B is equally responsible for cocreating this scene and that both players are advancing the action. A variation is to have the accepter (player A) make negative offers, the blocking of which (by player B) becomes positive:

A Hello, Mary!
B (brightly) I'm not Mary, I'm her sister Janet.
A Yes, you don't really sound alike.
B (reassuringly) Oh, yes we do. I happen to have a cold.
A You don't think I'll catch it from you, do you?
B (triumphantly) Why, yes, you will. My colds are infallibly contagious!
[etc.]

As Johnstone (1992) notes, there is pleasure in seeing the blocking "aggressor" being manipulated by the apparently submissive accepter. This will become clearer after learning more about status (Chapter 7).

NO, YOU DIDN'T

Here, A begins a fictitious first-person narrative. After about two sentences, B interjects "No, you didn't," "No it wasn't," or some other challenge to the content of A's story. A must at once accept the block and change his story to incorporate B's contradiction. B continues to interject a negation after every couple of sentences. A will find that B's interjections actually aid his imagination, *provided* he gives up the need to control the story (which is why this game won't work with a factual narrative).

BLOCKING OR ACCEPTING LISTS

In this game, two lists are drawn up, one consisting of verbal *blocking* statements (such as "No," "You must be joking," "Drop dead," etc.) and the other of *accepting* ones (such as, "Yes," "Sounds good to me," "I'll go along with that," etc.). One player is assigned one of these lists and gives *only* one or another of the items on his list as a response to whatever offer is made by the improvising other player.

This game is useful in training chronic yea-saying or nay-saying clients to play fully the opposite response as well as to free players from having to come up with verbal offers so they can attend to some other aspect of the enactment (such as body offers).

CLINICAL ASPECTS OF BLOCKING

The example of *Boris* illustrates one way that improv for therapeutic purposes diverges from stage performances: What an outside audience wants to see is not the decisive factor in determining the choices made when a game is used for clinical purposes. A problem in the use of improv games for theatrical performance, or wherever the reaction of observers is significant to the players, is that the audience often prefers to see the offerer blocked and frustrated, so the performers become reinforced by audience laughter or applause and engage in still more blocking. Eventually, this can degenerate into players becoming so competitive at being more clever than others that there is scarcely any acceptance of offers or narrative development in their scenes. In RfG, it is imperative that the therapist/director remain alert to early signs of such pandering (Johnstone [1993] also refers to it as "whoring for laughs") and gently discourage it (without crushing the playful spirit) in order to keep the work on purpose.

The principal clinical use of working on blocking and accepting offers is in relationship therapies (group, couple, and family therapies). Since only the full acceptance of offers will permit scenes to advance, characters to develop, and positive relationship energy to build, the therapist/director will need to encourage and demonstrate accepting offers and coach players to accept offers when they block—unless his sole purpose is to assess the degree of alignment and cooperation between the players. Even then, immediately side-coaching a player to accept an offer he just blocked usually permits the game/exercise/scene to continue and adds information regarding whether the blocking player can accept the therapist/director's coaching. When the aim includes training players in the use of improv principles and objectives, coaching also helps players realize both the extent of their blocking (which they are typically unaware of) and the resulting contrast in affect and energy between blocked and accepted offers.

Having clients report their experiences with games featuring blocking and accepting offers is also helpful to others. For example, Sam, a new man in a therapy group, cultivated a "prankster" persona. During the latter half of his first group session and throughout his second he acted as the group clown, entertaining other members but also irritating them by disrupting group process. When playing a scene he "hogged the show," mugging and gagging, refusing to accept fully the character offers of others. When in the audience he called out lines of dialogue that, while witty, disrupted the process of the players on stage. When the group members confronted Sam with their annoyance at his conduct, his demeanor changed strikingly. With eyes lowered and a soft, faraway voice, he responded that he felt too afraid to let others control him. This admission immediately led to a softening of the group anger that had been directed toward Sam and induced other members to voice their own problems with blocking and being blocked. One member feelingly described the demoralizing effect of having his offers blocked. Another spoke of her mixed feelings at being both entertained and ignored. In further processing it also became clear that Sam had relied on his "prankster" to adaptively "get by" in binding situations arising at least as far back as middle childhood in his family of origin. Later, when offered roles in which he could explore the safe acceptance of offers, Sam rapidly became a supportive group member, accepting offers about as well as most of the other group members.

When blocking clients report a feeling of vulnerability, or display distress at fully accepting the offer of another, it is a strong indication that they have something "at stake" in the exercise regarding their status (see Chapter 7). Possible status reasons for player A's blocking include: (a) to raise A's own status, either in relation to B or to onlookers; (b) to lower B's status, (that is, to invalidate B, or make B "look bad" in the eyes of onlookers; (c) to avoid the lowering of A's own status as distinct from (a); and (d) to demonstrate independence from/defiance of the therapist/director, thereby blocking the therapist's offer of "accepting offers."

Blocking that is manifested in improv often parallels the difficulties present in a relationship. Paul and Marcie, an engaged couple, were asked to try the game *One Word at a Time.* Paul spoke first, alternating words with Marcie; what follows is the verbatim story (Paul's words appearing in CAPITALS.)

I—am—COMING—home—TO—from (FROM? . . . yes)—THE—green—HOUSE—which—(pause) WILL—cover—UP—all—THESE—(pause) curtains—THAT—are—MINE.   You—CAN'T—hope—MY—mother—WILL—free—UP—any—DISTRAC-TION—that—SHE—brings—ME.

This was narrated in a tense, disjointed manner, with little eye contact. Immediately following the exercise Marcie complained that she had had to do all the hard work, that Paul had taken the "easy" words. For his part, Paul was condescending and irritated in explaining his attempts to "keep the story on track." Apart from the content pointing to a mother-in-law triangle it became clear that Paul and Marcie were having considerable difficulty in sharing control. (The more general issue of using improv exercises to assess relationships is discussed in Chapter 9.)

Through spontaneity we are re-formed into ourselves. It creates an explosion that for the moment frees us from handed-down frames of reference, memory choked with old facts and information and undigested theories and techniques of other people's findings.

—Viola Spolin (1963, p. 4)

The only thing that makes life possible is permanent, intolerable uncertainty; not knowing what comes next.

—Ursula LeGuin (cited in Anonymous, 1989, p. 86)

CHAPTER 5

Freeing the Imagination

Rfg IS, AT THE CORE, playful exploration of possibility in the service of personal growth. In life, what keeps us safe, but limited, is curtailing the use of imagination or censoring its products.

As already noted in Chapter 4, improv has clearly defined principles, the most important being the acceptance of all offers, including those that arise in one's own imagination. The difficulty that most of us have in accepting offers at least some of the time (and for some of us, nearly all the time) arises clearly when we attempt to improvise. One plausible explanation for this difficulty is—not surprisingly—prevalent childrearing practices. The typical socialization of children involves both negative, limit-setting rule-enforcement and adults "correcting" and redefining children's reality. By repeatedly invalidating the child's constructs and requiring conformity to their own reality, adults teach children two unfortunate lessons: (1) by their example, to invalidate (block) and ignore the offers of others; and (2) as a consequence of their influence, to doubt and censor the offers of imagination.

77

Blocking the offers of others, then, stems from the first unfortunate lesson. When we block, we feel powerful by thwarting others (as every two-year-old who exclaims "No!" discovers). Such power is achieved, however, at the expense of connection to others—it is only a defensive power resulting at best in being left alone. In real life, people not infrequently *refuse* to support others in order to look powerful. Improv training demonstrates how people can feel playful and powerful by attending to and supporting others, even by making *others* look good. In the play-world of RfG, a sequence of games and exercises is offered so that participants experience making each other look and feel powerful. The frequent shifting of power creates trust and ease with one another: I trust that I can fairly give you power now because I know you'll extend it to me soon.

As adults we have learned all too well the second unfortunate lesson: to censor our imaginations. A curtailed imagination seemingly does us no harm, but we unknowingly miss out on much of our potential for creative fulfillment and the playful enjoyment of life. Self-blocking makes us over-socialized, conventional, and defines us by our own perceived limitations— characteristics we rightly associate with being grown-up. Relative to our childhoods, we adults play less freely and less frequently. Moreover, play-fulness is often absent in games where "winning/losing" and "being good at/not good at" take precedence over "learning from" and "having fun at." As David Waters (1993) notes, almost no one "plays" tennis, in the sense of "being playful"; we compete at it. As a relearning experience, improv is at once play and training in accessing playfulness.

Since we adults tend to censor imagination automatically, in RfG we stay alert to the tendency to fall back on some piece of behavior, a character or witticism that worked for us in the past (following J. L. Moreno's [1934] construct of "cultural conserves," we might term these "personal conserves") and encourage players to act upon impulses spontaneously; that is, *before* thinking about them.* As Sperber (1974) puts it: "One gains the most when spontaneously reacting to the moment, searching always for new avenues of expression, avoiding the pattern that 'worked' successfully in the past" (pp. 2–3). Since improvising in RfG is done in a context of safety and permissiveness, we can repattern to bypass the learned behavior of "looking before we leap." The price of unlearning this caution is encountering the fear of risking our dignity. Yet, to the extent we release ourselves to uncensored spontaneity, we experience the delight and aliveness of childhood play. As an additional benefit, improvising then offers us choices to

---

*Moreno was explicitly critical of those who, like the acting teacher Stanislavsky, would use improvisation to activate memories of the past rather than achieve spontaneity in the present. See Moreno, 1983, pp. 101–102.

broaden the range and variety of whom we allow ourselves to be, as we once did as children.

On our way to becoming adults we learn to "get by" in life by staying with what we believe we are good at and by offering others only that side of ourselves that will convince them to accept what we are comfortable showing. Social politeness, of course, requires the same pretense of others: Don't challenge my mask and I won't challenge yours. Children, as we know, often subvert this collusive social arrangement; they will tactlessly point out that the emperor has no clothes. From the RfG viewpoint, children are not imperfectly socialized adults; rather adults are overly-tamed children who have lost much of their original zest and spontaneity.

> [I]t can sometimes be a heartbreaking struggle for us to arrive at a place where we are no longer afraid of the child inside us. We often fear that people won't take us seriously, or that they won't think us qualified enough. For the sake of being accepted, we can forget our source and put on one of the rigid masks of professionalism or conformity that society is continually offering us. The child-like part of us is the part that, like the Fool, simply does and says, without needing to qualify himself or strut his credentials. (Nachmanovitch, 1990, p. 50)

IMAGINARY SENSORY EXPLORATION

It is well-known that attending fully to sensory experience regularly enables adults to access imagery, emotion, childhood memories, as well as a heightened sense of being in the present moment (the here and now). What is less well-recognized is that activating the imagination will reliably access sense-memory and invention in the moment.

HANDS OUT

The players stand in a circle and one at a time walk to the center, then stop, put their hands out and "see" what they land on, describing the sensation or object out loud. If the player relaxes mind and hand, allowing the object to be felt to the touch, there is a wonderful sense of surprise and knowing; a picture, a sensation or a voice usually appears in the imagination. The therapist/director may guide this experience by asking such questions, as: "What color is it?" or "How old are you in this moment?" This practice in spontaneity is basic to learning that the imagination and creativity work easily if we practice getting our thinking out of the way.

BREAKING CONVENTIONAL LOGIC

> Do you remember, when you were born, everyone around you laughed while you were weeping? Resolve to live your life so that, at your death, others will weep while you laugh. (Traditional Persian Saying)

RfG is not merely a vehicle for allowing spontaneity; it is also a non-chemical means (though not a reliable technology) of accessing altered thinking patterns. Such changes in point of view unlock a higher wisdom, what the Russian mystic P. D. Ouspensky (1971) called "thinking in other categories."

In a less profound but still very useful way improv can challenge the assumptions and conventions that shape our narratives. One anecdotal example comes from Keith Johnstone (1988, p. 14). He asked a group of actors to improvise a deathbed scene with a dying father, daughter nursing him, and son arriving home with a new wife. The characters began the scene looking serious and unhappy, speaking in hushed tones, but the scene was so false that the class was soon laughing hysterically. Johnstone stopped the scene and apologized to the actors for setting them a trap.

ACTOR But what was so funny?

JOHNSTONE You were trying to show us how unhappy you were!

ACTOR But it's a deathbed scene!

JOHNSTONE Ah, but how do the characters know?

ACTOR Er . . . he's very ill. The doctor says he's dying!

JOHNSTONE But will he die in the next five minutes? In half an hour? Tomorrow? Next week? He may drag on for months!

Johnstone then asked them to suggest a purpose for each character. The actors offered: "to make Father comfortable," "to express her love," and so on.

JOHNSTONE Too monotonous and too sentimental! And you're all trying to look like nice considerate people — it's too predictable. How about the father's purpose being to cheer everyone up?

ACTOR But he's dying!

JOHNSTONE He doesn't know it's going to happen in the next five minutes, and people don't necessarily change character just because they're ill. Maybe Dad's always tried to cheer other people up! And let's add the daughter trying to get sympathy, the son trying to give everyone a bad time and the wife trying to make them think she's intelligent.

Johnstone then showed the actors how to construct and play *Behavioral Lists* (p. 137) — not only to create involving scenes but give them permission to expand their use of self.

It should be added that repeated practice at improvising in general heightens awareness regarding personal assumptions, unmasks fears, and increases tolerance for incongruity.

CALLING OBJECTS THE WRONG NAME

This is a very good warm-up for a group of players. Everyone at once runs from object to object in the room, points to each, and shouts its wrong name (i.e., any word other than that normally used to denote that object, such as calling a chair "democracy," an ear "ceiling," etc.). Sensory perceptions are heightened, colors get brighter, sounds sharper, and people report feeling refreshed.

BACKWARD SCENE

In this advanced and mind-bending game, a final tableau is established on stage, such as one player lying dead on the floor and the others in position as murderer, bereaved friend, medical expert, etc. The idea is to play the scene backward in steps separated by minimal pauses in the action. For example:

[Final Tableau: female player B lying on the floor, male players A and C kneeling sorrowfully over her.]

A Oh, no, Susan!! [all three stand up; A mimes pointing a gun at B and firing] Bang!

B Pete, don't do it! [positions C in her place, steps aside briefly and then jumps in front of C]

A I . . . I'll never give you up, Susan . . . and as for *you* . . . [mimes drawing a gun from waistband]

C [pulls B down to a lying position next to himself in lying position across room; sits up] Pete, its time you knew . . . we love each other.

A [walks up to B and C lying together on floor and stops, looking down in disbelief] I just came home because . . . Susan, what's going on here?

B [Mimes hiding C under covers] Oh my God, Walter, it's Pete! [sits up]

A [walks backward to opposite side of stage] Hi, Susan, I'm home! [mimes slamming door]

[etc.]

This looks impossible to do spontaneously, yet skilled improvisers can create a wonderful scene like this. For clinical purposes the result is not as important as the process, which usually provokes a lot of laughter as players get mixed up and do or say things out of correct (reverse) sequence. This game, therefore, acts as a diagnostic indicator of how important getting things right is to clients in couples, families, or groups.

EMOTIONAL SHORT-CIRCUIT

A nonimprov technique is the following Zen-like acting exercise: First, have the client(s) think of a happy time in their lives and physically cry over it, then have the client think of a terrifying or depressing incident and laugh out loud. I haven't heard a satisfactory description of how people manage this, but people often can at least fake the crying or laughing; as Annette Goodheart (personal communication, 1992) points out, the diaphragm doesn't know the difference between the fake and the real emotion, and soon the genuine emotion often supplants the faked one. The effects of doing this exercise are experienced as profound and far-reaching; people discover that their story about the incident is wide open to reinterpretation and that they have the power to "decouple" their emotional responses from the content. The following (more advanced) improv game serves a similar purpose.

MONSTERPIECE THEATER

In *Monsterpiece Theater*, also classified as a type of lists game, a common list of repulsive attributes or endowments—which can include emotional states, personal mannerisms, hygenic habits, ways of treating others, physical characteristics, etc.—is first created by the group. Next, the therapist/director selects the attributes (usually no more than three) that each player is to incorporate into her or his character during a given scene of any number of players (alternatively, the attributes may be selected at random). As a warm-up to the scene, or when working with less-experienced players, the therapist/director may have the players assume character with their attributes in a *Monster Party* in which they mill about, briefly pairing off with different partners just long enough to establish all their endowments before moving on to another partner. After the scene, players share reports of their inner difficulties and offer feedback to each other regarding the outer convincingness of the characterizations. In practice this game is easier to enact than *Play the Monster* (described on p. 139), since the player has been assigned endowments which are not necessarily his own worst nightmare.

GIBBERISH ENCOUNTER

Gibberish refers to nonsense speech; that is, syllables not intelligible in any language known to those present ("Cho buxta prembihana," for example). Gibberish is a very useful device in improv, as it gets players away from attending to speech content and focuses them on vocal expressiveness and body language. Warm-up exercises to familiarize clients with gibberish are given in Chapter 8 under *Gibberish Emotions*.

In the preliminary (warm-up) phase of this group exercise, created by Gloria Maddox, two players stand on opposite sides of the room, backs to each other. The therapist/director calls out a nationality, emotion, or occupation, whereupon the players turn and walk toward each other, simulating a meeting in the street between two persons sharing the given endowment, gesturing and speaking in gibberish to one another. In the next (main) phase, the players return to their original positions and are asked to think up a brief story about a new character (unrelated to who they were in the first phase), such as: "I'm a 45-year-old housewife who's feeling guilty that I've gained eight pounds and haven't been to the gym for a week." The players are told that when they turn around they will be on a street and will meet someone with whom they have a significant personal relationship; they will discover the identity of that person and what the relationship is only when they turn around. Once they "recognize" the other person they are to play a brief scene in gibberish with them. The therapist/director calls out "Start!" and the players turn, walk toward one another, and begin their scene. The therapist/director then ends the scene and asks the audience to say what they saw going on. Then, each player is asked to describe her or his character, who the significant other was to them, and what she or he thought was going on during the scene.

Suppose that player A, whose character was described above, sees player B as her ex-husband, with whom she still has an antagonistic relationship. Player B, meanwhile, has made his character a former businessman who has renounced the world and is now an Enlightened Being. He has just returned from a mountaintop to spread peace and joy to the world; to him, A is his former secretary and a potential first convert. As A sees B, her body stiffens; she glares and speaks angrily in gibberish. B, who has been gliding along with a beatific smile, speaks soothing gibberish and extends his hand to comfort this agitated soul. A sees this snake of an ex-husband as out to con her into forgiving his nonpayment of alimony, and her fury redoubles. B is puzzled by her conduct; he regards her conduct as a test of his compassion and vows to win her over by the power of divine love. The scene is ended as both of them further exaggerate their positions.

Players of this exercise get to experience the effects of dealing with their own inital disconfirmed expectations, as the other player will most often appear to behave quite strangely. However, players will almost always find a way to interpret the conduct of the other character as consistent with their original framing. In this way the scene corresponds to the structure of theatrical farce and illustrates how the mind actively and persistently construes the world according to its established frame of reference (psychological set). The audience members will most often get the point of view of one of the players, less frequently pick up both viewpoints accurately, and occasionally see something quite different from either player.

GIVING UP OVERCONTROL
(ATTAINING NONANXIOUS FLEXIBILITY)
OF BODY, IDEAS, AND EMOTIONS

Overcontrol refers to the dynamic whereby one or more persons strives to alter the behavior of others beyond what is functionally neccessary to their relationship. Overcontrol is a practically infallible sign of anxiety; all of us overcontrol others some of the time and some of us do so all of the time. At the core of the following games and exercises is the device of not allowing one player the use of a faculty that is under the control of another player. In order to play the scene the players must cooperate in an unfamiliar way, requiring them to experience a novel type of interdependence. This format is particularly useful for demonstrating the importance of underlying overcontrolling in an established relationship, since clients are usually unaware of its extent.

THE BLOB

This exercise is also known as *Speaking in One Voice.* Two or more players form a line by linking arms around each other's waists or shoulders and move and speak in unison as a single person (the blob), either to another blob or in response to questions from the audience. Blob members are instructed neither to lead nor follow but to speak simultaneously while maintaining eye contact with one another (although this instruction is an ideal rather than what actually happens most of the time). When the blob moves, all its members are part of its body, with the players on the ends supplying the arms and hands. This is an elementary improv exercise that, nonetheless, calls for the same elusive mutuality of *Mirrors* (p. 70), *Verbal Mirrors* (p. 70), and *Simultaneous Leaving* (p. 70).

The therapist/director should encourage the blob to speak more rapidly so that there are mix-ups in which some words are garbled. In doing so, this becomes a good exercise to decondition players from the fear of failure, since speaking different words simultaneously is no one player's fault. Screwing up good-naturedly in the company of others actually promotes a bonding experience among players and between players and the audience (who actually wants to see things screwed up).

POET'S CORNER

Two players, one a poet from another planet or country, and the other a translator, take the stage. The poet, speaking gibberish (as described earlier) while performing broad and varied body movements, pauses periodically to allow the second player to translate the poem. At first, the poet need not know anything and is free to move and make sounds at will; later, he attempts to incorporate the translation into his gesturing and vocalizing. The translator, taking abstract visual and sound cues from the poet, speaks whatever comes into her head, creating a poem of seemingly great philosophical depth and merit; both are loudly applauded for courage, if not for literary ability.

The satisfaction of this exercise lies in its capacity to please the audience (which includes the players themselves) by adopting a confident and vigorous stance. Actually, the players can hardly fail to create the event of a poem, since what an audience expects from a poetry reading requires a minimum of structure, and any apparent mismatch between the length of a turn of gibberish and its translation, or between the antics of the poet and the contents of the translation, adds to the amusement. When the exercise goes well, however, the players will experience that they have cocreated the story of the poem.

PUPPETS

One player (the puppeteer) moves the body of another (the puppet) who is giving a lecture on a supposed field of expertise, and who is incorporating these body offers into the talk. The puppet is not limp, but holds her or his body where it is put until the puppeteer changes the position. Any repetitive motion begun by the puppeteer is continued by the puppet until halted by the puppeteer. Both players influence each other and accept offers, thereby taking the burden off one another and freeing themselves from prepared ideas in order to respond to what is happening in the present moment. Scenes involving two puppets may also be played.

Children appear fascinated with this game, particularly when they get to manipulate their parents as puppets. I have found that children between the ages of four and nine nearly always try to get their parents in trouble, often by having the puppet put a finger up her or his nose.

One of the sociological functions of play is to sanction forbidden behavior by providing a special context for it (such as Days of Fools and Lords of Misrule in the highly hierarchical medieval societies); because of this play context, parental authority is not truly undermined in *Puppets*.

ARMS-THROUGH PUPPETS

This game features two players playing the part of one character. One player (A) stands or is seated with his hands behind his back while the other (B) stands, crouches, or kneels (depending on the players' relative heights) close behind and sticks her arms forward underneath his armpits to make the character's arms. In the simplest version, the character gives a speech to the audience as an expert on some topic. A controls everything except, of course, the arms and hands of the character. Player A attempts to play the scene normally at first, although his arms seem to have a life of their own, making inappropriate and/or distracting gestures, that have to be justified. It is B's job to break the routine of the speech by unusual behavior, which A has to justify (in stage performances, A is frequently given a jacket with small physical props in its pockets for B to use to complicate A's task). In more advanced versions, two or more characters (usually seated next to one another, as in an interview), play a scene in which the arms of each character can interact with the arms and body of the other character. More than most improvs, *Arms-Through Puppets* may occasion conventional body touching boundary violations; the therapist/director should be explicit in setting rules for touching and be discriminating about whom to use this game with.

DUBBING

In this game, the on-stage players have control of their bodies but their voices are supplied by another player off-stage; on-stage players lip-sync what their off-stage voices are saying. In the easier version, one on-stage and one off-stage player cotell a third-person narrative, starting from physical movement. In a more advanced version, a scene is played between two or more on-stage players, each with his own off-stage voice. A different variation (which is also more difficult) is for on-stage players to speak for one another; it is even possible for three players to do this, with A speaking for B, B speaking for C, and C speaking for A. As with other shared narratives, if the responsibility is shared all around there is spontaneity, ease, and the lightness of being in the moment. Thinking ahead of time what to say or do takes one out of the moment and follows a kind of logic largely devoid of intuition and inspiration.

There is a greater tendency for the voice player to offer sexual, scatological, or aggressive offers in *Dubbing* scenes than in games where the voice-player's body is on stage; the quasi-anonymity seems to bring out such naughtiness. Sometimes this is done playfully to get the body-player into trouble (see Chapter 6). *Dubbing* scenes in which the partners play one character are useful for real-life couples who can experience a different sort of shared control in their relationship.

LITTLE VOICE

One player on-stage (character A) is walking along when an off-stage player (character B) begins to speak to A. Startled, A cannot at first locate B (who is a small, talking creature or object) but then they connect. The further premise is that B has a favor to ask of A. Since B is only an off-stage voice A has to create B's physical location, size, and attributes for the audience. A variation is to reverse the sizes and have B become a Big Voice (God, a giant, planet Earth, etc.).

As in *Dubbing* scenes, this game (also called *Off-Stage Voice*) permits players who are inhibited about displaying themselves on-stage to play the role of character B. Since the premises insure the resulting scenes to be fantastic, both players have to contend with the unconventional (in contrast to many games in which the characters are living in a "normal" world, despite functioning under extraordinary constraints).

HE SAID/SHE SAID

In this narrative-voice game for two players, each controls his or her own speech and controls the other's body movements through instructions as the storyteller. For example, player A begins by speaking in character: "Well, Amanda, I'd better start looking for the treasure." At the end of A's speaking turn, player B says: " . . . he said, *picking up a shovel and digging a hole.*" B thereby names the action that A then mimes; B then speaks in character as Amanda: "I guess Grandpaw wanted you to be the rich one when he gave you that pirate map, Jed." A, continuing to dig, says: " . . . she said, *pointing a pistol at him and motioning him to hand over the treasure-chest.*" B then extends one hand as though pointing a gun while motioning toward her feet with the other hand, as A speaks in character as Jed: "Why, Amanda, I didn't know money meant so much to you!" B says: " . . . he said, *holding his hands straight over head, his eyes wide with terror,*" etc. Emotional states may be used as offers, (e.g., "he said unhappily") but there should always be at least one movement instruction on each "he/she said" turn.

To play this game coherently, active coaching may be needed at first. This form takes some getting used to, since inexperienced players will tend to forget (a) that they may only move when, and according to, the other's instruction, and (b) that they have to supply the movement instructions for the other player before they speak in character. Not only are the players collaborating closely to create a story, but both are making offers to one another's body which directly opens up their imaginations. This game is also great for getting the other player playfully in trouble by making offers like, " . . . she said, sticking out her tongue and waggling her hips," an offer that will often require ingenuity to justify within the scene and will usually result in a reciprocating getting-into-trouble offer.

BORING SCENE

The premise of this game (also known as *Serious Scene*) is for each player to follow, in a naturalistic way, the logic of the character and setting given at the beginning of the scene without being original, clever, or funny. This instruction gets players to focus more on being their character and attending to the relationship between the characters. Paradoxically, the resulting enactments are not usually boring to watch, as the choices made to advance the action stem from an inner consistency that can reveal each player's real-life choices and attitudes. A *Boring Scene*, by lessening performance pressure, reveals how interesting to the audience it can be to watch someone doing something, rather than indicating doing it. *Boring Scene* is similar to the use of improv in much of drama therapy. Players who have become accustomed to hiding behind comic exaggeration or making fantastic offers will find this game most worthwhile.

What matters is that lives do not serve as models; only stories do
that.

— Carolyn Heilbrun (1988, p. 37)

[T]he narrative metaphor proposes that persons live their lives by
stories — that these stories are shaping of life, and that they have
real, not imagined, effects — and that these stories provide the
structure of life.

— Michael White (1993, p. 36)

CHAPTER 6

Storymaking:
Cocreating New Realities

NARRATIVE, UNDERSTOOD as the process of the mind operating in the
narrative mode (Chapter 2), is a way of making sense of the totality of
experience. Out of this totality we select particular sets of events and construct our stories. Once constructed, these stories organize cognition, attention, and memory. All of us develop habitual patterns of self-referential
storytelling, leading to the impression of a consistent self-image; put into
theatrical terms, we develop one or more characters, operating within a
limited range of plot choices. The stories clients present in therapy about
themselves and their lives tend to be problem stories; that is, they are
dominated by themes of obstacles, limitations, restraints.

When these same individuals operate in other relationships and different
social contexts, different themes may emerge. Thus, each social encounter
entails a greater possibility for new perspectives, other self-images, and

different meanings to develop. However, relationships (of which therapy is an instance) develop their own patterns in which the partners mutually define the characters of self and other. By shifting the context of the relationship, as all psychotherapy attempts to do, change in the social reality of character and relationship becomes possible. RfG is a technique for shifting that relationship context, both in terms of the characters that participate and the rules of interaction, so that different stories emerge.

GOOD NARRATIVE TECHNIQUE:
STRUCTURE, NOT CONTENT

Just as there is a correspondence between adhering to principles and objectives of good improvising and good relationship functioning, stories that are aesthetically pleasing and dramatically absorbing correspond to those that define our reality in both a meaningful and healthful way. Within Bruner's paradigmatic mode of thought (described in Chapter 2) theories are judged as better to the extent that they are more elegant, more predictively powerful, and having a wider capacity to encompass other known facts. Within the narrative mode, a story is seen as more insightful when there is greater coherence in its structure, greater universality in its message, and greater artistry in its performance.

While clinicians working with therapeutic narrative are generally attentive to both the content and the affective components of client stories, they seldom attend to storytelling as performance and hence pay less attention to their presentation, organization, or structure. An exception is Roberts (1994), who has developed a number of ways of working with storytelling in family therapy and classifies narratives told by family members along a number of dimensions, among them: how the story is linked to the stories of other members; how the members divide up the narration or supplement the parts of the story that others have told; from which or whose perspective the story is told; to what extent stories resonate with, parallel, or contradict one another; how historically rooted or detailed a story is; to what extent the story points to a hidden text; how open the narrator of the story is to alternative meanings; how variable the stories are when retold.

As noted in Chapter 1, it is the *deixis* (pointing out/pointing to) and *ostension* (showing/displaying) that distinguishes dramatic performance from narrative. Traditional societies have employed storytelling as a method of promoting relatedness, preserving culture, and building a sense of community. In such settings the performance of storytelling is itself healing, in that the teller is not only locating self in role and in the characters of the story, but is also serving the community by taking up that role.

Psychotherapy is conducted within a framework that intentionally separates it from the rules of discourse that apply in public and communal life. Therapy is viewed as a semiprivate enterprise that offers clients an opportunity to drop their social masks, truthfully attending to and bringing forth aspects of self that would ordinarily render them vulnerable to shame and social rejection. In order to establish the safety of client self-revelation the therapeutic profession has not only appropriated the legal device of privileged communication but created a therapeutic persona that presents clients with a nonjudgmental, attentive, client-focused audience.

How an audience is affected by a storytelling performance, and what it desires to hear told, or to see enacted, is an influential yet relatively neglected dimension of therapeutic narrative. As audience, we are affected by the performer and the performance; as Coles (1990) puts it, "This is what we do as we hear a storyteller speak: let our own imagination, our past experiences, our various passions and problems, help form images that accompany the words we're hearing" (p. 334). In psychotherapy, the therapist, therapeutic team/system, or therapy group become an audience—at once catalyst, guide, and witness, yet constrained from interacting fully as an audience with an acknowledged right to be involved out of its own interest. I am not arguing that this is itself altogether undesirable, only that this position is limiting (another dimension of this issue, the therapist-as-performer with the client-as-audience, was mentioned in Chapter 1; the subject of therapist-as-performer with professional peers-as-audience is discussed in Chapter 13). In contrast to professionally conducted psychotherapy, the current fashion of retelling personal stories in a more public space (such as confessional celebrity books and interviews, television talk shows, and twelve-step testimonials) serves the dual functions of therapeutic (reparative) process and a means of creating a semblance of caring community.

A distinction should be made between narratives that are attempts to reconstruct and recount the remembered experience of the teller; those that are the retelling of second-hand stories; and those that are intended as inventions. However, these distinctions are not simply those between fact and fiction. As Nye (1993) explains,

> From the constructivist viewpoint, no objective veridical description of events is possible. All stories, all accounts, are elaborations of "reality" that are "constructed." The particular story that is told is the result of the interplay between experience and individual and cultural frames and meanings, which the teller selects (consciously or unconsciously) to employ at that moment, in that setting, for that audience. This description of the process of telling personal narratives is much closer to a description of the creative process. (p. 17)

As noted by early Gestalt experimental psychologists, the retelling of a story from memory, even one based upon recent and nontraumatic events, involves distortions, omissions, and transformations which are not random but follow principles of organization.

Beginning with psychoanalysis, psychotherapies rooted in historical truth have placed emphasis on the curative power of recalling and telling stories in the form of traumatic memories. Nye (1983), reviewing the literature, points out that narrative telling of traumatic memories can have two contrasting outcomes: (1) transformative telling, in which an active restorying process occurs, characterized by the creation of a more complete, emotionally integrated, and meaningful story; and (2) repetitive telling, in which the retelling is compulsive and literal, the narrative has a fixed, rigid form, and the story does not evolve with repetition. My experience shows that the process of cocreating improvised stories that are told and enacted, *even when the content appears unrelated to the facts or circumstances of a client's life*, has a transformative effect and serves as an effective resource in overcoming the stuckness of repetitive telling. An example of this transformative power of improv occurred in Case 1, "The Tough-Guy Within," described in Chapter 10.

Advancing the Action—Not Cancelling Offers

Improvised storytelling, unlike improvising as a form of witty entertaining without narrative, taps into a deeper, more universal recognition of the human condition. For persons unfamiliar with the experience of improvising it may come as a surprise that making up and enacting a story can be so involving and distressing as to evoke strong defensive processes. As Johnstone (1988) points out,

> Stories are always threatening to plunge the improviser into grief, or terror, or rage, or joy, or a lot of other things he's not prepared to experience in public. This brings him into conflict with the needs of the spectators: he may want to be admired for his good looks, but they may want him hunted down by psychotic killers . . . The average improviser tries to avoid "trouble" by using joke-behavior because once a scene becomes "silly" then the "monsters" can't get at you. It's normal to assume that improvisers kill stories in order to "be funny," but maybe they're "funny" in order to kill stories. (p. 10)

Johnstone (1987) discusses 12 ways that improvisers prevent narratives from developing. These are enumerated below as examples of what to avoid in good storytelling.

1. Cancelling, which nullifies the offer
2. Sidetracking, which offers the development of a side-plot instead of proceeding with the main story
3. Being original, which acts as a distraction from the mood or energy of the story
4. Wimping, a way of refusing to define what is present or emerging in the story

5. Conflict, which uses fighting (often in the form of argument) to sidetrack or freeze the action
6. Instant trouble, which ends the original story line by superimposing some dramatic but irrelevant event
7. Games, or agreed activities, which substitute routine interaction for development of the action
8. Hedging, which postpones the inevitable next step of story development by including "filler" material
9. Gossiping, which talks about something happening off-stage rather than develops the on-stage action
10. Blocking (discussed at great length in Chapter 4), which Johnstone defines as "anything that prevents the action from developing, or that wipes out your partner's premise" (1981, p. 97)
11. Negativity, which slows or stops the action by negative offers
12. Gagging, which uses jokes to shift the context away from *adventure within* the story toward *amusement at* it

TRUTH EXERCISE

In this modified Gloria Maddox exercise, a single player starts by standing with eyes closed, stretching, and taking a few deep breaths with sound on the exhale. After this relaxation and centering of attention she then opens her eyes and reports truthfully on any present experience, whether sensation, perception, or emotion (e.g., "My right elbow itches . . . there's a faint humming noise behind me . . . there's some paint that's peeling off that wall to my left . . . that's an ugly-looking dog across the street . . . I'm feeling sad . . . etc."). The therapist/director instructs the player to remain receptive to these experiences and gently directs the player to begin a third-person narrative that incorporates any current sensations, perceptions, and emotions. Whenever any such experience cannot be integrated into the story, the player is to step out of role briefly to report it in a theatrical aside and then return directly to the role of narrator. The therapist/director attends to the player's breathing, vocal inflection, body tension, and movement in order to remind the player to stay present (a problem of underinvolvement) or (rarely) to break a nightmare-like trance (a problem of overinvolvement). The story that results, puctuated occasionally by these asides, is usually quite cohesive; players readily become fully absorbed in their stories and typically report having had an abundance of details from current experiencing that supplied their imaginations.

This exercise offers players a profound inner adventure that vividly demonstrates how closely connected our ongoing, idiosyncratic experiencing is with our thematically universal life-story structures. Although not strictly within the scope of RfG methodology and therapeutic intent, it would be possible to use this single technique repeatedly as an important tool of self-discovery, especially when accompanied by journal-writing and group discussion.

DREAM STORY

Keith Johnstone created this exercise for any number of paired partners. It begins with one player (the dreamer) lying comfortably on the floor on his back with eyes shut; his partner (the listener) sits on the floor near him and makes light contact by putting a hand on the dreamer's shoulder (rarely, a dreamer may prefer not to be touched, in which case the listener sits nearby without physical contact). The lights are dimmed and the therapist/director leads the players through a brief relaxation exercise. The dreamer then tells a third-person story created by interweaving the imagery that came into his imagination during the relaxed state. The listener's task is to be there attentively for the dreamer; he speaks only if the dreamer gets into a distressing dream-story, indicated by its content, more shallow, rapid breathing, and strained vocal tone. In such cases, the listener makes suggestions that turn the story away from the source of distress. If this is not sufficient, the listener can ask the dreamer to open his eyes, give him a hug or rock him, and reassure him that the distress will soon pass. After four or five minutes the therapist/director announces that the dream will be over in one more minute, giving the dreamer notice to bring the story to an end.

This exercise, in addition to demonstrating that the imagination works without the effort of conscious thought, is chiefly valuable as practice in improvised storytelling. An important variation is *Cooperative Storytelling*, described below, which is especially useful for guarded dreamers or those who are convinced they cannot tell stories.

COOPERATIVE STORYTELLING

In this exercise, one player (Q) provides context through questions and the other player (A) provides content as answers. The players sit facing one another, knee-to-knee, looking into each other's eyes. For example:

Q You're in a dark place; where is it?
A An old, deserted factory building.
Q What time of day is it?
A Late afternoon. The sun's pretty low.
Q You go around to the front gate. Is it locked?
A No.
Q You push it open a bit and peer inside. What do you see?

A Huge, rusted machinery.
Q There's a sign on the machinery. What does it say?
A "Danger! High-speed . . . " the rest is rusted away.
Q You become aware of someone at the far end of the factory. Who is it?
A An old man in a guard's uniform.
[etc.]

This variation gets the questioner into the storyteller role along with the answerer with the result that they share the adventure and may become emotionally closer. As in other improvs, it is important that each accept the other's offers and keep the story moving forward. Notice that this is different from certain forms of guided imagery techniques in that the story is created in the moment and the questioner follows as well as leads at times.

RIVER EXERCISE

In this exercise the storyteller begins by standing with eyes closed while her partner, beside or behind her, provides frequent, brief, and gentle touches. These touches direct the storyteller to move his entire body quite slowly, fluidly, and continuously, moving in the direction indicated by the touches. The storyteller remains in control of her own movement and stays on her own balance throughout the exercise. The partner's job is to attend fully to the storyteller, whose eyes remain shut throughout the exercise, as well as provide specific and varied suggestions (offers) for movement, including touches behind the knees that guide the storyteller to kneel; it is helpful if the partner gets the storyteller to lie down, roll over, stand again, etc. After being in motion for only a short while the storyteller begins a third-person narrative, drawing on the indirect suggestions that her movement provides.

The experience for the storyteller is dream-like and often deeply emotional. The partner's presence is sometimes felt as an inner guide rather than as an external person. The continuous, slow, fluid motion seems to open the storyteller's imagination in ways that are not so familiar, with the result that the adventure of the story is experienced quite vividly. Although this exercise is similar to *Puppets* (p. 85) in that one player moves the storytelling other player, the resemblence ends there; stories in a *River Exercise* are told more for the storyteller herself rather than for an external audience and are apt to differ markedly in mood, tempo, and content.

STORIES FROM FEELINGS

Developed by Gloria Maddox and related to *Dream Story*, *Stories From Feelings* is a simple, valuable technique when a client, whether initially in-role or not, becomes emotionally distressed in the stuck, repetitive sense. The therapist/director wishing to assist the client out of this state asks him to focus on his emotional state, using it as a springboard to begin a third-person fictional narrative. The client is instructed to allow the story to come, to not "steer" it, but to let the principles of good storytelling operate. If the storyteller gets stuck, the therapist/director may interject "Suddenly, . . . " to help him advance the action. The typical result is a story that begins with a character in the client's emotional distress who has an adventure that ends on an emotionally positive note (although the story need not have a happy ending).

I view the process of such storymaking as "transformative interaction" rather than as dissipating emotive energy or relying on distraction to relieve distress. Clients report feeling better not only because they have moved themselves to a better emotional state but also because they have expended energy to create something positive and of value for others (the audience of the therapist/director and any other clients present). They are also freed to be with others socially, rather than be withdrawn inside their own distress, and have acquired a resource for handling future distress that imparts confidence.

SOAP SCENE

This exercise uses a brief and banal script around which the two players, by their choices of movement, timing, vocal inflection, etc., improvise the status (defined in Chapter 7), intentions, and relationship between their characters. The script may go something like this:

A Hi!
B Hello.
A Go anywhere last night?
B No. How about you?
A Stayed home and watched a little TV.
B Anything good on?
A No, not really.
B Well, gotta go.
A See you.

This scene can be played in a well-nigh infinite number of ways and is useful clinically to heighten clients' (and trainees') awareness of the many possibilities people have to cocreate meaning in their relationships. It can be combined with *Emotional Lists* (p. 131) or *Status Transfer* (p. 116) to highlight the emotional or status features without the variability or distraction of improvised dialogue.

EXCUSES

Two players with arms around each other's shoulders role-play a scenario in which they are two young children. When confronted by an off-stage parental voice, saying, for example, "How did chocolate ice cream get all over the upholstery?" they have to create a story that will avert their getting a spanking. They are indeed guilty but must make up a fantastic story, using acts of God or superheroes and lots of imagination to get out of a tight spot. They must support each other as brave, make each other right, display lots of sibling harmony and thereby make the parent look good for having created such exemplary children. It is possible to advance the action effortlessly when each player is so approving of the other and the responsibility for advancing the action passes frequently back and forth.

It is also possible to have the players be adults (e.g., a married couple in a tax-audit, or two robbery suspects in a police interrogation), although the adult will be an on-stage player and the choices then include playing it straight (trying to concoct a plausible story) or absurd (relying on fantasy). The point of the game is to cocreate the experience of a genuine mutually supportive relationship out of a shared fictional danger.

FAMILY STORY

This game is useful for actual families or for unrelated groups of players who play the parts of extended family members. The game is started by one member introducing a fictional event involving a fictional family member (e.g., "Do you remember the time Uncle Bruce showed up at our house with no shoes?"). Other members play the parts of family members (actual or fictional) and take turns adding details and furthering the story, often becoming major characters in the story itself. There are only two rules: (1) everyone gets a chance to contribute, and (2) no blocking (objections, denials, or negation) of anything already said is allowed. Since the story is made up on the spot, no one actually knows more than anyone else. One result is every member's contribution is important — the story is owned by all.

Creating and Breaking Routines

A routine is a predictable sequence of actions. The routine of driving a car, for example, begins with the action sequence unlocking the door — sitting at the wheel — adjusting the rear-view mirror — turning the ignition key — releasing the emergency brake — etc. A routine, no matter how unusual, has little narrative value until it is interrupted or broken. Breaking a routine generates narrative. Completed routines serve as introductions ("platforms") for routines that will not be completed.

In the unstated contract of storytelling, the audience believes that the storyteller is presenting them with an action that she or he intends to develop (that is, a routine to be broken) and gives the storyteller their attention with that expectation. All elements introduced in a story are expected to be brought back into the story (reincorporated). In essence, the audience's attention is a loan to be repaid by the storyteller's adherence to these rules. For this reason, storytellers are influenced by this contract to present even factual accounts within this format.

FORTUNATELY/UNFORTUNATELY

This is an improvised first-person narrative told mainly by one player. The storyteller's partner serves both as audience and as a shifter of the narrator's point of view, which is accomplished by alternatively interjecting "Fortunately," or "Unfortunately," after every sentence or two of the story. The narrator takes this as the first word of his next sentence, which he then completes. This frees up the imagination of the narrator as he proceeds, since he now has to justify the incorporation of the attitude implied by either word. This game is also useful for including bashful players, since the role makes minimal demands (and no improvising), yet is a speaking part. Of course, in working with equivalently adventurous players, the roles can be exchanged in another round of the game.

NARRATIVE/COLOR

Similar in form to *Fortunately/Unfortunately*, the improvised story can be told in any person or tense. The partner's role is to call out "Narrative!" as a signal to the narrator to advance the action whenever the story line appears stalled, and "Color!" when the story appears to need more description. For example, the narrator begins: "Jake ran to the edge of the cliff and looked down. Flavia screamed at him to stop, but Jake dove off the cliff anyway . . . " At this point the partner wants more description and calls "Color!" The narrator continues: "Jake's body was arched, his arms held in tightly to his sides. He appeared to Flavia intent on smashing head-first onto the rocks below. The cliff looked to be 150 feet high; large grey boulders were jutting from the teeming, dark waves below . . . " At this point, having had enough description and wishing the story to advance, the partner calls "Narrative!" etc. In contrast to *Fortunately/Unfortunately*, the partner exercises more judgment and plays a significant part in the cocreation of the story; at times it may be necessary for the partner to repeat "Narrative!" or "Color!" when the narrator does not shift at the first instruction.

This game highlights an important feature of narrative performance: People avoid the uncomfortable telling or retelling of stories by either advancing the action so rapidly that they "get it over with" without dwelling on those descriptive features that might evoke emotional underdistance (all narrative, no color) or dilate with description, forestalling "getting to the danger" (all color, no narrative) equivalent to "hedging" as described above.

Reincorporation: Looking Backward

As previously noted, the audience expects elements introduced in a narrative to be brought back into the story, a process termed "reincorporation." Keith Johnstone (1981) offers this analogy:

> The improviser has to be like a man walking backwards. He sees where he has been, but he pays no attention to the future. His story can take him anywhere, but he must still "balance" it, and give it shape by remembering incidents that have been shelved and reincorporating them. (p. 116)

Stories are ways of relating the past to the present; reincorporation is feeding the past into the present.

THE TRIAL

In this group game, each player gives character to one central player, who then reincorporates the information in a final monologue. As an example, player A sits on a chair at stage center while players B, C, and D stand alongside. The therapist/director or audience offers the character the name "Cynthia," who is an alcoholic housewife secretly writing a novel. Player B begins by addressing A in character as follows: "Cynthia! It's me, Mrs. Willits, your fourth-grade teacher! I remember when you wrote that essay on your neighbor's dog . . . " Players C and D then step forward, perhaps as Cynthia's high-school sweetheart and as her older sister, offering character to themselves and to player A. Finally, Cynthia stands and addresses each of the other players in turn, reincorporating the information from B, C, and D in a brief monologue to the audience.

One therapeutic use of this game is to give the central player a chance to answer back to those others who defined her in "life." This can be very empowering for clients who find it hard to construct comprehensive stories in a coherent fashion, but who can readily reply "face-to-face." When used with autobiographical material this game is similar to psychodramatic technique.

SPOON RIVER GAME

This three-person game (also called *Voices from the Grave* or *Tapestries*) gets its name from Edgar Lee Masterson's *Spoon River Anthology* and is a verbal analog to *Simultaneous Leaving* (p. 70). Three players are seated in a row, looking straight out into the audience. Each is given an occupation, a mood or attitude, and a physical endowment. The premise is that all three are dead, speaking from the grave, and constructing, in the past tense, the story of how they each died in the same place and at about the same time as the other two characters. At first, each character speaks in turn, establishing his or her identity. As the story unfolds, the players, speaking in any order, interweave their narratives so that the other players' characters enter and become central in their own stories. By the last turn, each story must end with the death of the narrator's character, in the same location as the other characters, and at about the same time.

This game teaches players to advance the action with others. When the stories interweave and come to their conclusion, players need to utilize reincorporation of both their own previous offers and those of the other characters.

Creating Character

A central feature of the way we locate meaning in stories is in the creation and taking of character at different levels: the characters within the story, the character of the storymaker, the character of the audience. In improv more obviously than in life, the players are constantly engaged in the creation, development, and depiction of their own and other players' character, constantly shaping one another's expectations and identities. Both the story's narrative content and the performance of storytelling involve the formation and shaping of character within and across the above-mentioned levels. This process is of importance not only to clinicians engaged in helping clients restory their lives but also in understanding how the therapist and client mutually shape their relationship, giving character to one another throughout the therapeutic endeavor.

GIVING CHARACTER

This is a training exercise for making offers that endow others with character and that is good preparation for *One Knows, The Other Doesn't* and *Endowment Lists* (both described below). First, player A is given or selects an endowment for player B that is unlike him. Examples include: *emotion* (bitterness, sexual arousal, condescension); *occupation* (dentist, truck-driver, farmer) *physical trait* (bad breath, lame, very tall) *present or recent transaction* (is cheating, just now insulted, has been flattered by A's character). Then, A makes an offer to B, treating him as a person with the chosen endowment. A accomplishes this by herself becoming the person affected by B's endowment: for example, A's eyes widen and her body tenses; she backs away from B, open palms out in front of herself, saying nervously, "Now Joe, just be reasonable. I'm sure we can work it out." (Note that description should NOT be used; this would be "indicating."

For example: A stands alongside B, saying, "You sure are aggressive. You shouldn't have hit me.")

B responds by becoming endowed by A's offer—NOT by attempting to guess what A has made him into. Continuing the example above, B might glower, advancing on A with a raised fist, saying, "Next time you touch my kid, I'll kill you!" Or, mechanically smiling with arms folded tightly across his chest, speaking in an insincerely soothing voice, B might say, "Jean, really, I *like* you—just come over here so we can talk things over."

The exercise may end here or A and B may play the emerging scene further, improvising other circumstances and dialogue. More advanced players might be invited to play a scene while fulfilling other conditions imposed in advance by the therapist/director (such as, falling in love, having one character die, bringing up some appropriate reference to New Orleans, or even all three!).

ONE KNOWS, THE OTHER DOESN'T

One player is sent out of the room while the second is given exact details of character and situation for both. For instance, Judy, (who is out of earshot) is the aging mother being sent to a nursing home against her will; she has fallen several times and cannot be left alone. The second player is the daughter whose husband won't have the mother live with them; they are upper middle class, the mother is 80 years old, the daughter, 50. In the easier version, the second player is given a character that matches his/her actual age and gender; in the more difficult one, no restriction applies to the second player's character.

When Judy returns to play the scene she knows nothing; she could be male or female, younger or older than her real age—all clues for her identity and the details of character and situation must come from her partner. The burden is on the other (knowing) player to treat her in such a way that she will "get it" and take on the characteristics communicated without verbally indicating any details directly. If Judy misunderstands and begins to act like a three-year-old, the partner might say, "It's just this kind of childish behavior that proves you can't live alone any more." (but NOT, "Mother, you're 80 now; act your age!" which would be "indicating"). The comedy or drama of this exercise depends on the nature of the circumstances given. It is excellent for teaching the acceptance of offers and drives the creative imagination of the knowing player to communicate clearly.

ENDOWMENT LISTS

In this more advanced game, two or more players are each privately given a list of endowments that they use to give character to each of the

other players. The lists of endowments can, but need not be, identical.
For example, suppose a four-player game in which all players receive the
following list: "Smart/Sexy/Funny." Each player now selects which of the
other three players gets which one of the above three endowments and plays
the scene by giving character to each accordingly. It is important that players behave within a socially normal range in order to keep the scene and the
characterizations realistic. At the end of the scene the players are asked to
point in turn to the one they made smart, sexy, and funny.

What makes this especially interesting is that player A will say or do
something that is taken differently by the others; B and C may react as
though A has just been funny, while D will react as though she was being
sexy. It can be challenging fun to play the scene without blocking the other
players' different attributions. What players discover is that behavior takes
on meaning from the way it is construed by others.

GOING ON ADVENTURES – TOGETHER

The essence of play is the creating, sustaining, furthering, and, eventually, the ending of adventure. The chief dramatic form of adventuring or
storymaking in improv is the scene. One reason that blocking is to be
avoided is that blocks divert energy from the flow of an adventure. Like a
relationship, an adventure takes on a life-force which must be fed constantly by the involvement of the player(s).

DIRECTED STORY

Also called *Options*, this game is essentially an enacted scene in which
the action is advanced by offers made by outside sources during the scene.
These outside sources may come not only from the therapist/director but
from any off-stage spectator. As with player-generated offers, outside offers can include new or revealed circumstances, endowments, dialogue,
props, secrets, states of mind — anything that advances the action. For example, a scene is begun in a diner between a morose truck driver and a
cheerful waitress. The waitress is putting a cup of coffee in front of the
seated truck driver when the scene is frozen and the therapist/director says,
"The coffee is spiked with vodka." The scene continues with the players
incorporating the offer of the spiked coffee. A little later in the scene, the
now-drunk and energized truck driver has discovered that his wallet is
missing and says, "I must've left it back in the truck. I'll just . . . " the
action is frozen again and the therapist/director supplies the rest of the line:
" . . . give you my high-school class ring in payment."

Directed Story can be used with inexperienced or inhibited players as a bridge from the mere following of instructions to full improvising. This can be accomplished by having the therapist/director making fewer interventions as players become more capable. Alternatively, the therapist/director can freeze the stage action at any point and ask an audience member for a suggestion. In the above example, for instance, the therapist/director would call "Freeze!" and then turn to the audience and say, "Something unusual was put in the coffee. What was it?" The audience would supply "vodka" (or "a giant cockroach," "a severed human thumb," "a magical potion that makes the drinker invisible," etc.). This device not only heightens audience involvement but prepares onlookers for their own future enactment. In family therapy, when certain children (or, on occasion, one of the parents) may be too shy at first to participate in enactment, I will have other family members begin a scene, freeze the action and ask the shy, nonparticipating member for a suggestion. Shortly after the players continue the scene I freeze the action again and ask the member who made the suggestion whether it played to her satisfaction. If it did not, I have a pretext for inviting the suggestion-maker on stage to show how it should have been done.

HOW WE MET

Two people are instructed to tell the story of how they first met, which they do. When the people have a real-life relationship this becomes a non-improvised exercise in telling a true story together; it has some value as a means to assess their relationship by the way they approach the task. (Watzlawick, Bavelas, & Jackson [1967] report using this interview technique.) What is more useful is to have the players improvise a fictional story of how they met, in which they can explore other status positions, accept all offers, and create a new story together. I have also asked marital couples to tell the story of some future event (retirement, a trip around the world, taking a yet-unborn grandchild for the summer) for that same purpose. Naturally, for unacquainted partners *How We Met* is is an improv exercise as given.

Making Risky Choices

Inexperienced improvisers do not allow anything to happen; more experienced ones invoke a danger, but then avoid it. Courageous improvisers go on thrilling adventures. As noted in Chapter 4, blocking is a way of preventing adventures from commencing. Johnstone (1981) observes:

> There are people who prefer to say "Yes" and there are people who prefer to say "No." Those who say "Yes" are rewarded by the adventures they have, and those who say "No" are rewarded by the safety they attain. There are far more "No"

sayers around than "Yes" sayers, but you can train one type to behave like the other. (p. 92)

This typology is equivalent to Couch and Kenniston's (1960) distinction of yea-sayers (who desire and actively search for emotional excitement in their external environment) and nay-sayers (who aim for inner equilibrium and regulate impulses in order to maintain control).

Risk is not complexity, but uncertainty. Any choice that is experienced as risky will stretch that player's role repertoire—if attempted. Good improvisers respond spontaneously in and to the present moment. Bad improvisers look into the future to avoid mistakes and the vulnerability of the unknown.

MORAL CHOICES

This category encompasses games in which the characters are offered dilemmas or temptations requiring a clear moral choice. While any scene might develop in this direction, *Directed Story* (p. 102) could be utilized to develop a moral choice, as could a *Little Voice* (p. 86) scene where the off-stage voice personifies the on-stage character's conscience. For a *Moral Choice* scene to be impactful, the player facing the choice must be aware, in the moment, of the plausibility of more than one alternative. The resulting experience is interesting both dramatically and psychologically, since the player often will experience the choice in the scene as resonating to some real-life personal moral choice.

Keeping the Action On-Stage

One diagnostic sign of an improv scene losing its power to evoke immediacy and adventure is that the players shift the focus from interaction and action to events occuring off-stage (interaction is one person being altered by another; action is the change of events caused by the interaction). When this occurs scenes get "talky"; players stop moving and "stay in their heads." There is a tendency to go off-stage for props (they can be mimed as being on hand), dilate about the past or future, gossip about a character off-stage, or react to danger or a circumstance that is off-stage. These are all attempts to avoid being in the here and now. Coaching is then needed to bring players back to the here and now, to play the scene fully.

Acting teacher and director Jean Eskow points out that improvisation can be used to test whether a theatrical idea is valid, instead of relying solely on thought to predict what will happen.

> Truth can be discovered or predicted; discovery comes through improvisation. . . . There lies the great value of improvisation; to expose the fact that we often

predict actions that we never take. We tell ourselves things that we would, but never do. The object of an actor using improvisational technique is to get away from his head, so he is no longer dictating responses to it. He doesn't analyze the action out of existence by predicting it. (cited in Sperber, 1974, pp. 98–100)

When the action is on-stage the "truth" of the adventure unfolds and discoveries are made.

Making the Other Person(s) Look Good

One of the distinctive features of Johnstone's version of theater improv is the emphasis given to being supportive to others. As noted in the Introduction, RfG evolved as a way of utilizing improv because of the correspondence between good improvising and good relationship functioning. A fascinating change occurs when players stop concerning themselves with how good they themselves look while improvising and instead pay attention to supporting their stage partners to look powerful, clever, and interesting; the characters come into focus, the players enter into a creative flow where imaginative choices are made and the scene works in terms of both aesthetics and personal satisfaction. Supporting the other person to look good entails paying full attention to everything about that person in the present moment and accepting fully her or his offers. "Looking good" does not mean "wonderful according to my values"; if the other player's character is established as a villain, his or her villainy must be supported to the fullest. Being fully supported and made to look good is a highly positive experience, although clients with chronically low self-esteem may become disconcerted.

PRESENTS

Two players face one another. One (the giver) holds out her hands with open palms in a gesture of offering a present. It is important that the giver have no preconceived notion of what the present is, but simply offers it in a neutral way. The receiver looks at the giver's extended empty palms and allows a desirable present from her imagination to appear there. The receiver then mimes picking up (no unwrapping necessary!) and using the present, and ends the turn by expressing great gratitude to the giver for such a wonderful present. Even though the receiver is accepting his own imagination's offer the giver receives the real present of the receiver's thanks. The players then exchange roles and the next turn begins with the offer of another present.

Presents is a simple exercise that I use in most conjoint therapy in order to promote use of the imagination in a way that reliably results in positive feelings between the players. It is also an easy way to get players to experience making their partner look good (in this case, by having given them a wonderful present).

CRAZY EDDIE

Named after a now-defunct chain of retail electronics stores noted for ads with high-pressure, mile-a-minute-talking salesmen, this exercise is an excellent way to train clients in a group setting to take the risk of jumping out on stage when totally unprepared in order to rescue a teammate who is faltering.

Three or more players line up across the back half of the stage and face the audience. The therapist/director places an object (e.g., a paper cup) on the front center stage and one player steps forward to pick it up. When he does so, he becomes an intense, high-pressure salesman of the cup to the audience, verbally and physically demonstrating how it can be used in many, many ways: "And with this wonderful cup you can scoop up dog poop (demonstrating), you can wear it on your ear to remind you of the ocean, you can even open doorknobs without getting germs on your hands, etc." The other players, the "chorus line," mimicking his movements in unison behind the foreground player, lip-syncing to his patter. Sooner or later the speaking player runs out of new ideas and begins to stall, repeat himself, or stretches out the latest idea. As this begins to happen, one of the other players, *with or without an idea* for a new use of the cup, jumps forward, tapping the speaker's shoulder and takes the speaker's place (the old speaker replaces the new speaker on the "chorus line"). This continues so that every player gets to speak at least once.

The valuable part of this exercise is the rescuing that takes place when one player taps out the other; clients are stretched by taking the risk to rescue and thereby build camaraderie with one another. Not infrequently, the rescued player has strong delayed reactions to having been rescued, ranging from gratitude to embarassment to anger.

TAG IMPROV

In this group exercise a two-player scene is begun. As the scene progresses, a succession of off-stage players come on stage, tapping the shoulder of either one of the players, assuming the same posture and continuing the scene as that character. When the replacements come on in rapid succession (less than every ten seconds, even every two seconds) the effect is that of a "standing wave" where the characters are constant and the players are interchangeable. Before the scene gets too frenetic each player may get to appear onstage two or three times.

This exercise is a high-energy group warm-up that has the additional advantage of having the entire group create the scene without pressure on individual members. Players are also freer to make bold offers, since they won't be around as that character to reap the consequences of how they advanced the action!

Using Whatever Happens (Justifying)

As noted in the Introduction, one of the definitions of spontaneity is an ability to respond externally to new situations in an immediate, creative, and appropriate manner. *Justifying* is employing spontaneity in the service of stage reality by incorporating everything that occurs into the scene. For example, if a player smiles, his character must find a reason to be smiling in the scene at that moment, saying, as the character, "I just thought of this joke," or even, "I don't know why I'm smiling just now." Should an off-stage noise occur during a scene it may be ignored, but a "better" response would be to include it as an event within the scene at the moment. The opposite of justifying is breaking character, allowing the outside event to create a sense of incongruity with the stage reality such that the outside world contaminates or destroys the pretense.

SLO-MO COMMENTATOR

In this game an athlete on-stage moves extremely slowly while an off-stage sports-style commentator gives significance to the minimal stage activity ("He's using the Von Schlaubenheim knee-bend here—hasn't been used since Englehart won a silver medal in the '56 Interzonals—Wait! his right foot is turned inward—he's losing control!!—etc.). The activity may be utterly prosaic (e.g., "Olympic chair-sitting"), yet the commentator's spiel imparts drama to the event. It is possible to have two athletes on-stage, and/or to use two commentators (one commentator and one "color" person, or sidekick), or stylistically contrasting commentators (such as sympathetic/unsympathetic, emotional/intellectual, bored/excited).

The commentator idea can be applied to any scene and is a good way to involve clients who are reluctant to be on-stage players. To be effective, commentators must appear to be visibly and strongly affected by the minimal action on stage and to focus on what the on-stage player is doing. At the same time, the commentator can coach by anticipating (e.g., "He's about to touch that chair") and can advance action by calling blocks, looping, canceling ideas, etc. Commentators don't evaluate so much as describe (and implicitly explain) action, thereby telling and shaping the story.

Commentators can be made part of most other improv games so long as they don't dominate or usurp the on-stage action. Commentators who shine (show-off) are competing for laughs with the on-stage players; improv scenes don't need frenetic or constant commentary. Therapist/directors may use a commentator role in order to teach principles and objectives such as status, blocking/accepting, or advancing the action.

Sharing Control and Mutuality

Since contemporary American culture glorifies individualism at the expense of fully subordinating the individual's will to that of the relationship, team, or group, it is plausible to expect that exercises that teach the sharing of control will be experienced as more challenging or even threatening to Americans than to people acculturated in less individualistic societies (e.g., Japanese culture). I have had insufficient experience to test this hypothesis; what I have observed is that, surprisingly, the *skill* with which enmeshed family members share control is no greater than that of members from disengaged families, although their reported *ease* is somewhat greater. Coached practice at improv noticeably improves both reported ease and skill at sharing control in further improvising but practice alone appears insufficient to transfer skill at sharing control to out-of-therapy relationship interaction; therapeutic progress in other categories also is needed.

Many improv games (e.g., *One Word at a Time*, p. 65) reveal how players exercise overcontrol, often by rules that distribute some faculties or information across players, such that they cannot succeed without cooperating with one another. In a broader sense, scenes involving two or more players require the cooperation of those within the playspace to make offers, accept offers, and advance the action. Mutuality, defined as coordinated interaction without leadership, is implicitly present in the way people ordinarily adjust their status, physical positioning, body movement, and turn-taking speech, among other social behaviors. The mutuality that is explicitly called for in exercises like *Mirrors* (p. 69) takes place in a state of mind where each player is fully aware of the other's behavior and unaware of one's own willfullness. Mutuality is typically intermittent; players go in and out of a mutual state when they strive consciously to attain it.

Playfully Getting Others in Trouble

It might appear that getting others into trouble, even playfully, is antithetical to the spirit of support, cooperation, and making others look good. In fact, once a playful context is established and the boundaries of what is signified as play are defined, there arises a need for stimulation to counterbalance the tendency to stagnate in safety and triviality. As noted in Chapter 2, Huizinga (1949) saw play as a universal human activity precisely because, throughout history and across all areas of human endeavor, people have gone beyond the merely functional, direct way of meeting their basic needs in order to embellish living with arbitrary-yet-challenging rules and actions.

Miller's (1973) term "galumping," developed out of her observations of baboons, refers to a "patterned, voluntary elaboration or complication of process, where the pattern is not under the dominant control of goals" (p. 92). Galumping in humans is a functionally inefficient, playful mode of action that is most obvious in the behavior of children, who adorn routines with absorption, surplus energy, experimentation, and (often) unselfconscious risk-taking (e.g., hopping on one foot while avoiding sidewalk cracks, instead of merely walking). Playfully getting others in trouble is, of course, a fundamental aspect of competitive games, where the presence of an adversary provides the stimulus for challenging oneself to the fullest extent. Competition is associated with nonplayful conflict as well as with games, with the result that play (particularly, the games of adults) is contaminated with a need to win and to look good (as noted in Chapters 2 and 4).

In one sense, since improv games and exercises challenge players to go beyond the habitual or conventional ways of carrying out tasks, the invitation of the therapist/director to improvise could itself be classified as a way of getting players into trouble! What makes improv games and exercises absorbing to audiences is that they want to see others dealing spontaneously with the unexpected and unfamiliar; the elements of danger, of failure, and consequent loss of face are significant factors. At the same time, the players get to experience the risks and glory of putting themselves on the edge, in contrast to the usual ways that we protect ourselves from taking chances (Remember, the RfG the motto is "Face Fear Through Fun"). Improv games and exercises have premises and rules that promote a galumping frame of mind, often by taking away a faculty or restricting choices; paradoxically, this typically has the effect of freeing imaginations and heightening the vividness of experiencing. Imposing further conditions on the players (such as playing a scene in verse or with a German accent) makes things still more difficult — but more rewarding for performers and audience alike. Paradoxically, committment to rules (as in a game) frees one to play more vigorously. The composer Igor Stravinsky wrote, "the more contraints one imposes, the more one frees oneself of the chains that shackle the spirit . . . and the arbitrariness serves only to obtain precision of execution" (1942). (See Appendix B for conditions that may be added to most improv scenes.)

The game described below is one of many stage games in which its structure encourages players to playfully get their partners into trouble.

HAT GAME

This is an advanced improv game with a competitive premise. Two players, each wearing a not-too-tightly-fitting brimmed hat, attempt to snatch the hat of the other while playing an improv scene in which all offers must be accepted. In an earlier version of this game, the rules prevent players from holding their own hats. An unsuccessful attempt to snatch the other's hat loses a point, as does having one's hat snatched. After a point has been scored the players start a new scene. This game may be played in groups where a winning player remains on stage with a new challenger until defeated.

Getting the other player into trouble occurs when an offer puts the other player in a vulnerable position to having his hat snatched off. If player A, in character as a priest, says to player B (his parishoner): "Yes, my son, your sins are great, but God pardons those who repent. Kneel before me now and I will pray over you," B must accept the offer and kneel. He may, however, say: "Yes, Father, and kneel with me in my hour of need," thereby equalizing their physical positions.

Keith Johnstone's concept of the *Hat Game* has gone through an evolution. Playing this game well used to be thought a function of agility or of cleverly maneuvering one's partner into a physically vulnerable position; more recently, this game has been conceived of as Zen-like training in staying mentally present in the moment. Since it is virtually impossible for a player to take the hat from another player who both has her in his field of vision and is aware of her intention at the moment she decides to make her move, the more "spiritual" version of *Hat Game* permits one to hold the brim, or temporarily remove one's own hat, whenever the other player moves outside one's visual field. Instead of such crude maneuvers, successfully taking the hat occurs when a player becomes distracted from the present danger (usually by becoming engrossed in anticipating where the scene is headed). In such cases, the hat can be lifted quite slowly, rather than snatched. Good improvisers are usually skilled at this game because they remain present-centered throughout a scene.

If a gentleman comes to your house and you tell him with warmth and interest that you 'are glad to see him,' he will be pleased with the attention and will probably thank you; but if he hears you say the same thing to twenty other people, he will not only perceive that your courtesy was worth nothing, but he will feel some resentment at having been imposed on.

—Anonymous (cited in Goffman, 1959, p. 87)

In heaven an angel is nobody in particular.

—G. B. Shaw (cited in Daintith et al., 1989, p. 276)

CHAPTER 7

Status: Improvisation and Power

A CONSTRUCT OF GREAT UTILITY to improv and of considerable value to therapists is status, which may be defined as the importance a person is perceived as having in relation to someone, or something (i.e., objects and places), else. Following the usage of Johnstone (1981), status refers to what people do, or play, akin to dominance and submission. Thus, a waitress may play high status (condescension) while her customer, a physician, may play low status (awkwardness) despite their opposite social standing. Note that this definition differs fom using status to describe anything (intelligence, ability, taste, strength, habits, wealth, or social position) that makes a person inferior or superior to others (James & Williams, 1984), thereby confusing the result with the means used to produce it.

STATUS AND SELF-ESTEEM:
PLAYING AND HAVING STATUS

When Johnstone began teaching actors to create minimal status differences (maximal differences usually produce absurd, comic effects) their work ceased to be stagey.

111

> The scenes became "authentic" and actors seemed marvelously observant. Suddenly we understood that every inflection and movement implies a status and that no action is due to chance, or really "motiveless." It was hysterically funny, but at the same time very alarming. All our secret maneuverings were exposed. If someone asked a question we didn't bother to answer it, we concentrated on why it had been asked. No one could make an "innocuous" remark without everyone instantly grasping what lay behind it. Normally we are "forbidden" to see status transactions except when there's a conflict. In reality status transactions continue all the time. In the park we'll notice the ducks squabbling, but not how carefully they keep their distances when they are not. (1981, p. 33)

Seen in this way, human interaction is never status-neutral; we are all constantly adjusting status in relation to our surroundings and to others. Many of the games described in transactional analysis, as well as the ploys and gambits humorously described by Leacock (1981) are maneuvers designed to obtain the desired status relationship between self and others. Further, status transactions are territorial, involving the use of space, gesture, posture, vocal inflection, as well as verbal content. Family therapists in particular, whose use of live and videotaped observation of clinical sessions puts them in a position to appreciate the richness of nonverbal communication, will find that awareness of status transactions will further enrich their grasp of family dynamics. In my experience, shifts in status regularly accompany significant changes in family interaction; such shifts are always noticed, even when not being acknowledged.

Another useful observation concerning status is that many people are generally more comfortable playing one status position than another, although contexts exist in which they will play a nonpreferred position. Flexibility in shifting one's status position is valuable in life in general and in the practice of psychotherapy in particular. People who can only play one status position are in a position comparable to the dilemma many of us face in a shoe store: whether to look good or be comfortable. I surmise that people assume the same predominant status position as they held in their families of origin and thereafter maneuver to replicate that position in other systems. Since status is relational it would follow that people maneuver to get others to assume (mostly) complementary status, thereby "giving" status to, and receiving status from, others.

Despite the apparent simplicity of this construct, status transactions are more complex than they at first appear. People are frequently unaware of the status they are playing and are even convinced sometimes they are playing opposite to their actual status. Johnstone (1981) uses his own experience to illustrate this point.

> In my own case I was astounded to find that when I thought I was being friendly, I was actually being hostile! If someone had said "I like your play," I would have said "Oh, it's not up to much," perceiving myself as "charmingly modest." In reality I would have been implying that my admirer had bad taste. I

experience the opposite situation when people come up, looking friendly and supportive, and say, "We did enjoy the end of Act One," leaving me to wonder what was wrong with the rest. (p. 36)

Matters become still more involved when we realize that people both *have* status (which corresponds to their opinion of themselves or self-esteem) as well as *play* status (which represents their adaptive choice in the present social context). Not infrequently, people attempt to conceal the status they have by playing opposite to the status they are experiencing; usually this is unconvincing and, for low-status players attempting to play high, invites aggression against themselves. Goffman (1959) gives numerous detailed examples of the intricacies of misleading status performances. Status games can also be played by agreement, which marks them as playfully intended, such as when friends display familiarity by insulting one another. Social groupings of humans and numerous other species display status hierarchies, both inside their own group ("pecking-orders") and as a group in relation to other groups. While these have been studied extensively, families in particular appear to have many diverse and subtle ways of maintaining hierarchy that are not readily apparent to nonmembers, even to nonmembers with the same class and ethnic background as that of the family.

Status can be *complementary*, when each player acts in conformity to the status expectations of all the others, and *conflictual*, when a player's actions give or take status that is unacceptable to any of the others. Two or more players can play high status in a complementary fashion when they all agree on their mutual worthiness; human nature being what it is, it is likely that this state of affairs will soon give way to conflictual transactions over whom is more worthy. Triangling in others (whether actually present or referred to), who can be assigned "unworthy" status, deflects such competition between the "worthies"; family therapists will have no difficulty recognizing this pattern. Above all, people resist having their status involuntarily lowered by others; even when they are assuming low status they prefer to do it themselves. This principle is illustrated in the following joke: A wife demonstrates to her friends her domination of her husband by ordering him to crawl under their dining table, which he does without hesitation. After some time, she orders him to come out from under the table, whereupon he says, "No, I won't! I'll show you who's boss in this family!"

Another familiar principle is that the presence of an audience mediates the interaction among the players; for example, when player A attacks the status of player B in order to get the support of player C for A's own status, a coalition may develop between A and C against B, or between B and C against A. To a considerable extent, the norms of social reference groups (such as the professions) influence the ways in which status is to be displayed. For example, professional therapists are often of higher social status than their clients, yet professionalism demands that the client is entitled to the respectful attention of the therapist (the word "therapist," incidentally, is derived from the Greek word for "servant"). A therapist may play high status to her client, so long as it is "benevolent high status." The Roman Catholic Pope is referred to as "the servant of the servants of God," which can be interpreted in light of the high status awarded to humility in Christianity. Yet another influencing factor in groups and hierarchies is the style of status-maintenence modelled by the status leadership: scapegoating low-status players, or playing benevolent high status, for example. Waiters in exclusive restaurants, with the encouragement of the management, may act condescendingly high status toward customers whose attire fails to meet desired standards, despite the waiter functioning as a servant. In sum, status transactions in real life are often the result of complex, shifting factors.

UTILIZING STATUS TRANSACTIONS:
GAMES AND EXERCISES

As there are significant cultural and historical differences in the ways that status is and has been conveyed, the following descriptions are offered as generalizations that are valid only within contemporary Western societies. It should be noted that different cultures differ not only in how they signal status, but also how overtly important status differences are shown to be. For instance, Americans socially join with strangers by overtly offering and playing equal status, even though they are covertly quite interested in their relative social ranking. Even after inequality in social rank has been established, Americans generally continue to offer equal status. In Indian society, by contrast, people on first acquaintance are not at ease until they have determined who is of greater importance, whereupon they unselfconsciously take up and display their respective status positions, continuing indefinitely to maintain these unequal status positions.

Eye contact is important when playing status. High-status persons hold direct and steady contact while low-status persons frequently look away, giving them a shifty-eyed appearance. When introducing this concept to a group, ask the players to pick a partner and practice eye contact, playing alternately high and low. Often there will be a clear preference for one or the other and a great difficulty in playing the less familiar status; it feels like putting the wrong shoe on each foot. People will also have a judgment that one or the other status is wrong; it is important to point out that for a living being, playing and shifting status is as natural and unavoidable as breathing. Even the highest status person at times plays low status to someone or something, and vice versa.

Persons lacking experience with intentional status transactions not infrequently assume that high status is always a position of advantage and power, and that there is something inferior, disadvantageous, or degrading about assuming a low-status position. In part this is a result of failing to make the above-mentioned distinction between *having* status (which may be ascribed, relatively fixed, and not within a person's control) and *playing* status (which is a fluid, contextually meaningful choice). It can be helpful for the therapist/director to praise expert low-status performance as a way of desensitizing the common aversion to taking a low-status position.* This can be accomplished by direct coaching or from an off-stage commentator (see *Slo-mo Commentator*, p. 107).

Body language is another way of showing status. To play low status, a player would take up as little space as possible, crouch, slouch, and hold his limbs tightly in toward his body; he would make frequent little gestures like pulling at his hair, rubbing his face, and "fixing himself up"; he would also speak with a "small mouth" and in a tentative way, qualifying his assertions constantly, making little, ineffectual noises, and ending his sentences with a questioning inflection. High-status players take up maximum space, have erect but not stiff posture, move in an unhurried way, and are relatively inactive.

Physical status cues are readily demonstrated to groups by having two persons act as models (either stationary or in simple, repetitive movement) so that the others can observe how the smallest change in posture or gesture affects their status relationship. Of course, the models experience these effects, too.

Status transactions are to some extent correlated with blocking and accepting offers, since high-status players tend to block offers in order to maintain control and low-status ones tend to accept them in order to avoid the appearance of themselves having power relative to those of higher status. One can, however, accept offers in a high-status way or block them without raising one's low status.

IMPOSING STATUS

This exercise teaches players to make and accept verbal status offers. Player A starts by speaking to player B, using tone of voice as well as content to make clear which is higher and which lower (posture and movement may be added). Player B is to accept the status positions implied by the status offer, replying to confirm A's offer, and take up the opposite (complementary) position. For example, A begins (speaking humbly): "Excuse me, Sir, could you spare some change?" B now recognizes that A is playing low status to his high and responds haughtily, "Why don't you get a job?" The conversation continues with two or three turns apiece, the players maintaining their initial status positions. Then B starts a new conversation by making the initial status offer, which A accepts.

---

*Or perhaps being seen in a low-status position by others. Nonimprovisers frequently (yet erroneously) assume that playing low status indicates stupidity.

One variation is to have players establish a relationship by posture and movement, without speaking until the status relationship is clear (when they begin speaking they will discover whether they were in agreement with their partners). Another variation is to have player B respond with the most minimal status difference from player A's position of which he is capable. In the above-mentioned example, B might reply, "I really wish I could, but I'm having some troubles of my own right now," indicating an only slightly higher status than A. This tends to produce more realistic scenes and gives players who are already experienced with status transactions an opportunity to develop more nuanced status maneuvers. Care should be taken to distinguish these complementary status transactions from competitive ones, such as those developed in *Status Conflict* below.

STATUS CONFLICT

In *Status Conflict*, two players are each given enough information to start a scene (character, occupation, setting, etc.) with the further instruction that each play lower (or higher) than the other. The conflict is immediately palpable to all observing; the effect of playing the conflict to the hilt is absurd and comic. The value of this game lies in discovering what it takes to fully commit to a status position. One variation, comparable to the motion of two hands first ascending and then descending a ladder, is to get to an extreme status position by steps, each player going further than the other. A player reverses the status direction at the point where he cannot go further, whereupon the other player also switches direction competitively.

STATUS TRANSFER

This status exploration usually releases a lot of laughter and good fun as people become more conscious of their daily habits. One player assumes a high-status role while a second player assumes a low one; the players then transfer gradually to the other's status. The transfer is useful because it gives each player the chance to experience the changing of status. Once the concept is introduced, two players can experiment with a scene in front of the group. The therapist/director assigns status, gives the players character and place (e.g., a high-status criminal and a low-status policeman, or a low-status king and a high-status court jester, etc.), and asks them to play a scene in which they justify a status transfer.

There are many variations on this type of two-person status scene. The transfer may be justified by a change of circumstance or new information (e.g., one player reveals he has a gun or has just won the lottery); the transfer may occur rapidly or very gradually; the therapist/director may assign one or both players specific needs that they attempt to fulfil (e.g., get permission to borrow the family car, be praised by the other for one's good work). These needs can be assigned openly or be conveyed privately to each player. In general, needing something from the other player will lower a player's having status, but not necessarily limit the choices for playing status.

STATUS PERCEPTION

In this game, developed by Gloria Maddox, two players face one another, looking into each other's eyes without speaking or moving for between 10 and 30 seconds. The players concentrate on the feeling of the status relationship; on a signal from the therapist/director they begin to move and speak based on their felt sense of relative status. It is possible for the first spoken line to be scripted (i.e., decided in advance); the way the line is delivered conveys the speaker's status position.

One intriguing and useful feature of this game is that, since there are no preexisting criteria by which to assign status positions, a frequent result is that the players find afterward that there were unexpected features to their partner's response, even though the ensuing scene might have gone well. Complementary transactions are an indication of matched expectations, while conflictual ones point to unmet expectations. Asking players to report on their perceptions/projections of status during the initial 30-second period can lead to a therapeutically productive discussion of what their status expectations were based upon, how they reacted when their expectations were confirmed or disconfirmed, and what judgments arose toward their partner.

HIDDEN PECKING ORDER

This is one of a number of status games that three or four people can play. At the beginning, players are assigned role relationships and a setting (e.g., family members at a picnic). Each player privately chooses his own status rank and the scene is played. At the end, or after a few minutes of interaction, the players in the same role and setting pick a new status rank and repeat the scene, attempting to keep the same content.

UNKNOWN STATUS

In this three- or four-person game, similar in form to *Hidden Pecking Order*, each player privately assigns a status ranking to himself or herself *and* to each of the other players, treating each according to the number given. For instance, A may assign himself the number 4; B will be his number 1, C his number 2, and D his number 3. During the scene A will defer to all his partners but to varying degrees. B, of course, will have his unwavering deference, no matter how she behaves. B may also have assigned herself the number 4 position and will try to raise A's status, much to his dismay. This sort of status battle creates a lively and often funny scene that is also experienced as emotionally realistic.

Games such as *Hidden Pecking Order* and *Unknown Status* can be used to analyze the subtleties of status transactions in greater detail and therefore have considerable use in clinical training (see Chapter 14).

EXCLUSION

In this game, each of the three or four players, speaking in gibberish, tries to avoid becoming "iced out" (excluded) by the rest of the players. The effort to stay connected with the majority and avoid exclusion activates the players to attempt all manner of negotiations and maneuvers. In a variation, roles and intelligible dialogue may be improvised; this is frequently experienced as unpleasantly realistic and often activates vivid early memories of being excluded or of excluding another.

The "danger" of being excluded shifts from person to person until the majority ices someone out. The game isn't over until the isolated player accepts his or her exclusion; some capitulate quickly, some never do. This game is an excellent teaching device for learning the formation of status hierarchy.

STATUS TRIANGULATION

Each player in this three-person status game is assigned an intention that carries status implications for each of the other players. For example, player A is instructed to elevate his own status in relation to player B (by boasting) while lowering player C's status (by ignoring or belittling C's opinions). Player B, meanwhile, is to play high status toward A (by showing that he's just as important) and low status toward C (by deferring to C's opinions). At the same time, C plays low status to A (by trying to win A's approval) and equal status to B (by seeking sympathy for the treatment he is receiving from A). The scene can be played as a social gathering of friends, a business meeting, a love triangle, etc., and is useful for the effect it produces on the players' felt self-status. For more intensive relationship- or clinical-training it is instructive to replay this game with the players rotating the roles of A, B, and C so that the same status positions can be experienced from different perspectives.

STATUS PARTY

In a group of four or more, each player privately creates a character (with a fictional name, occupation, and life ambition, for example) and mills around the room, greeting and briefly interacting with other characters while assuming a variety of status positions (benevolent high, oppressive high, friendly equal, shy equal, submissive low, hurt low, to name a few). This packs a lot of experiencing of status into a short amount of time and allows for less self-conscious exploration of status (since there is a lot of movement and rapid change and a fictional identity to lead with). It also teaches that status is independent of occupational title, consisting instead of the way a character is played.

MASTER/SERVANT GAMES

This category of games, described in detail by Johnstone (1981), includes numerous variations that all feature the premise of overt formal social status inequality. Since American society (except for such institutions as the military) downplays the display of differences in social importance, these games heighten the effects of inequalities in rank. Examples include: noblemen/courtiers, masters or mistresses/servants, employers/employees, and teachers/students. These scenes may be played with the possibility of anomalous status configurations, such as a high-status servant with a low-status master or a status transfer occuring during the scene. There can be more than one master with the same servant(s), more than one servant with the same master(s), and servants themselves having servants or subordinates. Numerous examples of such configurations occur in classical comedies, such as by Shakespeare and Moliere.

One variation of particular clinical usefulness, *Overconfessing Servant*, is an example of how to get away with wrongdoing by assuming a defenseless, low-status stance. In the following scene, the mistress questions the servant, who not only readily admits to her culpability but refers to even greater misdeeds.

MISTRESS Have you finished making the beds, Marie?
SERVANT Oh, no, ma'am, I haven't done any work all morning, on account of my hangover, ma'am.
MISTRESS What? Have you been drinking on the job again?
SERVANT Yes, ma'am, I just had to have a drop after I felt so bad for scorching your evening gown while ironing it.
MISTRESS WHAT?? My Dior gown?? I ought to fire you on the spot!
SERVANT I know I deserve to be sacked, ma'am, especially after I then dropped the iron on the carpet, burning a hole in it.
MISTRESS No!!! Not the priceless Oriental!!!
[etc.]

As Johnstone points out, the more abject and defenseless (i.e., low-status) the servant is, the more difficult it is for the mistress to retaliate, probably because doing so would lessen or even level their status distinction (in cultured social circles, if a high-status person has to resort to overt threats or violence in order to maintain the upper hand, her control is shaky, indeed). Overconfessing can be explored as a passive-aggessive strat- egem by people who suffer from low self-esteem when experiencing condi- tions of relative powerlessness.

Another variation of the *Master/Servant Games* is called *The King Game*. The premise of this game, for three or more players, is that one character is an absolute despot, with power of life and death over the others, who play servants. The king (or queen) is very difficult to please; at the slightest provocation he points his finger at the offending servant (who is trying to placate and survive) and says, "Die!" The targetted servant promptly expires on the spot, perhaps moving unobtrusively off-stage a few moments later to appear as another servant further on in the scene.

One more useful variation, sometimes called *Making Faces*, has the king figure be an employer with the power to fire any of his employees whom he catches mocking him, which of course they begin to do as soon as he takes his eyes off of them (it helps to have more than one employee on stage at a time). If caught in some disrespectful gesture or face, the employee can save his job only by coming up with a justification on the spot (e.g., if caught sticking out his tongue at the employer during an office scene the employee might mime bringing an envelope flap to his mouth and explain that he was licking it shut). Unlike the king in the first variation, who kills off servants purely on whim, the employer should relent if offered a plausible justifica- tion, but his decision to fire is final.

Another related variation is the *Stealing Game*, in which player A starts a scene in a room where it is established that he is the owner of numerous physical props there (e.g., he is a doctor in an office containing his supplies and instruments). Player B enters, wearing a long, oversized coat (B could be a patient). As the scene is played, A finds a number of pretexts to turn away from B; whenever he does so, B grabs a prop or two and stuffs it under his coat. A's job is to allow B to steal, but will try to catch him; A will turn back abruptly and demand to know what B is doing with his arms wrapped around himself, why something is bulging under (or stick- ing out from) the coat, etc. B attempts to justify his actions or the suspicious circumstances, yet continues to take every opportunity to keep stealing more. What makes this scene so funny is B's insane persistence in stealing.

In both *Making Faces* and *Stealing Game* the player in the antisocial role can be encouraged to take greater chances of being caught (and will be caught, eventually). The therapeutic benefit of doing so lies in playfully taking risks, instead of "playing it safe" in order to win or avoid danger.

The King Game is most useful for helping chronic low-status and socially inhibited clients experience an aggressive form of high-status play and the expression of hostility; the therapist/director may need to coach the king to be more autocratic and arbitrary in order to desensitize clients overconcerned about hurting others' feelings. The servants get to play abject and terrified low-status roles; their task is to learn how not to call attention to themselves, keep activities going, not invade the monarch's space, and avoid bringing about a situation in which the king has to think about anything (since this nearly always results in the "death" of the servant). In the employer variation, the main fun is had by the employees, who shift rapidly between deferential behavior to the employer's face and vulgar mockery behind his back. Such lowering of the status of the powerful by the downtrodden, while being at risk, has universal appeal and is satisfying to an audience as well.

TUG-OF-WAR

This is one of the most clinically useful improv exercises. In one simple, brief enactment, *Tug-of-War* teaches many of the RfG principles and objectives: cocreating a reality, making others look good, accepting (body) offers, paying attention to your partner(s), giving up overcontrol, being aware of status clues. Clinically, *Tug-of-War* has great utility in assessing several qualities of connection between relationship partners; between unrelated partners also, as in classes, group therapy and workshops, *Tug-of-War* helps reveal assumptions, judgments and attitudes, especially toward power issues.

As in all RfG games and exercises, participants are offered the exercise as a voluntary activity, told that it involves physical movement, asked to take responsibility for any physical limitation they might have (e.g., sprained wrists, bad backs), and to inform their partner(s) of such limitations. It is preferable for participants to wear casual clothing with women wearing slacks and removing shoes with any heel elevation. The usual instructions are to position two persons facing one another, three to six feet apart, with some room behind each of them. The participants are told that there is an imaginary rope on the ground between them and that, on the therapist/director's signal, they are to pick up the rope and have a tug-of-war with their partner. The players need to treat the rope as a reality of their interaction; one's hauling in rope implies the other's being pulled toward the center. Blocking often takes the form of a "rubber rope" which is seen as stretching or going slack when the players are inattentive.

Often, I instruct players to make eye contact, make sounds without using words, and to have there be a winner within 30 seconds. Following whatever outcome, I then often have them repeat the game twice, with the predetermined outcome of each participant winning once and losing once.

In this way, the exercise is transformed from a contest into a scripted theatrical performance, where the aim now becomes to make the enactment convincing.

Tug-of-War helps reveal assumptions, judgments, and attitudes, especially toward power issues. Players may reveal their willingness to lose, to win, or to permit a decisive outcome by the way they approach this exercise. As in RfG generally, regardless of the way the participants play *Tug-of-War*, the therapist/director needs to remain supportive and nonjudgmental, offering feedback and suggestions in a way that conveys that all concerned are here to learn and play together.

The primary issue of clinical interest is whether the couple is involved with cocreating the reality of the rope and of the struggle. Assuming that the exercise is attempted, a further issue concerns whether the couple can create a decisive, hard-fought outcome, or whether one member will either prematurely give in, or will refuse to permit either a win or loss. As this exercise implies the creation of a competitive reality, the partners bring to the *Tug-of-War* their own proclivities and assumptions regarding competition. When done with a man-woman pairing, for example, not infrequently the woman assumes she is no match for the man in an apparently physical contest, overlooking that mental intensity, not physical strength or size, is relevant here. Even more often, "not being defeated," "not winning," or maintaining control by "letting the other win" emerge as motives. Observe also how the partners use body language—some convey great involvement by grimacing and straining, while others smile and appear minimally involved.

Asking participants about their experience following the initial round usually reveals each partner's issues with the enactment, whereupon the instructor may repeat the exercise after further instructions. For example, the report of a man who gave in to his female partner revealed a fear of being perceived a bully, while the woman experienced humiliation at being patronized. The therapist/director reminded them of the goal to create a convincing struggle and invited them to repeat the exercise, with the man asked to lose only after putting up a good fight, the woman asked to win after almost losing, and both reminded to make frequent eye contact. The result was a far more convincing *Tug-of-War*, after which both participants reported feeling energized and more connected with one another.

In groups, it is possible to have teams on each side of the rope, although this usually becomes more of a high-energy warm-up than a clinically useful exercise. An exception is men vs. women, where the peer pressure highlights gender schisms (men particularly will scapegoat one of their own who doesn't show the team spirit). In groups we have found it helpful to have one couple enact *Tug-of-War* while half the members root for each partner, heightening the felt significance of the contest.

CLINICAL USE OF STATUS

The intentional use of status transactions in therapy does not require that they be used in conjunction with improv, although improv is an ideal way of learning about and developing proficiency at such maneuvers. An instructive example of effective use of self by means of status change is provided by Aponte (1977). As the therapist conducting an initial interview with a low-income, single-parent family, his efforts to join the family were impeded by several factors: their reluctance to attend the interview, their annoyance at his lateness in conjunction with their early arrival, the pressure he felt to conduct the interview competently as a demonstration for observing clinicians. Out of his own discomfort Aponte began defensively, maintaining his high status.

> THERAPIST I'm the director of the clinic here and what I have is a group of clinicians who can see you here . . .
> MRS. J People who?
> THERAPIST . . . psychologists, social workers, you know [Mrs. J makes an expression of displeasure] . . . you have an attitude about . . . you don't like that?
> MRS. J I really don't.
> RAYMOND I don't either.
> THERAPIST You don't . . . alright. Then maybe I should have somebody else see you because I have to do this for them. This is like . . . we have conferences and we show each other the work that we do. It's up to you; I mean, nobody is putting pressure on you.

> I was in a bind. They threatened to refuse the taping and I countered with the threat to withdraw myself after having announced I was the director. In the waiting area, they had already threatened me with not accepting me and left me feeling insecure. I felt excluded by them, treated by them as an alien to them and their circumstances. That hurt and irritated me but it did not show. I looked deliberately relaxed and in control as I sipped coffee. A forced retreat would not have brought me any closer to them. They conceded ground. (pp. 103–104)

The initial resentment and protectiveness exhibited by the family represent their attempts to obtain high status by lowering the status of the therapist, the setting, and perhaps the entire enterprise of therapy. Aponte recognizes the desirability of their attaining high status (he is keenly aware of the disempowering acceptance of low status), yet he is in a bind: he needs their cooperation but does not wish to lower his own status by relinquishing control.

> I felt connected with them and yet, that day, our positions and current circumstances put great distance between us and I felt it. They treated me like a member of the oppressive society that overawed me as a child. I understood their initial resentment and protectiveness but also resented them for not recognizing themselves in me. I knew I had to reach them on their terms but I also could not compromise mine as their therapist and the teacher of a group of clinicians who were observing. (p. 112)

Observing that Raymond, the oldest son, functions as the boundary guard of the family, Aponte makes the choice to maintain his own high status while offering high status to Raymond. He next works to equalize status with Raymond by connecting around boxing as a way of joining with the family:

THERAPIST Are you interested in sports?
RAYMOND Just boxing.
THERAPIST Just boxing . . . how interested are you in boxing?
RAYMOND Very interested in boxing [shifts in his chair, looks with a grin at the ceiling and then at me].
THERAPIST I mean . . .
RAYMOND I want to be a boxer one day . . . yeah . . .
THERAPIST Have you done any boxing?
RAYMOND Uh, huh.
THERAPIST Where have you done boxing?
RAYMOND At the PAL Center on Manchester Street.
THERAPIST Have you been in any kind of amateur bouts or are you just training?
RAYMOND Just training.
THERAPIST Uh, huh . . . how much do you weigh?
RAYMOND About 195 . . . light heavyweight.
THERAPIST Oh, no . . . you would be a heavyweight.
RAYMOND Light heavyweight.
THERAPIST Light heavyweight?
RAYMOND . . . I just started gaining weight, really.
THERAPIST Do you think you would be fighting at 175 or something like that?
RAYMOND 178. [I let the 3 pound discrepancy pass.]

Raymond and I, here, find ground on which we can both meet and compete. I, too, am interested in boxing and we dispute each other about whether or not he is a light heavyweight (the light heavyweight limit is 175 pounds). I engage him on this issue. I want him to like me and so we would continue to talk about boxing, but, I want him to respect me, so I am reluctant to back down in our disagreement. This discussion is a metaphor of the struggle between Raymond and myself as I believe he attempts to protect the family. If I can gain ground with Raymond the odds improve to win with the family, but while I try to join him, I must not shrink from him. If I do, I will lose status in my own eyes and possibly his. If I do not feel in control of the situation, I will become inhibited. The tension in me heightens at this point. I struggle between being accommodating and striking back. Being aware of that helped. Did he feel similarly? (p. 106)

The struggle Aponte highlights here is common to a vast array of social and clinical situations. At this point in the session Aponte raises Raymond's status by displaying his interest in Raymond's boxing activities; however, if he challenges Raymond's misinformation about the light heavyweight weight limit he upholds his own high status but lowers Raymond's. On the other hand, if he agrees with Raymond he equalizes status but risks lowering his own. By asking questions Aponte brings the misinformation indirectly to Raymond's notice, giving him the opportunity for a mutually face-saving compromise in front of each of their reference groups (the family and the onlooking clinicians). Interestingly, this maneuver is often used by low-status players to avoid challenging high-status players, such as when a subordinate wishing to bring his superior's notice to a mistake committed by the superior respectfully inquires as to whether things are as they should be.

> THERAPIST Do you ever go see the fights at the Spectrum or the Arena?
> RAYMOND Sometimes.
> THERAPIST When was the last time you went?
> RAYMOND It was two ladies . . . I forget.
> THERAPIST Two ladies [sniggering]. Oh, I wouldn't have gone to see that. Are you going to the Briscoe-Hart fight?
> RAYMOND Ain't that tonight?
> THERAPIST That's the sixth . . . I think that it's next week, next Tuesday night. Are you going?
> RAYMOND Yeah, I was thinking about going. [He uncrosses his arms for a moment and passes his hand behind his head.]
> THERAPIST The tickets are pretty expensive . . . I thought I was going to go, but I think I am not going to go.

I had kidded Raymond about his going to see two ladies fighting which was joining him in a one-up position. His gesture of discomfort in answering about attending the Briscoe-Hart fight made me think he was not going. I retreated to join him in a one-down position by acknowledging that I probably would not go to the fight because it was expensive, which was true. He conceded me a small smile at the end of this interchange. I thought his defense loosened a bit. (pp. 106–107)

Note Aponte's lowering of status, in the last line, in order to join Raymond despite his determination not to lose status in his own eyes. When a person intentionally shifts her or his status, his self-esteem is not thereby at risk. Thus, therapists can be trained both to recognize their own habitual status patterns and to learn to vary those they play. Just as there are problems encountered when committed to playing high status (as in Aponte's example), chronic low-status players also run into difficulties as therapists. A therapist who can raise and lower status of both self and others convincingly will be able to deal resourcefully with the widest range of clinical opportunities.

A breakthrough for the inhibited actor cannot be hoped for except in improvisation. If the emotionally bound-up actor merely rehearses and performs, almost inevitably he will merely continue in patterns of inexpressiveness.

—Lee Strasberg (cited in Hothman, 1965, p. 226)

CHAPTER 8

Expanding Emotional Expressiveness

ONE OF THE THERAPEUTIC purposes served by improv exercises is to free clients from the often constricted range of emotional expressivity displayed in a specific context (such as a marital relationship) or throughout life itself. Because psychotherapy is itself a specific social context, strongly influenced by the therapist's own preferred emotional style, therapists often have an incomplete or distorted assessment of their clients' emotional range (when they have considered the issue at all). For example, suppose a therapist with an emotionally calm, cerebral style is working with an intellectualized, angry client. The client picks up on the therapist's comfort with rational discourse and keeps from experiencing or expressing anger, even when anger is the topic in focus during therapeutic sessions. The therapist, while noting the intellectualized style of the client, may well be unaware of how limited the client's expression of anger is.

For many clients, improv enactments teach an emotional vocabulary, point up how others signal emotion, and permit comparisons both within and across scenes on how nuances of emotive expression powerfully shape social reality. Improv enactments also lend themselves to a suspension of the constraints that regularly inhibit acting "out of character" by offering fictional characters through which to live. Despite such permission, clients frequently discover that they cannot bring themselves to fully enter the stage reality of their character. They either break character altogether or underexpress the emotion called for in the moment (yet another variation is to offer a caricature of the emotion which is recognizably incongruous for that stage character). What is of primary interest in RfG is the expression of emotion that accesses a character or part of self in the moment, rather than emotional amplitude or intensity for its own sake. Within the acting profession there is a widely taught technique of locating and reexperiencing a personal emotional reaction in order to present a convincing emotional performance. Spolin (1963) believed that the actor should play emotions freshly derived from present experience instead of evoking them by dredging up memories of previous experiences, a process she termed "psychodrama."

Johnstone borrows the concept of "heat" (passionate expression that betokens emotional involvement) from staged wrestling (which he sees as a form of working-class theater) to guide Theatresports performances. He thus stands in the tradition of theater artists like Antonin Artaud and Peter Brook who desire to rescue contemporary theater from the stultifying alliance between an overdistanced, "educated" audience and a dull, "cultured" performance. As Shepher (1992) observes, "An audience that is not bound by accepted rules reacts more spontaneously, and it would seem that the less 'cultured' an audience, the more spontaneous it may show itself to be" (p. 186). Similarly, in improv group therapy the degree to which spectators are involved with the enactments of other group members is a measure of how cohesive and empathic the group is, as well as how spontaneous the players are. The human need for catharsis, to shout en masse, is not experienced by "lit-crit" audiences, nor by therapy groups that function only at the level of observing and analyzing.

GAMES AND EXERCISES
FOR INCREASING EXPRESSIVENESS

While all improv games and exercises offer opportunities for emotional work, the following games, listed roughly in order of difficulty, have proved directly useful for exploring and expanding emotional expressiveness. A frequent result for players in these games is the recognition that their emotional responses are a matter of how they choose to approach or construe a situation; thus, these games experientially teach this major tenet of cognitive therapy.

It should also be noted that most of the other games and exercises already described (particularly *Overaccepting Together*) will evoke or facilitate emotional expressiveness, both as a consequence of playfulness and the dynamism of enacted characters.

GIBBERISH EMOTIONS

In the simplest variation, *Free-form Gibberish*, paired players have a gibberish conversation, experimenting with their inflections to express emotions of different quality and intensity while picking up on the expressions of their partners. In another variation, *Gibberish Lists*, the therapist/director prepares a list of four to seven successively contrasting moods or emotions and calls out each in turn every half-minute or so. The players continue a dialogue, preferably with plenty of gesturing, expressing the most recently called-out emotion. Another variation is described below under *Volume Control*.

A significant minority of players find it difficult to speak in gibberish. They will vocalize sounds without consonants, repeat the same syllable pattern over and over (for instance, "bibble-bibble-bibble-bibble") or completely freeze up. About half of these players will readily respond to brief private coaching; the others may require gradual exposure before venturing into gibberish scenes and exercises.

CIRCLE GIBBERISH

In *Circle Gibberish*, three or more players in a circle have a group "discussion," gesturing and reacting in no particular order to one another's gibberish as though the content was understood. This is one exercise in which it is preferable for the therapist/director to initiate the discussion among the players. In this way the therapist/director can draw in players who are less active. Of course, as in improv generally, whenever a gibberish utterance (or any offer) is reacted to with great emotionality the speaker is made to appear influential and validated. *Circle Gibberish* may be used as a group or family warm-up, as it creates a more expressive and cohesive group atmosphere.

One useful variation is to have the gibberish offer made in turn going around the circle, with each player first receiving an offer in gibberish, next responding with gibberish to the offerer while matching the emotion, and then turning to the next player, making a gibberish offer in a contrasting emotion. This game can also be played making minimal emotional offers rather than broad ones; this sharpens the players' perceptions and develops more subtle and varied vocal inflections and gestures.

GIBBERISH GROUP STORY

Best attempted following *Circle Gibberish*, this game has seated players go around the circle in turn, speaking gibberish and using gestures and mimed objects to build upon previous players' offers to tell a collective story. This game helps players attend to one another, reincorporate (see Chapter 6) the gibberish utterances and gestures of others, and experience a relatively low-risk form of expressiveness in front of a group. At the end of the "story" I often invite players, in turn, to describe what the story was when it reached their turn and what their added part was. While the discrepancy between players' accounts is usually great (and amusing!), it is also suprising how players pick up on one another's offers in some particulars and how the mood of the story is accurately sustained.

YOU WILL/I WON'T

In this simple exercise, borrowed from Gestalt therapy, two players face one another and repeat the dialogue (A: You will. B: I won't) with a variety of inflections and gestures. After several rounds, A and B trade scripts and repeat the exercise. While this exercise might be classified as an exercise with a blocking premise (since it demonstrates how opposition, here the premise of opposing wills, can be used to create a scene) it is more usefully employed to explore emotional intensity and variety. Often, feedback between partners elicits useful information concerning the effect of one's partner's emotion on the other's (frustration, pleasure at frustrating the other, seduction, etc.).

VOLUME CONTROL

I devised this set of exercises to assist players in overcoming their reticence to express, or to have others express, more intense emotion. While not, of course, synonymous with intensity, volume does carry messages of intensity, intimacy, and self-control. In the most basic variation, the therapist/director calls out "Soft!" "Normal!" or "Loud!" at frequent, random intervals while an ordinary dyadic or group conversation is held by the players. Upon hearing the call, the speaking player instantly shifts to the volume level named; the conversation continues at this level until the next call. Numerous variations (for dyads) may be used:

1. There may be more than three volume levels.
2. Players can be assigned fixed volume positions.
3. A rule can be employed that one responds to soft with normal, to normal with loud, and to loud with soft.

4. One player can be instructed while the other player varies volume spontaneously.
5. Both players can vary their own levels spontaneously.
6. Gibberish can be substituted for some or all of the meaningful words in the conversation (see *Gibberish Lists*, and *Insults*, p. 132).

Another kind of exercise is to give players control over one another's volume level. This can be done by having the player hold up a number of fingers at or near the end of his or her speaking turn. For example, if a five-point volume scale is used, player A holds up two fingers, signifying that player B is to speak softer than normal; B, near the end of his turn, holds up one finger for A to whisper; A holds up five fingers, indicating that B is to shout. For anxious players paired with less-anxious ones, it is helpful initially to give the anxious one control of the other player's volume but not to be controlled by the other player(s). After doing this exercise for a short while the anxious player can be invited to hold up a number of fingers for his own turn as well as the turn of his partner, followed by each controlling the other's volume.

Volume control can be used in conjunction with games like *Emotional Lists* (below) in order to explore the expressive range available to a client around a specific emotion (particularly anger). When combined with status exercises (see Chapter 7) players can explore how volume influences, but does not determine, status. Such use of volume is an example of how exercises may be combined in order to customize improv interventions as well as to create new improv forms (see Appendix B).

HITCHHIKER

This beginning group exercise is useful for helping players accept emotional offers. Four chairs are set in two rows to simulate the seating of a car. Four players sit in the car, miming going on a drive and having a conversation, with all four displaying the same mood (which is supplied initially by the therapist/director). Other group members line up on the "side of the road"; the player at the front of the line puts out his thumb and flags down the car, which stops for him. Any one of the players in the car finds a reason to get out of the car (miming opening and closing his door) which makes room for the hitchhiker. When the hitchhiker enters the car he establishes a contrasting mood or attitude; the other three players give him their attention and all take on the same mood or attitude. All four maintain this attitude until the next hitchhiker changes it again.

EMOTIONAL LISTS

This game is related to *Hitchhiker*. Two players begin an improvised scene, both playing an emotion supplied by a therapist/director from a list of emotions drawn up in advance. At various points the scene is frozen, a new emotion supplied, and the scene continued with both players taking up the new emotion. Throughout, the players must continue playing the scene while justifying their emotions. This game is usually lively and often stimulates players to expand their variety of emotional expression.

This game can also be played in a somewhat more difficult version where the players are given different concurrent emotions to play. For example, A plays "sadness" while B plays "anger"; then, A is switched to "fear" while B is to play "boredom." Another version has A assume B's emotion when B is switched to a new one. The challenge in all three versions is twofold: first, to play the emotion authentically; second, to justify the current emotion in relation to what has gone before in the scene.

EMOTIONAL ZONES

The stage area is divided into two or more zones, each of which is given the name of a contrasting emotion. During a scene, any player moving into a different zone must play his part and justify that emotion for as long as he remains in that zone. It is helpful to instruct players to play their emotion immediately upon entering or leaving a zone, and to physicalize in addition to indicating emotion verbally. Since the main interest in this game is to experience and justify abrupt contrasts in emotion, players have an incentive to advance the action so that they, or another player, gets to move into other zones.

COUPLES WITH CONTRASTING EMOTIONS

This game, also known as *Family Masks*, is for four players, divided into two pairs. The scene is set by the therapist/director, who assigns players the roles of two marital couples, each with a contrasting emotional mood, and who are meeting socially (e.g., "The Grumps" meet "The Cheerfuls," "The Anguisheds" meet "The Boreds," or "The Haughties" meet "The Humbles"). Each couple in turn plays a short scene in their assigned mood before playing the main scene, in which the couples meet. The couples' relationship could be that of friends, strangers, business partners, neighbors, siblings, etc., while the setting could be over dinner, on a double-date, in a lifeboat, on a tennis court, etc. During the main scene players should be coached to remain in their mood, whether with their partner or in interaction with the other couple.

This game will be useful for players who have no real-life relationship with their scene partner, but it is especially valuable to actual couples (I regularly use this game in relationship workshops with couples). What happens often is that each player experiences being reinforced in maintaining the assigned mood by his or her partner so that there is a feeling of playing on a team, an experience familiar to most actual couples. When there is competition or hostility between the partners this team spirit breaks down or does not arise (see Chapter 11).

I have also used a variation of this game with families in which the family ensemble plays the same emotion and I take the role of an interviewer, guest in their home, tour guide, etc., with a contrasting mood or attitude. As with the couples variation, this game promotes a team spirit that is often lacking for the whole nuclear family.

INSULTS

In my version of this Keith Johnstone game, a brief, commonplace scenario is first enacted between two players. Then, the same scenario is repeated, but with a gibberish word added at the end of each line. This gibberish word is treated as an insult by the other player, who reacts with astonishment and annoyance, repeating the word before delivering his next line (which also ends in a gibberish word-insult). The first player now repeats the insult while reacting strongly and going on to deliver his next line, ending with a gibberish insult, etc.

As the scene advances the insults become greater so the reactions to them magnify to disbelief and outrage, climaxing in all-but-speechless fury. When the players pace themselves and remember to complete the scene (not always easy to do!) this game produces wonderfully satisfying results for players and onlookers alike. Following is an example of an *Insults* scene.   .

[Player A is given the role of shopkeeper; player B is a customer. The scenario is for B to enter A's shop, buy a hat, and leave.]
A Good morning, prizig.
B Prizig? I'd like a hat, black, size seven, darbostari.
A Darbostari!? . . . Yes, here's one you might like, mashoo!
B What! Mashoo!?! You . . . ah, how much is it, Zopnish!
A ZOPNISH!!! Fifteen ninety-five for you, BROOLBAH!!
B *BROOLBAH*?!?! You call ME Broolbah? I'll . . . I'll take it, you . . . Vonnerflub!!
A *VONNERFLUB*!!! You . . . you . . . Here's your change and I hope you enjoy the hat . . . FLINIGPOTZ!!!
B FLINIGPOTZ??? *FLINIGPOTZ*!!!! . . . Good Day!

As Johnstone (1981) points out, we are not so interested in insulting, but rather in seeing someone insulted. "The interest we have in custard pies is in seeing them hit people" (p. 54). Johnstone uses other variations of this game primarily to free the actors he trains from self-consciousness and defensiveness; once someone can accept being insulted, he explains, that person then feels safe and experiences great elation. In our work a "high" is often experienced following such an emotional "full-out" enactment. Therapist/directors should also attend to the accompanying freedom of gesture and body position of which the players will, most likely, be unaware.

TEAM INSULTS

This Johnstone game involves a group divided into two teams standing in facing lines. One player steps forward and flings a verbal insult to the opposing team as a whole, with the insult-word in gibberish and accompanied by appropriate gestures — for example, "You're just a bunch of *Roonaps!*" delivered in a sneering manner. He is cheered on and congratulated by his teammates, while the insulted team reacts visibly — incensed, perhaps shocked. Then one member of the just-insulted team steps forward and, to the delight of her team, similarly insults the first team ("Oh yeah? Well, *you're* all SPIGBLOKERS!!"). The intensity of these exchanges, amplified by the teams, grows to the point where teams may have to mock-restrain their members from charging at the opposing team; the therapist/director must stay alert to the possibility that things may escalate to the point where players forget that they are in-role (if the insults change from gibberish words to actual insults, for example) and stop the action promptly.

I have used this game with a mixed-sex group that was discussing gender issues in a restrained, overintellectualized fashion, having men on one team and women on the other. It cleared the air and the discussion proceeded in a more direct and emotionally honest manner. It may also be helpful in weakening existing alliances in groups to have allies play on opposing teams.

IT'S TUESDAY

The first of two players makes a simple statement that the second player reacts to in some specific emotional way and continues to build to the extreme beyond coherence, and ultimately to a comic death. This game works best when people have built trust and feel safe to take big risks together. The player who has just "died" revives and then makes a simple statement to which her partner responds with a different emotion, but in like manner. There is license given to break all the rules against making noise and losing emotional control, the result of which is most often glee on the part of the players and those watching. Follows is an example of an *It's Tuesday* scene.

A That's a nice watch you're wearing.
B (rather softly at first) Yes, it is rather nice. Do you know how I got it? (warming up and speaking louder) For 38 years I worked for the Canarsie Railway. Rain or shine, I was there. (impassioned now) Slaved for them, really. (louder still, with anger) I GAVE THEM THE BEST YEARS OF MY LIFE! (yelling and waving fists) *AND TWO WEEKS BEFORE RETIREMENT THEY CUT OFF MY PENSION AND GAVE ME THIS STINKING WATCH INSTEAD!!* (shrieking while thrashing and rolling on the floor) **The Bastards!!! I'll kill them all!!! ARRRRRRGH!!** (B "dies." A brief pause. B sits up and says to A) Blue has always been my favorite color.
[etc.]

It's Tuesday, though conceptually straightforward, can be a difficult game to play convincingly, as few of us are so spontaneous as to be able to take matters to their full emotional extreme. Since many, if not most, players will hold themselves back at some point, the therapist/director can praise the players for having gone as far as they did and later explore verbally what stopped them from going further. Another version of *It's Tuesday*, related also to *Emotional Lists* (p. 131), has the therapist/director call out a contrasting extreme emotion for each player on every turn or two, so that the players, in effect, overaccept each other's offer. The game works best when the final remark in each player's turn is neutral or innocuous, so that the overacceptance can stand in greater emotional contrast.

WALLPAPER DRAMA

In this curiously named, four-person game created by Keith Johnstone, the players are assigned a location where a number of people might meet and are instructed to begin an emotionally neutral scene between two on-stage players. At some point the therapist/director calls out "Positive!" and the players *gradually* shift the emotional tone of the scene in this direction. The therapist/director calls out changes from time to time, switching the emotional tone through neutral from positive to negative and back again. The four players enter or leave the scene so that there are never more than two characters on stage for more than a moment during exits and entrances. The players have the option to time the shifts of emotional tone to coincide with an exit or entrance.

This game heightens players' sensitivity to the minimal cues present in offers upon which emotional/attitudinal choices to shift tone may be made. When used to sharpen observational skills, an entire scene may be videotaped and immediately replayed, with the therapist/director "freeze-framing" at transition points to highlight the choice made, and to invite alternatives. While this interruption can be done during the actual enactment as well, such a disruption of the scene will wipe out the emotional tone and a new scene should be begun rather than continue with the interrupted one.

STEPS TOWARD ENACTING ANOTHER SELF

In classical Greek theater the actors wore masks; the word "person" is derived from the Latin *persona*, meaning mask. As Landy (1991) points out,

> At the heart of the dramatic experience . . . is the principle of impersonation, the ability of the person to take on a persona, or role. The dramatic experience is one of paradox: I am me and not-me at the same time. It is one of engagement and separation: I take on a role and then I separate from it . . . In its present form, role is persona rather than person, character rather than full-blown human being, part rather than whole. It is that which holds two realities, the everyday and the imaginative, in a paradoxical relationship to one another. Without role there can be no drama. (p. 29)

The following games and exercises further the exploration of taking on and/or deepening the enactment of a persona.

MANTRA

This exercise is one in which the players are instructed to mentally repeat a phrase that focuses their character's intention toward the other character during the playing of a two-person scene. The mantra may be "I love you," "I hate you," "I hate you but want to sleep with you," "I'm afraid of you," etc. The mantra, which should always be phrased in the affirmative, is to be repeated throughout the scene but is said out loud only if it can be said truthfully. Players may have the same or different mantras from one another, only one may use a mantra, or the dialogue can be in gibberish.

The content of the scene may start out as unrelated to the mantra; the precise nature of the mantra, when given privately, may be unclear to the other player but the presence of its intention invariably makes itself felt to the audience and the other player during the scene. Scenes done with mantras take on a dramatic intensity as the players are more involved emotionally with one another than is ordinarily the case.

This exercise is clinically useful for training clients to alter a recurrent position they take up with a relative or other significant person; it will work best when the therapy has prepared the client to stand in a different position with the significant other and when the actual encounter involves just the two of them. The other person will, quite often, display attitudes and behaviors that are atypical of the client's prior experience with them, to the surprise of both.

FAMILY LEGEND

This group game, a variation on the form of *The Trial* (p. 99), is based on a story involving an actual (often long-dead) ancestor in one client's family tree. The client tells as much of the story as he knows (which may be merely a description of a single trait or event) and then sits in a chair in the center of the group. From this point on the client acts the role of this ancestor. The other group members, who are standing, take on improvised characters; these characters may be freely invented and need not be relatives, yet are based on the given story. Each character in turn approaches the ancestor, addressing him or her in character. During this speech the ancestor "takes in," but does not react or reply. After all characters have spoken, the ancestor gets out of the chair and replies, as the ancestor, to each character in turn; the characters now "take in," but do not react or reply. The family has now invested drama into the legend; they may then be encouraged to discuss the meaning and impact of their newly fleshed-out legend.

CHARACTER RELAY

In this group game (which was developed by David Shepherd, the founder of Improvisational Olympics), each of the players is supplied with one physical prop as well as an identity and relationship to the other character(s). The players begin a two-person scene which is frozen by the therapist/director calling "Switch!" At this point, the players exchange props and roles and continue the scene as the character with whom they have switched, imitating the voice, movement, and character of the player who originated the role.

In a considerably more complex version, more than two characters are used; then, the players are not switched until each character has been established in a two-person scene which is connected to the story line of the previous scene(s). The story line is developed and advanced by different pairings, round-robin style, after which it may be possible to have scenes with three or more players. The physical prop helps to anchor each character for the players. This game trains players in assuming character "from the outside" and sharpens observational skills.

BEHAVIORAL LISTS

In this group game, the therapist/director writes down, on a separate card for each, three to seven attributes or social postures (such as "athletic/intellectual/wealthy/sexy," etc.) that represent some of the ways that people *try to appear* to others. For each, the group contributes a list of *behaviors* that help convey the attribute. For instance, the "To Be Seen as Athletic" list might include "doing push-ups/slapping people on the butt," etc., while the "To Be Thought Wealthy" list could contain "mentioning luxury items owned/referring to servants," etc. Once every list has at least five items (and a list can have 30) the therapist/director sets up a scene with two or more players in a specified location and has the players draw a card randomly for their character to play the attribute on that card. Players are instructed to play the scene in character, referring to the card in order to include any of the behaviors on the list, in whatever order, that can be justified and truthfully played. This last point is important, since a player intent on "getting through" list items will not attend to others or the logic of the scene. It is also helpful for the therapist/director to coach players to try something else on their lists every 20 seconds or so, in order to provide transitions for the scene. A variation has players exchanging lists and replaying the scene; it is instructive to note how different players attempt making the same list work.

This Keith Johnstone game teaches players to develop vivid characters by grounding their performance in specific behavioral characteristics, rather than merely having a "purpose" or "intention." Characters become interesting when they play their lists, regardless of whether or not they achieve their purpose. *Behavioral Lists* is a valuable resource in RfG; it provides an easy and effective way for players to extend themselves and play "against type"; that is, to not play the character(s) they normally play, on-stage and off. Not only does this exercise give clients permission to play unfamiliar characterizations with minimal social risk, it also facilitates behavioral rehearsal of certain social skills, offering options that may be internalized to promote changes in real life. Conceptually, enactment in *Behavioral Lists* lies between free improv and scripted drama and does for improvisers what improv does for not-in-role clients: it lowers (or further displaces) accountability for one's stage behavior as representing one's "real-life" character. As Johnstone (1988) observes, *Behavioral Lists* corresponds to Virginia Satir's scenario, in which a family consisting of a blamer ("To Make Guilty"), a placater ("To Accept Guilt"), a distracter ("To Be a Confuser") and an intellectualizer ("To Be a Computer") interact.

Clinicians will also benefit from this game to focus on what "list" a client is playing. Any list may be applied to any dramatic text (such as a *Soap Scene*, p. 96) or to any real-life situation as well, although naturally there are consequences to be considered in doing so. Still, persons who apply lists to shaping their self-presentation, such as clinicians in training (see Chapter 14), will expand their skills and open up further possibilities for adventures in social interaction.

COMBINED LISTS

In this advanced variation of *Behavioral Lists* three or more players enact a scene in which each player plays a different list to each of the other players. Suppose, for instance, that player A is playing "To Convince Others that You're Normal" toward player B while playing "To Get Sympathy" from player C. At the same time, B may be playing "To Give People a Good Time" toward A and "To Give People a Hard Time" toward C. Meanwhile, C is playing "To Be Thought Beautiful By Others" toward A and "To Be Thought Wealthy" toward B. Players in this game discover how richly layered social interaction can be.

INVITING A CHARACTER

This series of steps, developed by Gloria Maddox, constitutes a methodical and thorough improvisational approach to exploring a character "from the inside" that is unlike one's everyday persona. The therapist/director begins by asking each of the players, who are seated, to focus on some character attribute that has a particular "charge" to that person. This could be an attribute that the player is repulsed by, has some significant judgment about, holds dear, etc. The therapist/director then invites players to close their eyes and allow that attribute to inhabit their bodies and take them over, to become another character. Players are then asked to stand and begin moving slowly as their new character, exploring the physicality of their character's body and giving their character a name, age, gender, occupation, country of origin, circumstances, how they dress, etc. Next, the players are instructed to give their character a line of dialogue, to see the world through their character's eyes, to get in touch with their character's needs, and to begin to interact with other players' characters in order to get their own character's needs fulfilled.

After a brief amount of time during which the players in character interact with a few other characters, they are instructed to be seated again, shut their eyes, breathe deeply, bring up the opposite characteristic in themselves and repeat the process described above as their new character. Then, some players are invited to interact in pairs, in character, in front of the rest while the rest are asked to be observers as one of the two characters they had just explored. The pairs do a *Boring Scene* (p. 87), beginning the scene as one of their characters and transforming into the opposite character by the end of the scene.

This complex exercise is richly layered in the levels of pretense and reality that players encounter. When taking on the chosen attribute, a player first focuses on the general emotive transformation occasioned by one's identity being changed.*

Next, there is a physical and cognitive shift in orientation as movement and specific social identity features are added. With the addition of dialogue and social interaction, the player explores the character in a dynamic aspect, improvising from a deeper perspective.† After this, for both those playing a scene and those being a spectator in character, the dimension of theatrical performance is added, creating meta-theater (see p. 3). Finally, the evocation of the opposite characteristic and the transformation from one to the other character during the enacted scene demonstrate the wealth of possible identity choices we all possess.

Unlike games and exercises, which are relatively brief in execution and which engage only a superficial or limited aspect of client functioning, *Invite a Character* is lengthy and taps into profound and broad-ranging therapeutic issues. As when using most games and exercises, the therapist/ director employing *Invite a Character* needs to tailor the amount and depth of ensuing discussion to both the group's purpose and to its level of sophistication (see Improvisation as a Clinical Tool, p. 144).

PLAY THE MONSTER

In this emotionally involving game, one player selects one, two, or three endowments that are personally repugnant and describes and/or demonstrates these briefly to a partner. It should be clearly understood that the endowments offered are not attributes that the selecting player detects in, or projects onto, his partner but are ones that are difficult for himself to play. At this point the partner has the option of refusing the offer to play any or all of the endowments, in which case the rejected endowments are dropped from the scene, and the first player offers acceptable alternatives. These agreed-upon unwelcome endowments — physical, emotional, and psychological — are then incorporated into both players' characters in an improvised scene. Depending upon the purpose to which this game is put, it

---

*There is a lot of commonality between the altered state of consciousness fostered by this exercise, mask/trance stage work, and ritual. In all three, there exists a simultaneous awareness of one's normal social identity as well as a distinct, alternative one. This state of consciousness differs, however, from that of being "possessed" or taken over by an alternative identity, since one's awareness of normal identity remains present in the background of consciousness.

†Note the correspondence between improvisation in this exercise and the preparation of an actor taking on a dramatic role, as referred to by Gloria Maddox (p. 14).

may be desirable to approach the formation of characters using the methods described in *Inviting a Character*. Following the scene, players generally have a great deal to share about their enactment and perceptions of the endowment in each's choices.

What makes this game particularly valuable is the experience of exploring a relationship in which these repugnant endowments are shared with another, rather than defining one's character merely by contrasting its endowments with those of another. Paradoxically, scenes developed within this game may seem to outside observers to be focused on the endowments (because these are indicated and referred to a good deal), yet the reported experience of the players is often one of intimacy with one's partner and a greatly reduced distancing from these endowments in others in real life. When used in conjunction with other therapeutic tools, *Play the Monster* contributes both to increased toleration of differences in others and to a reintegration of excluded parts of the self (Schwartz, 1992).

Another way of using this game is to have two or more players share the role, either by substituting for one another during the enactment of a scene or in the manner of *Couples with Contrasting Emotions* (p. 131). As Pat Watts (1992) points out, this device can reduce the psychological risk of playing monsters that feel too threatening to the individual, particularly in the case of malevolent or angry characters.

PART III

Pragmatics: Applying Improv to Clinical Practice and Training

I think that this is how magicians should be: first, they should do their magic to enchant us, then they should teach us their tricks.

—Augusto Boal (1992, p. 29)

CHAPTER 9

Technique

Mу practice of using improv games and exercises for therapeutic purposes developed following considerable experience with their recreaional use. There may be a temptation to treat the descriptions of improv games and exercises as a sufficient instruction for applying them to psychotherapy. For several reasons, I strongly encourage therapists to enter the world of improv personally before offering these games and exercises to their clients. First, the experience of playing these games gives the therapist an appreciation of their impact, particularly the discomfort that one invariably encounters at first. Second, the selection or creation of games in clinical situations is itself improvisatory and cannot be skillfully applied without being warmed up to the play context. Yet another reason is that introducing these games succesfully only occurs when clients experience the safety of being free from the consequences of being judged; a therapist, however well-trained, who has not experienced the process will make interpretations reflecting an outside, judgmental viewpoint. Indeed, in order to enter the play context, many clients need to see the therapist struggle and even fail occasionally in order to be sufficiently reassured. Lastly, the therapist must be available to demonstrate, model, and (often) enter the improv enactment in order to achieve her or his goals.

I encourage therapists interested in developing proficiency in RfG technique to take part in my trainer certification program and also to form peer play/study groups in which to explore and experiment with games and exercises. Another way to benefit from improv training is to learn from actors who improvise on stage. I strongly recommend seeking out groups that perform Theatresports (which are in most large and some medium-sized North American, Northern European, and Australian cities), as these improvisers work according to Keith Johnstone's principles, something not always true for other performance improvisers.

My experience is that RfG techniques are applicable to a broad range of clinical situations and that they work well within and alongside a wide variety of approaches. RfG is a way of accomplishing a number of therapeutic objectives: clarifying the role each person plays in the drama of others (imago therapy); enacting hopes and fears (Chasin's psychodramatic family therapy); trying out new stories to expand the limitations of existing self-narrative (narrative family therapy); etc.

LEVELS OF RFG APPLICATION AND INVOLVEMENT

1. Enrichment of the Therapist's Own Life

At the initial level, therapists are attracted to improv in order to refresh and enhance their use of self: using one's playfulness, enjoying the rediscovery of imagination, and appreciating the absurdity of breaking conventional logic and getting past social convention (particularly, getting to be "bad"). A related aspect of improv games and exercises is the stretching of our faculties, such that we cannot take our usual functioning for granted. An example would be *Calling Objects the Wrong Name* (p. 81), which makes the habitually-familiar world novel again, reinduces the vividness of sensation and absorption of attention from childhood, and effectively counteracts therapist burnout.

2. Improvisation as a Clinical Tool

At the next level, therapists apply the improv games and exercises that they have experienced to their clinical work. Here, the therapist becomes an improv director, introducing and coaching clients in the enactment of improv exercises for one or more of the following purposes:

- experiencing the same benefits as therapists at the above-mentioned level
- identifying defenses and limitations of individual clients

- asessing relationships — how clients interpret the task
- assessing how well clients function in an exercise (e.g., emotional range, use of body)
- noting differences in functioning during an excercise with one, rather than with another, person (group member, therapist/director, family member, stranger, etc.)
- discovering how flexibly a performance can change with coaching
- teaching principles of good relationship functioning: cooperation/support, giving up overcontrol, going on shared adventures, playfully getting others in trouble
- making interventions to change relationship functioning: expand emotional range, heighten empathy, experience new possibilities (which might be termed "expanding dramatic range")

3. Improvisation as a Systemic Intervention

At yet a deeper level, the therapist makes use of improv games and exercises to empower a shift in the therapeutic context — to change mood, energy, and status relationships during sessions by means of self-enacted changes in the therapeutic role. The therapist who operates at this level ventures beyond her or his habitual range of taking risks and spontaneity. The primary difference between this level and the previous one is that the therapist is the initial focus of the change, rather than standing outside and observing or inducing client change.

4. Improvisation as Therapeutic Artistry

At the final level, called "artistry," the therapist improvises novel scenarios that advance the therapeutic work. For artistry to occur the therapist has to be both versed in the technique of using improv and warmed up to her or his own spontaneity. The esssence of artistry cannot be captured by technique alone, for it entails an intuitive grasp of the possibilities for change in the moment as well as a vision of how the present context might be shifted. These issues are elaborated upon further in Chapter 13.

One caveat should be made clear: Unlike the therapist improvising in a recreational or training setting, when in his social role as therapist he does not ethically have license to act spontaneously upon any and all impulses which arise toward clients. As stated previously, it is practically and ethically necessary to establish a boundary that separates play from therapy and it is mandatory that the therapist remain aware of its location, behaves appropriately with respect to it, communicates its location to clients when needed, and regulates that boundary in interaction between clients. The therapist aspiring to artistry will need to attend to her or his own senses of boredom, danger, and playfulness (to name but a few), as well as to screen carefully intuitive choices in cases where she or he has known counter-transferential issues with the client(s).

PRACTICAL CONSIDERATIONS IN CLINICAL USE

It should be emphasized that the games and exercises described in this book are not offered with the expectation that a therapist can take these "off the shelf" at any time and apply them successfully as a clinical technique. Just as improv works when people accept offers, the therapist's offer of improv will need to be accepted by the client. Joining with the client, it need hardly be said, is an essential prerequisite for successfully introducing improv, yet more is needed. The therapist needs to establish a context within the session that is safe enough to support experimentation and yet which encourages risk-taking. Indeed, unless the therapist establishes a play context and is prepared to model playful interaction, these games will be of limited clinical value.

Except under the conditions specified in the next paragraph, I do not bring improv techniques into therapy during the initial session. Clients first need to learn what therapy is like and to get a sense of themselves within the present therapy context. Accordingly, it is useful to time the introduction of improv techniques to a moment when some humor, boredom, or obvious impasse in the therapy work exists—a point when both client and therapist are optimally receptive to novelty. This point often lies between those times when things are tolerable in life (and when therapy is perceived as working) and a point when things are going badly, when the client is in pain and wants immediate relief rather than change. I have found it helpful to preface the introduction of improv with, "It might be helpful to see what happens if . . . " or, "Just for fun, let's see what it would be like to . . . " Anxiety over looking foolish or doing poorly can be lessened by reminding the client that "this is just a rehearsal," a reframing that distinguishes this enactment from some unspecified, yet consequential, "performance."

I will use improv in the first session sometimes under the following conditions:

1. When dealing with very intellectualized clients who are highly experienced with therapy (such as "professional clients" or clients who themselves are therapists). In such cases, the novelty and immediacy of improv enactments offer effective alternatives to what might otherwise become an overly familiar procedure.

2. When clients enter therapy in a warmed-up or spontaneous state (usually an indication of above-average psychological health or are coming with the purpose of experiencing action techniques). In this circumstance I discuss the RfG approach and discover their expectations before moving to enactment.

3. When clients are unwilling to enter the therapeutic process (such as resentful or wary dragged-along spouses, most adolescents seen in family therapy, or court-mandated referrals). In these cases it

seems clear that there is little or nothing to lose by shifting the context of therapy from "work on you" to "play with you" and I attempt to engage them by offering myself to play with them.

When offering exercises and games it is usually best to "stretch" people gradually, offering them tasks and roles that are initially within their "comfort zone" and only later, when they have had successful experiences, offer more risky ones (an experienced improviser can usually estimate the level of both perceived and actual difficulty of an improv game or exercise). Once one member has a successful improv experience, this has the effect of "warming up" other members to attempt improv. As in psychodrama groups, the members that are the most warmed up are those to work with first, sometimes by participating in improv with those members and having the rest of the clients as an audience. To be effective as an improv director the therapist needs to appreciate the timing for offering improv exercises and be willing to allow for unpredictability without making the client(s) feel as if she or he is doing something wrong!

A number of options are available to ease players into improv enactment. One of the most useful is to have reluctant or inhibited clients serve as "understudies" to other, more able players in enactments, whereby each stands behind a player during a rehearsal scene, imitating the player's posture and movements. The therapist/director "freezes" the scene periodically; the understudy supplies a line of dialogue which is repeated by the player as the scene continues (this is similar in structure, though not in function, to psychodramatic doubling*). The next step is to have the player and understudy reverse positions and direct the players to supply the dialogue while the understudy acts the body character in the scene (essentially, a *Dubbing* game [p. 86]). A further step is then to have the understudy play both the body and voice of the character, but with the option of calling "Prompt!" if she or he gets stuck, at which point the (original) player supplies the next line or stage direction. For scenes involving emotional expression beyond the range of the understudy, the original player may repeat the understudy's last line with slightly greater emotional intensity (rather like an amplifying double in psychodrama†) or tap the understudy on the shoulder to step aside, whereupon the player performs a somewhat more forceful movement. This last technique should only be used when the players are sufficiently skilled and mature enough to intervene for the support and encouragement of the understudies without supplanting or upstaging them.

---

*In psychodrama, doubling refers to the function of voicing the inner thoughts or feelings of the central player (the protagonist).

†An amplifying double repeats the substance of the protagonist's speech, but with greater emotional intensity (using stronger language, heightened expressiveness, and/or in a louder voice).

It can be counterproductive to tell players to "do their best" since this injunction typically "raises the stakes," making them self-conscious and purposively striving. When they're not trying, people walk normally on a foot-wide plank that is resting on the ground; when that same plank is suspended one hundred feet above ground, people are intent on "doing their best" in order to survive. The result is that their bodies are so wracked with tension they can barely inch across. Likewise, coaxing reluctant clients by telling them, "It's easy!" or predicting, "It'll be fun!" is bad pedagogy, as these statements tell others what you expect their experience to be.

The role of the therapist/director during an improv is to be an observer and coach, to supply needed offers, and to intervene in order to make the scene work. Most often the therapist/director's interventions will be in the service of furthering the scene (such as when one player has blocked or broken a rule of the game), but occasionally it may be of overriding importance to interrupt the scene, particularly when the enactment has produced a breaking of character. These events do not necessarily represent a failure of the process and can become opportunities to uncover undealt-with clinical issues (see Chapter 12).

It is necessary for the therapist to have first established a rapport with clients that creates a basis for their trusting that there exists a safe and stable non-play context that can be departed from and returned to after playing. This includes establishing not only the rules and therapeutic rationale for play but also that the therapist is responsible, sensitive, and competent — in sum, trustworthy. Otherwise, the boundaries demarcating the play context will be unclear and the therapist may be perceived as a someone who has a careless attitude toward the feelings and perceptions that the clients are attached to, that they experience as an authentic or necessary part of their life. The way I establish boundaries in therapy is to establish in advance a time for "debriefing" during which the players return to their conventional personae and share their reactions and judgments to the improv, to their own performance, and to the performances of others.

Psychological as well as physical safety is a precondition for permitting oneself to play fully. Satir (1987), a therapist who believed firmly in the reality of an authentic self, rightly pointed out that

> [if] patients feel that they are at risk because they feel 'one down' in relation to the therapist, they will not report their distressed feelings and will develop defenses against the therapist. The therapist in turn, not knowing about this, can easily misunderstand the patient's response as resistance, instead of legitimate self-protection against the therapist's incongruence. (p. 21)

As noted above, the therapeutic value of play in RfG is rooted in the safety of players' knowing that "this is play" and that, within behavioral limits, they are free to enact roles without real-life consequences. However, even supposing an accepting therapist, this freedom from consequences is relative, not absolute, posing a particular dilemma for psychotherapy sessions with couples and families. The obvious problem, common to all forms of conjoint couples or family therapy, is that any factual information divulged during sessions may well have out-of-session consequences; this may be handled by constructing improvs that avoid using biographical material. The more difficult problem to resolve is that even when employing fictional roles there is still no way that players can be entirely exempted from being judged for their enacted choices of character and action. For example, suppose an improv scene in which a wife's character behaves meanly to her husband's character. Is that to be taken by him to mean that she is exploring a "shadow" side of herself without regard to her general feelings toward him? Or might he justifiably construe the enactment as a pretext for venting her dislike of him behind the facade of it being a pretense? Now anticipating this, might the wife choose to avoid or supress her character's acting meanly to his character, or perhaps temper the extent of any displayed meanness? A clinical example of this problem is discussed further in Chapter 12.

In my training of therapists in using RfG, I do not often find that the therapist is judgmental or insensitive to the feelings, strivings, and vulnerabilities of the client. Nor is there likely to be a problem for therapists with clients who are reluctant to initiate play, or who play timidly. Rather, I find it an occasional problem that a therapist will not be fully open to play and is unprepared for the freedom, opportunity, and paradoxical danger arising from initiating play. In these cases, the therapist usually has a specific agenda for play and will be intolerant of the exuberence or egocentrism of the playing client, thus becoming anxious, punitive, and/or restrictive. Of course, it is necessary for the therapist to be clear and complete in setting boundaries for play experience, but she or he must then be prepared and willing to go on an adventure in which "anything goes" within those boundaries.

Most experienced therapists have had the experience of clients (particularly in group or family therapy) challenging the therapist by disrupting the therapeutic process or by attempting to use the rules to pursue a competitive agenda. This phenomenon occurs in a distinctive way in RfG insofar as indulging in "bad behavior" may be condoned, even encouraged, in-role. Afterward, the client may not de-role readily or willingly. I have found that using another name for the player's character makes it more effective when I address the client by name, differentiating him from his role and stage identity and firmly, though not harshly, holding him accountable for his off-stage social behavior.

As noted earlier, it is a distinct advantage for the client to see that the therapist can also engage in play and that she or he can also be on the edge and at risk of failing to do well in an improv, as well as manifesting craziness, silliness, or immature behavior. This offsets the client's tendency to project onto a passive observer-therapist qualities of aloofness, retaining power, and being judgmental and encourages the client to let go and play fully. By seeing their therapist at play, clients also view improv as playful, not just as therapeutic technique. This raises the question as to who is in charge if everyone is playing; I solve this by working in therapy groups and workshops with a cotherapist, and by clearly marking my moving in and out of role as a participant when working solo. In this solo position, however, I am not free to immerse myself fully in the playfulness of the improv, since a part of my attention needs to remain "on duty" as a watchful grown-up.

David Johnson, a drama therapist, marks six positions on a continuum of increasing involvement of the therapist with the playspace (the context for establishing dramatic enactment; see Chapter 2):

1. Witness or Mirror, in which the therapist functions as the client's observer and provider of feedback after the enactment
2. Director, in which the therapist functions as a theatrical director, active before and during the enactment, but remaining off-stage
3. Sidecoach, in which the therapist contributes to the enactment by providing off-stage voices, sound effects, and lines in addition to directorial functions
4. Leader, in which the therapist participates in-role on-stage while avoiding both central roles and total participation
5. Guide, in which the in-role therapist invites the clients to use him as a projective medium for the development of the drama, thus assuming a position of centrality among the in-role client(s)
6. Shaman, in which the therapist, in order to induce an altered state in the client, enacts the images and roles of the drama while the client remains off-stage as audience.

The therapist/director in RfG participates from positions across the entire continuum, though more infrequently at either extreme (witness or shaman).

It is important to keep the improv principles and objectives described in the Introduction in mind so that exercises don't drift into parlor games. Although very entertaining, it is best to play down that aspect in training, or people will begin to focus on cleverness and feel the pressure to be funny, which defeats the purpose. Also, it is best to mime all props (except for chairs, which are occasionally used) and the removal of clothing, which helps to create greater freedom for the imagination. As improvising usually involves physical enactment, it is important that players be instructed to remain aware of any physical limitations of their bodies so that they do not injure themselves. It is also important that players notify their partners of any physical conditions that might be affected by contact (e.g., "I have a sprained right wrist, so don't shake my hand").

Improv can be done anywhere, yet it is an advantage to have a space large enough for players to move around in freely, and to have full visual and auditory privacy. Where possible, it is helpful to have control over the illumination so that the room lighting can be dimmed during improvs; different colored lighting to set or intensify the mood is ideal (see Appendix B regarding external resources). Selective use of video feedback is highly valuable for working on movement skills and altering self-image (especially around status transactions), although indiscriminate use of this medium can dilute the impact of improv experience by overfocusing on or analyzing what was, rather than staying in the present.

It is also a good idea to reserve or mark out a "stage" area that is used only for enactment or storytelling. This is the creation of the temenos, the ancient Greek idea of a "sacred space within which special rules apply and in which extrodinary events are free to occur" (Nachmanovitch, 1990, p. 75). When clients are encouraged to perform improvs as homework they should also be asked to agree with their partner(s) on a stage area (e.g., their living room, backyard, or a public beach) in advance of the enactment.

The therapist/director needs to attend to the emotional climate through-out the process in order to determine the pacing of the improv and the desirability of going further (building on the intensity of what has just occurred) versus consolidating and subsiding (moving out of enactment into discussion). One of the tactical skills needed to be an effective therapist/director is sensing when to end a scene; generally a scene should end when a major action is completed. Usually there is either a comic or dramatic point which is the right time to call "Black-out!" or a time when reincorporation of material or repetition of pattern within the scene signals a "Fade-out!" call. Inexperienced therapist/directors tend to allow a scene to run on too long, with the result that players become stuck or begin to lose interest in the enactment. Most improv scenes are best ended after only two or three minutes.

For scenes that involve the release of anger through physical expression, keeping elongated balloons (though not the skinny ones that twist into party animals) on hand works well. The way I have seen balloon-hitting used is in *Master/Servant Games* (p. 119): When the master's frustration rises, it is as though the balloon itself wants to hit; the hit is done "through" the body (one forceful blow, not repeated ones) — the angry energy is dissipated completely by that one blow; the servant thanks the master and the master apologizes for hitting the servant; the scene continues, perhaps leading to a return of the entire sequence. When players follow this pattern, the anger seems to remain confined to the characters and doesn't affect the players.

In RfG, the usual intention is to play the scene forward and not to allow it to be set aside while the character becomes absorbed by expressing his rage to the exclusion of all else. Of course, this is a quite different practice from using Battacas or cushions in physicalizing anger for ventilative purposes.

Clear gender differences show up in enactments of stage violence. Women players will usually display aggression in their characters only if the circumstances are extremely different from real-life or if their stage characters are quite dissimilar to their own. Men will frequently maneuver to create justification for including violence in their scenes and seldom display distress at enacting it. This is consistent with the argument that, since women are consistently socialized to control impulses toward violence, women's aggression is seen as a failure of self-control, which lowers their status; men, by contrast, are taught to display aggressiveness as a legitimate means of establishing control, which raises their status.

After improv enactment there are a number of choices available to the therapist/director: repeating all or part of the just-completed improv, with or without reversing roles; moving on to further improvs (see "Sequencing and Repeating Improvisations," below); verbal processing of the experience among the players (which should generally precede other interchanges between players and others); sharing of solely personal reactions with players by audience clients (during which analysis and criticism are not permitted); descriptive feedback by the therapist/director (directed mainly to the performance features of the enactment); dialogue between players and the therapist/director regarding players' personal reactions during and following the improv; and discussing connections between improv performance and real-world functioning.

USING IMPROVISATION FOR ASSESSMENT

The therapist using improv exercises and games will find, as in therapy generally, that there is a reciprocal relationship between assessment and intervention. That is, the questions and enactments designed to discover or elicit clinically useful information produce some learning or change in the therapeutic system, while the effects of words or actions intended to bring about change provide further information (feedback) about that system.

From the outset, the therapist needs to be clear as to whether, at any one time, her or his focus is on the assessment of individual client(s) or of the interaction between clients; both have their uses. Although therapists trained in systemic thinking will have an easier time focusing on interaction than individual-oriented ones, all clinicians using RfG will find it advantageous to adopt each focus at different times.

Applied to couples and families, the use of games and exercises for purposes of assessment will reveal how rigid (literal and serious) or flexible (receptive to play) family structure is by testing what rules the family will break or refuse to break, what status inequalities exist among family members, and what the emotional range and climate is; broadly, the therapist may obtain an overall impression of the strengths and limitations of the family and of the degree that she or he is trusted by the family group. In group therapy, RfG methods can help reveal the degree of cohesiveness, cooperation, and playfulness available within the group as a whole and among subgroups of members; in individual therapy they are helpful in finding out how willing and ready the client is to use metaphor, access playfulness, give up overcontrol, express different emotions in the presence of the therapist, and cocreate alternative realities.

In all modalities, rigidity and limitation is revealed by the blocking of offers, the inability or unwillingness to shift status, long hesitations indicative of overcontrol instead of spontaneity, emotionality that is contextually unjustified or inhibited, and by difficulty in entering or leaving the play context. How instructions are interpreted is as much a part of assessment as the content, style, or skill level of the improv enactment itself.

The use of RfG for assessment in conjoint couples therapy can be directed most broadly to the couples' capacity to play together in a way that both partners experience as satisfying. If their play is competitive but mutually enjoyable, their rules can be inferred to promote competition, whereas competitive play that results in dissatisfaction for one or both will most often be signalled by blocking and indicates a refusal to accept competitiveness in that context.

A cautionary word should be said regarding interpretations of improv performances as revealing individual personality traits or preferred ego-defense mechanisms. I do not have sufficient data to warrant a firm conclusion. Although I have used improv with some of my clients whom I know well from our contact during long-term, intensive individual psychotherapy, and have experience with group therapy clients in using sequences and repetitions of improv, I have not found there to be any simple or invariant relationship between improvisational behavior and supposedly enduring individual clinical features. The reasons for this, I believe, are twofold: First, improvisation performance draws upon people's capacity to expand their range of possible emotions, attitudes, and behaviors, with the result that initial limitations in range or style (used to categorize or diagnose clients) can be transcended subsequently by full participation in the play and pretense of improv; second, the responses of the same client to any improv game or sequence of games are quite variable and contingent on subtle contextual features that are seldom replicable. What does appear to be true is that limitations in a client's initial improvising are likely to be present in further improvising, particularly when no coaching is offered. Whether coaching will help overcome these limitations can only be determined by attempting it. (See Chapter 12 for cases illustrating the effects of coaching.)

This is not to deny that individual clients will, in the short term, display patterned or even predictable behaviors in their improvising. For one thing, there exists for any one time a client's skill level of improvising, though that generally improves with practice. Also, clients making repeated use of specific characterizations or devices will be less spontaneous and more predictable. Status performances, particularly playing opposite to the client's more familiar position, tend to be enacted in a characteristic fashion; for specific emotions, expressed intensity will be predictably limited in certain clients. More importantly, clients often approach improv situations with an attitudinal set (such as not-losing, wanting to be thought of as clever, or keeping one's cool at all times) that bears directly on their relationship functioning outside of improvising. RfG assessment, when focused on individuals, consists, first, of observing improv performance behavior as it bears upon such broad and clinically significant issues as: self-esteem, self-image, expectations from others, need for success, need for control, need for the therapist's approval, etc. Next, the therapist considers the possible correspondences between outside-of-therapy data and these observations, treating these connections as provisional hypotheses or as presumptive but not conclusive evidence of patterns (indeed, whenever do clinicians justly regard their ideas as proven?). Then, further information may be gathered and/or additional improvs staged in order to test these hypotheses. The last stage is to design interventions that enable clients to overcome assessed limitations.

On the other hand, when clients in a significant relationship improvise together, interpretations of their improv interaction *are* clinically useful in assessing certain aspects of their relationship (more on which aspects is presented below). Most likely, the reason for such correspondences is that who, and how, we get to be is strongly influenced by the context of relationship. That we show variability at all in interacting within relationships is due chiefly to two factors: (1) that our significant relationships are sufficiently complex to encompass a considerable variety of responses, and (2) that the play context offsets the tendency to remain confined entirely to habitual patterns.

Improvisation and Clinical Inference

The seven characteristics listed below represent the *absence* of the good improvising signs (which were listed in the Introduction, pp. xix–xx), and provisionally correspond to the clinical inferences listed after each.

1. Players fail to make and/or do not respect clear boundaries defining the play context and what is permissible in playing. They are unclear with themselves and one another regarding the distinction between player-as-person and player-as-character.

When, during unstructured play or in the negotiation and signalling of play, there exists disagreement or ambiguity regarding what is playful, or how, whether, or when to play, there is a lack of trust and safety, often taking the form of fear of self-exposure, which precludes genuine play. Players who are too invested (underdistanced) in their characters are not fully free to improvise, since they are too invested in controlling what happens to their character.

2. There is a markedly unequal contribution from each player and a lack of give-and-take or reciprocity. Players are frequently unobservant and nonresponsive to the offers of one another; they don't listen well and talk over one another.

A tendency to either "hog the scene" or to remain aloof and peripheral to its enactment indicate an unwillingness to extend, or an unawareness of the opportunity for, an equal partnership of responsibility and mutual respect. Not infrequently, there is a competitive undertone to the players' relationship and an anxious quality to their interaction.

3. Players manifest difficulty in giving and fully accepting character. They attempt to make themselves look good by imposing conditions on how they interpret their characters (e.g., clever, heroic, sexy, high-status, central to the scene, etc.) and how they handle their role as actors (e.g., showing off or hiding out) regardless of what this does to the improv scene. They are unsupportive of making their partner(s) look good.

These behaviors point to a strong individual tendency toward overcontrol wherein one player insecurely attempts to make himself more interesting. These players' partners are likely to interpret them as controlling, whereas they typically see themselves as being helpful.

4. Players seldom physicalize in a grounded way corresponding to the story; they use limited expressive range, often expressing themselves at cross-purposes to the spirit of the situation.

Often, these behaviors are characteristic of clients who are too much "in their heads" and are inhibited or out of touch with their bodies and emotions. Since these are also common features of inexperienced improvising, the differential test is whether these characteristics abate with practice.

5. Players do not stay in the present moment when they are unsure of what is happening or when their imaginations are blank. They often become defensively self-conscious or utilize familiar protective behaviors (i.e., breaking character to apologize to the audience, panicking, quitting the scene, or blaming other players), and are incapable of playfully incorporating such actions into the scene.

It takes a fairly secure person to take ambiguity, uncertainty, or apparent failure in stride; experience with improvising, particularly combined with observing other players modelling nondefensiveness, helps a great deal. Clients who are perfectionistically self-critical and those who are defensive, high-status "specialists" have a harder time remaining present-focused. Therapists can provisionally hypothesize that the style and tactics of self-defensiveness displayed in such moments are the same choices present in that client's dealings with stressful social situations.

6. Players are often unenthusiastic or displeased by the outcome of the scene; after the improv they have difficulty acknowledging the positive contributions of the other player(s). They do not readily accept and learn from what occurred and find it hard to let go of judgments of self and of others.

The above-described conduct following an improv enactment is often exhibited by the same individual inferred in the previous item. On the interactive level, there is usually dissatisfaction with the mutually unsuccessful attempts to control one's partner, sometimes accompanied by an attempt to distance one's identity from the partner's and a competitive struggle over credit and blame for the quality of the improv's outcome. This reveals an absence or loss of perspective of improv-as-play and interpretation of the outcome as reflecting the player's worth in some fashion.

7. Players frequently reject the first idea(s) offered and censor both obvious and irrational or unconventional offers. Should such offers enter the scene via others, they have difficulty making these work in the scene. Players are "in their heads," i.e., planning ahead; they fail to remember where they have been, with the frequent result that the story wanders inconclusively.

It may take coaching and encouragement by the therapist/director to help players overcome the habitual attitude that what comes easily or spontaneously is either not good enough or dangerous. Consequently, players have acquired the habit of second-guessing themselves and seeking validation from others rather than trusting themselves and their partner(s). Healthy creativity requires the self-confidence to trust one's imagination and the willingness to persist in carrying it into action. In improv, a good idea is any one that is developed.

Role Hunger and Role Nausea

Social life has the tendency to attach a specific role to a specific person, so that this role becomes the prevailing one into which the individual is folded . . . But the individual craves to embody far more roles than those he is allowed to act out in life. It is from the active pressure which these multiple units exert upon the manifest official role that a feeling of anxiety is produced. Role playing is then a method of liberating and structuring these unofficial roles. (Moreno, 1934, pp. 325–326)

Psychodramatists speak of role hunger, a disposition or readiness to take on a role that is insufficiently available in that person's life. Role hunger can be inferred from attending to the stories (narratives) people tell about themselves in therapy. For example, embedded in a person's description of how she or he handled some situation might be the role of "Goodheartedbut-Naive Victim," or of "Fearless Hero." It has been my experience that players will opt for roles consistent with their role hunger but that the mere enactment of that hungered-for role, though usually gratifying, appears not to be particularly growthful for that person, nor does it provide that person's significant others with a novel experience of interaction. Instead, the enactment of the hungered-for role is effective in producing change when it occurs in a context of making a difference to someone else or to the outcome of the situation. The therapist should be reminded that not all role hungers, identified or suspected, are best enacted in sessions (e.g., murderous or incestuous impulses). It can be useful, however, to ask "as if" questions (such as, "If you were going to kill your husband, how would you do it?") in order to model the use of fantasy alternatives to real life stress. This is also advocated by Whitaker and Keith (1981): "Teaching the use of fantasy permits expansion of the emotional life without the threat of real violence or real sexual acting-out" (p. 212).

Sometimes, role hunger is a prominent feature of a person's life-style and emerges consistently in action. Warren, age 36 and recently separated from his wife, was a "frustrated professor" who delighted in holding forth on various subjects to family, coworkers, and perfect strangers in the local bar. His job as a postal sorter gave Warren scant opportunity for fulfillment of this role, a circumstance he unsuccessfully offered as a justification to his estranged wife, Anne, and beloved nine-year-old daughter, Julie (who, he reported, were both quite fed up with his "lectures").

Warren had come for therapy as part of Anne's condition for his return to their household. It appeared that escalating friction and competitiveness over who got attention had contributed to their separation; this pointed to status conflict as an underlying factor. While I saw this case as best conducted by means of family therapy, scheduling difficulties resulted in my seeing the three nuclear family members together only four times during eight months of treatment. During earlier sessions of our predominantly individual therapy Warren had proven an enthusiastic improviser; with my encouragement he reported successfully playing our in-session improvs (*Presents* [p. 105], *One-Word-at-a-Time Stories* [p. 65], *No, You Didn't* [p. 74], and *Mirrors* [p. 69]) with Anne and Julie during visits at their home. From his reports and observation of their enactments during the second of the conjoint family sessions, I saw that these improvs were helpful in creating an experience of mutuality and cocontrol.

What interested me more as a clinical goal than overcoming the antipathy reported toward Warren's "lecturing" was increasing role and status flexibility that the family could display around who got attention and admiration. As noted, the above-mentioned improvs were helpful toward that end, but the decisive intervention occurred during the last of their conjoint family sessions when I had Warren play a *Status Transfer* (p. 116) within a scene in which he, in his role as "pompous expert," started out high-status to Julie's low-status "interviewer." The stretching occurred when he succeeded at lowering his own status and raising that of his daughter, while she was equivalently stretched as she lowered him and elevated herself. At the conclusion of this exercise both of them were uncharacteristically complimentary of one another; their rivalry had subsided. Anne, who had watched this improv, exclaimed that she now saw clearly how stylistically alike Julie and Warren were.

At the following session Warren reported that he was moving back home that weekend since the tension between him and Anne had diminished sharply. Even though Anne had been only an observer, she had become hopeful upon seeing him lower his status during the improv with Julie; over the telephone she confirmed directly to me that this event had shifted her perception of Warren as someone who was capable of yielding to others. Therapy with Warren terminated the next week; to my knowledge, Anne and Warren are still together.

Sometimes the opposite pattern, what might be termed "role nausea," occurs, where a player is offered an overfamiliar role or one that is embarrassing, painful, or noxious. Beginning improvisers, enamored by the license afforded by the pretend context, regularly are drawn to exploring sexual, violent, and excremental themes. (Stage improvisers are familiar with the related problem of accepting offers from audience members who invariably want to see scenes involving proctologists or set in public lavatories.) Such offers may be repugnant to other players, who nonetheless may feel obliged to accept all offers. However, the consequence of forcing oneself into playing scenes that evoke such role nausea are counterproductive; players will then find improvising to seem the antithesis of play and will decline further opportunity to improvise at all. For this reason, I make it clear that any player, at any time, has the right to decline to continue with any scene, without any obligation to explain oneself. As therapist/director I also reserve the right to censor offers that I see as contrary to the spirit of play or that appear exploitative of others.

Occasionally, a player accepts an offer and begins to develop a scene, only to regret her earlier choice. A group client, Diane, found herself in such a situation when her character, a pleasant-mannered archeologist who had just discovered the fossilized remains of the Assyrian Elvis, was summoned to a nearby cave by her colleague. When she got there the character of the colleague mimed sexually exposing himself to her. Diane was taken aback but swiftly recovered; her character primly took out a magnifying glass and examined his genital area, gravely informing his character that the degree of fossilization indicated "its erection in the early Monolithic period." This brought down the house in great laughter and ended the scene. Instead of joining in the laughter and accepting congratulations for her wit from the group, Diane was angry and upset that she had complied in any way with an offensive suggestion. In further group discussion of the scene, Diane reported that being confronted sexually within the improv had "snapped her out of playfulness" and that in the moment she had been reminded of two real events in which she had had to contend with unwelcome sexual advances. What Diane found particularly upsetting was that she had passed up the opportunity to let herself enact the aggressive impulses she felt and had chosen to play the scene for comedy, thereby trivializing her justified anger.

The choices a player makes, particularly habitual choices that emerge from repeated improv exercises, provide valuable clinical data pointing toward underlying patterns of interpersonal style. Take, for instance, an *Emotional Lists* scene (p. 131) being played at a bus stop. The therapist/director has just called "Anger!" signalling the players to have their characters become angry while justifying anger within the scene. Player A says (angrily), "This damn 'Q' bus is always late! My boss is gonna be in my face again!" Among the many choices player B may respond with, consider these three: (1) "Yeah, you'd think the city would fire those drivers!" (2) "Well, I'd've made the earlier bus except my wife couldn't have my breakfast ready by 7:45!" (3) "Why don't you quiet down, buddy; yelling won't get the bus here any faster." All three responses meet the requirements for adequate improvising: they accept the premise of the scene established by player A, advance the action, and follow the instructions of the therapist/director. Assuming that these are habitual choices, the first suggests a player who joins with others by blaming or gossiping about third parties; the second, a player who locates the justification of emotion entirely in his own life; and the third, a player who takes the reactions of others personally. The therapist can use his observations to repeat or offer new improvs to test his hypotheses.

USING IMPROVISATION FOR INTERVENTION

As a clinician and a person with my own point of view, I retain a sense or judgment of what might constitute an improvement in the relationship life of my clients, yet I do not see my job as shaping them toward my own preferences. Rather, I encourage them to find their own way while inviting them to explore playfully some alternatives that they haven't tried which I think might prove useful. Perhaps they will like these alternatives and perhaps they won't; that is their choice. When we cocreate a stage reality both the client and I are open to the possibility of a change. Not only is the client subject to changes in her or his sense of what is possible but my sense of what she or he is capable of and has a talent for undergoes a change; how I am affected by the presence of the alternative reality we have just cocreated leads me to change my asessment and experience of the possibilities of our encounter.

Improvised Role-Play

While improv games make use of creating and enacting roles, there are fundamental differences between role-play in RfG and the more familiar uses of role-play, here termed structured role-play (SRP). SRP is a widely-used psychotherapeutic technique which also makes use of improv — for rehearsing behaviors that are of practical importance in the role-player's life (e.g., assertiveness training), for reexperiencing emotionally charged past or present life-situations, and for enhancing understanding or empathy with another's experience (as in role-reversals). Even when SRP is used for enacting subjectively experienced states (as in psychodrama or family reconstruction), the role-player is attempting to match his portrayal of the role with felt and/or remembered experience. Although RfG may utilize assigned roles it does so not to simulate realistic behavior but rather to encourage fantasy and exploration of alternative possibilities. Whereas SRP might be used to coach an anxious job applicant for an actual, impending interview, the therapist/director of an RfG improv might propose the enactment of a totally inept (or overwhelmingly arrogant) interviewee, or that the interviewer also be played as conventionally inappropriate, or only suggest the status positions of the players. The therapist/director may choose to set up a specific scenario rather than a more open-ended improv game (in which only a location, a character, or a relationship is specified) in order to facilitate or enlarge the players' social and emotional repertoire.

In such improvised role-plays the players, freed from having to "do it right," need only concern themselves with fully playing the scene by following the improv principles and objectives. Outwardly, such a performance is likely to be imaginative, humorous, absurd, even bizarre; yet the players frequently experience a great deal of tension stemming from blocks in their own spontaneity as well as blocking one another. When removed from familiar routines (roles, settings, social rules), even in play, the players' attention shifts to hitherto undernoticed cues: their own body position and sensations, the gestures of others, the promptings of their own imagination.

What frequently emerges from the experience of improvised role-playing is a more profound grasp of both the contextual features of a simulated situation and an appreciation of what is emotionally at stake for oneself in the actual situation. Rather than being coached on changing specific tactics and behaviors, as in SRP, improvised role players learn to use themselves more effectively by trying out and developing their own novel ways of dealing with both familiar and unexpected conditions.

Shifting Status as a Therapeutic Intervention

Changing status is an intervention that regularly impacts strongly on relationship functioning and self-image. As noted in Chapter 7, improv provides an ideal way of learning about and developing proficiency at status maneuvers. There are three broad categories of status change that are clinically useful:

1. Focusing on expanding the status range of individual clients. This may be coached individually but is always applied in interpersonal contexts; it is typically an explicitly instructional process whereby the therapist imparts skills and provides modelling and coaching to the client.

2. Shifting relationship patterns by intervening to alter relative status positions. As with (1), this can be instructional, but may also be an unacknowledged maneuver by the therapist, such as occurs in unbalancing operations within structural family therapy (Minuchin & Fishman, 1981).

3. Changing the therapist's status in relation to clients as a means of improving effectiveness. This is really the foundation for generally enhancing the influence of the therapist within the therapeutic context. As noted in Chapter 14, most clinical training socializes therapists to display confidence, knowledgability, and emotional self-control. This is not neccessarily a bad thing, but is quite limiting if the therapist assumes that this high-status manner of playing the helping professional role is always "correct." A therapist who invariably takes either a personally authoratative or an expert stance is playing high status to the client(s) and invites one of four likely client responses:

   a. A compliant low-status positioning: "I'm/we're so glad you are in charge. (And it's solely your responsibility to get results.)"

   b. A reproachful low-status positioning: "I am/we are still unhappy; why aren't you helping more? (It's your fault things haven't improved enough.)"

   c. A covertly conflictual high-status positioning: "You don't really understand me/us. (If you did, you'd realize I'm/we're right, and that it's your fault.)"

   d. A defensive, even overtly conflictual high-status positioning: "I/we told you that wouldn't work. (You're incompetent, insensitive, etc.)"

Were the therapist to shift toward a low- or equal-status position on occasion she or he could empower greater self-disclosure, higher self-esteem, and responsibility for the outcome in the client(s). Expressing warmth and accurate empathy is a status-equalizing move, while asking the client for help in understanding—or inviting the client to teach the therapist—moves her or him to a low-status position. In multiple-client therapies the therapist's differential use of status in relation to different clients greatly aids in promoting relationship shifts, as mentioned in (2) above.

IMPROVISATION IN AFFECTIVE EDUCATION

Affective education is an approach to teaching and learning that focuses on content that includes the nonverbal, the emotive, and the nontangible; its methods emphasize action, emotion, nonlogical cognition, intuition, and use of the body (Seeman, 1976). RfG improv can be employed readily to further affective learning, both in its content and by using it as a process of training. On an individual level, RfG offers people coaching in relearning to be playful, freeing imagination, and accessing spontaneity. On an interpersonal level, RfG helps train people to: cooperate with, attend to, and accommodate one another, improving their relationship functioning; heighten awareness of body cues and status maneuvers, giving them greater insight into the subtleties and complexities of social interaction; and experiment safely with different presentations of self, offering alternative choices to broaden effective use of self. The nontherapy workshops I offer to the public are a form of affective education. Moreover, RfG instruction operates without reliance upon didactic methods or indeed largely outside of verbal/aural channels, thus more effectively reaching the many persons who are not effective learners in this modality (according to Neuro-Linguistic Programming practitioners).

Creative Dramatics

This use of RfG overlaps somewhat with creative dramatics (CD), which is an educational program making considerable use of improv (which distinguishes it from formal dramatics) for personal growth in a nontherapeutic context. For young children (four- to nine-year-olds) stories, selected for a definite story line, strong characterization, expressed emotions and dramatic action, are first told and then enacted. The emphasis is on encouraging the child to act like another creature or person within the framework of the story. CD thus teaches children the expression of feelings, working with others and acting (improvising) within the framework of loose instructions (Carlson, 1973). Most CD leaders are schoolteachers whose experience with inducing pretending and enacting a story with groups of children can be valuable to therapists. Carlson notes, "The leader, or director, must urge the most reluctant child to take part without forcing him to do so. The leader must keep the story line moving without seeming to direct the players, and must stir up enthusiasm by example, either as a member of the audience or as a member of the acting group" (p. 21).

With young adolescents, CD teaches theater games; a more technique-oriented approach is taken (such as training players to use movement and voice-tone to express mood, age, and temperment of a character); to select objectives for their characters; and to fabricate obstacles that stand in the way of their characters' objectives. Presumably because adolescents are still in the process of mastering the adult containment of fantasy, Novello (1985) describes two games as particularly useful: *One Situation/Three-Ways Scene*, in which a scene is played first in pantomime, next with dialogue, and last in some totally unnatural way; and *If-I-Had-It-My-Way Scene*, in which a scene is first played the way it happens in everyday life and then is reenacted as one player's wildest fantasy. Given the high degree of adolescent self-consciousness in public and the likely inhibitory effect on untrammeled imagination of the adolescent peer group, I am skeptical of how freely this latter scene gets played out.

Another CD approach for older adults (Telander, Quinlan, & Verson, 1982) uses sensory recall, guided imagery, and autobiographical storytelling as preliminary activities leading to the creation and enactment of improvised stories. One exercise these authors describe goes as follows: One player brings a family snapshot and serves as a narrator/director by "interviewing" the other players as to the who/what/where/when/why of their roles. Once all the players have developed their characters, a scene is started that ends in the tableau of the snapshot. This game resembles *Spoon River Game* (p. 99) and can be usefully applied to therapy groups.

New Games

Begun in the early 1970s by Stewart Brand, Pat Farrington, and others, New Games cultivate an attitude toward play that explores creativity, community, and personal empowerment. New Games are created and played to provide challenge more than competition, to establish trust as the basis of play, and to attend to the safety of its players as the responsibility of all (Fluegelman, 1981). New Games are themselves modified and improvised during play, in keeping with their spirit of playfulness. The ones described in print are predominantly physical and frequently competitive, calling for agility, speed, and strength as well as quick wits. While deemphasizing the athletic component, RfG embodies a similar spirit and can readily make use of New Games, especially for group therapy and relationship enhancement. For example, in *Fox and Squirrel* (Fluegelman, 1976), a circle of players pass two larger balls (the foxes) and a smaller one (the squirrel) rapidly around a circle, abruptly reversing the direction of the passes occasionally. "The object of the game is for the foxes to catch the squirrel by tagging whoever is holding the squirrel ball with one (or both) of the fox balls . . . you can only *pass* the foxes to the player next to you, but you can *throw* the squirrel across the circle. To keep everyone alert, call out 'Fox' or 'Squirrel' each time you pass one of the balls" (p. 59). This game is competitive, in a way, yet it is difficult to say who you are playing with and who against. Another New Game, *Yurt Circle* (Fluegelman, 1981), is a physically cooperative group game in which an even number of players hold hands in a circle facing inward. Players alternate calling themselves off as "In" and "Out."

> Then we count to three, and the Ins lean toward the center of the circle while the Outs lean back. We all keep our feet stationary and support ourselves with our held hands. With a bit of practice we can lean amazingly far forward and backward without falling. (p. 123)

The Ins and Outs can switch roles in rhythm, enjoyably demonstrating how each part supports the whole through an interplay of simultaneous oppositional and harmonious forces.

Art of Play

Blatner and Blatner (1988) have created Art of Play groups to stimulate adult play for recreation and artistic expression. To facilitate Art of Play sessions, one person serves as a nonparticipating director, whose role "serves as a symbolic 'observing self' for the group, providing a stabilizing and consistent reminder that the roles being enacted are playful and not real" (p. 47). Their methods, rooted in psychodrama and sociodrama, make use of improvisation guided by the director. The challenge for players is to select unfamiliar roles and create scenes in which they explore enacted fantasies, usually from the perspective of a main character or protagonist.

RfG for Fun

Working in partnership with my wife Gloria Maddox, I occasionally offer RfG workshops to the lay-public, similar in intention to Art of Play groups. Our workshops are almost identical to theater improvisation training, the only difference being that our main objective is playful exploration for the group as a whole, rather than training players to become skillful improvisers. Accordingly, we keep the difficulty level of the games and exercises fairly low, though not to the point where people lack a sense of risk and challenge. This is how we brief our participants:

> Improv games provide a way of exploring the fantasy worlds inside of all of us, not just in thought but through action. When playing these games with other improvisers (players) you will discover the involvement of play. You will feel stretched in odd ways, too—at times it is hard to follow through on what you are aware comes next, you may go blank, feel absurd, embarassed, or self-conscious. Afterward, you may discover that you were unaware of what the other players were doing, or saying, or that they missed your signals. You will probably find yourself evaluating your own performance: Was I clever enough? Quick enough? Authentic?
>
> Our advice is: Don't listen too seriously to the critic inside who would discourage you; these games show us what self-judgments we harbor as well as

many limitations we were previously unaware of. The value of improvising lies in staying with what is created in the moment, rather than relying on memory of past experience.

We have found that participants not only enjoy playing these games, but that they frequently and spontaneously make comments regarding personal insights that occur to them during these workshops. Hard as it is for my therapist self, we acknowledge these comments but do not invite further discussion or analysis, since doing so would move people out of playful action into earnest contemplation.

SEQUENCING AND REPEATING IMPROVISATIONS

The impression created by my presentation of improv games and exercises to this point may be that each one is presented separately and independently of the others and that each stands as an independent tool for inducing playfulness, for assessment, and/or intervention. While isolated improvs can be used to clinical advantage, more benefit derives from using them sequentially and repeatedly.

Sequences of improv exercises are used in order to build up play skills, usually by adding exercises that are successively more challenging or that increase the degree of complexity required. Sequences can also be used to teach the same principles and objectives in both verbal and physical modalities, such as teaching mutuality by means of *Verbal Mirrors* (p. 70) and *Mirrors* (p. 69). When this is done it becomes possible to compare the performances of the same players across modalities or between player partners.

Repetition of improvs frees players from the need to focus on instructions and to play rather than attend chiefly to the form of the improv. When clients are first introduced to improv in the context of therapy they are likely to be guarded ("Why are we doing this?" and "What's expected of me?" are common responses). Once past this holding back, players repeating the same improv also get to explore different choices and to experience the range of play available to themselves with their partner(s). Therapist/ directors can better assess the degree to which a performance outcome was due to confusion regarding instructions, lack of willingness to accept the therapist/director's offer, or to inability to perform some aspect.

Repetitions with different partners have rich implications for assessment in group and family therapy; with couples therapy the therapist/director can compare a dyadic improv conducted between the spouses with one in which he or she participates with each partner. This occurred with Paul and Marcie, an engaged couple mentioned at the end of Chapter 4. After they had played *One Word at a Time* with one another (p. 65), performing in a tense, disjointed manner, they began to blame one another for their unsatisfactory (to them) performance. I then asked Marcie to play the game with me (in Paul's presence) which resulted in a conventional but freely flowing narrative of four sentences. Paul began to evaluate the improv critically almost as soon as it was over; I interrupted him to invite him to do one with me, which went fairly well despite lengthy pauses by Paul and his penchant for inserting unusual words. I now invited each of them to critique their own experience of participating in and observing these stories; while both were aware that their own game with me as partner had gone better than with one another, their focus was fixed on which of them was better at playing the game, renewing their hostile and competitive high-status battle. I observed that the improvement in their second story could have been a result of greater cooperation and suggested we play a further game with all three of us cocreating the story. However, as I didn't want to present either of them with an opportunity to be critical of a word presented by one's spouse, I explained that I would say every other word (thus, Marcie-myself-Paul-myself). When this was agreed to and attempted the result was a coherent, humorous story to which both took evident pleasure in contributing. Although these exercises conducted near the beginning of therapy scarcely changed the competitive quality of their relationship in other areas, I was able to make use of this success at a number of points in subsequent sessions to evoke cooperation and greater tolerance for differences.

When repeating improvs, it regularly happens that habitual choices are made with the result that the player recreates a recognizable and "stable" character that possesses a memory of its appearances in previous improvs and that resists offers that define it in other than the now-established way. Such character-formation is used in the theater, where actors may start with an improvisatory process and go on to create scripted pieces out of the characters, dialogue, and circumstances that develop. This phenomenon appears to be related to the development of subpersonalities or parts of self (Schwartz, 1992). In my work I make use of such emerging parts of self as formative characters in further improvs, using a mixture of drama therapy, psychodrama, and improv techniques. One example is using soliloquy, or inner monologue, as a prologue (or occasionally as an epilogue) to improv enactment (soliloquy during an improv scene will nearly always sidetrack the action). Since RfG aims to enhance relationship functioning I prefer to have family or group members do this work in tandem where possible; the emerging relationships between such formative characters are fascinating to watch and are rich in clinically useful material.

The choices of character made by or offered to a player may be classified along a dimension of familiarity. At one extreme, the player is so familiar with the character and the circumstances of the scene that he experiences the improv as a reenactment of real life, while at the other extreme he simply cannot relate to the character and hence cannot play the scene. More often, the player who experiences being unable to play a character is afraid either of doing it wrong or of losing control of his or her presentation of self, such as when he or she negatively judges the character and is reluctant to acknowledge any similarity or affinity between them.

The therapist/director who engages in improvising will have occasion to observe some of his own patterning. One of my trainees, a well-adjusted, intelligent psychologist, asked me why I regularly began scenes with him by giving myself the character of a rural Southerner (he actually said, "dumb farmer"). I had been totally unaware of doing so, yet recognized the pattern as soon as he pointed it out. On reflection I recognized that I felt friendly yet intellectually competitive with him, so I was attempting to create a play context that was very distinct (and distant) from our actual social and professional identities.

Full entry into an "as if" or imaginary world . . . can increase the possibility of entering a domain of experience in which the conceptions of the past are alive and inexhaustibly rich in untapped meaning, where the future is undetermined, and where the present is the creative nexus between the changeable past and the changeful future.

—Sallyann Roth and Richard Chasin (1994, p. 2)

CHAPTER 10

Applications to Group and Individual Therapy

I HAVE DIVIDED my presentation of case material into those cases where the focus is primarily on the drama of the individual client, presented in this chapter, and those where relationships are central, presented in the following chapter. While there is little difference conceptually between using RfG techniques to work with clients in individual or in group therapy, the latter offers considerably more resources and is to be preferred for the advantages summarized in the following section. For this reason, I encourage many of my individual therapy clients to participate concurrently in improvisational group therapy (as I did with Micky, in Case 1 below). For clients exclusively in individual therapy, RfG offers a variety of action techniques to enhance a narrative approach, as demonstrated in Cases 2 and 3 below.

APPLICATIONS TO GROUP THERAPY

RfG techniques are well-suited for applications within the format of group therapy. Many groups offer a heterogeneous mix of personalities and problems, which makes repeating improvs with different partners more interesting and invites fruitful comparisons of performance differences. The size of most therapy groups also affords flexibility in the choices of games and exercises. As group therapy participants usually do not have significant roles in each other's lives outside of sessions, players are freer to explore impulses and to redefine themselves and their partners than are clients in family and couples therapy.

The presence of others facilitates greater exploration of expressiveness, probably because there is simply more energy available when people are responding to another's emotional expression. Of equal value to the inner experience of expressing emotion is the discovery of the impact that our expressiveness has on others, a discovery that helps clients overcome inhibitions based on overgeneralizations from their family of origin experiences. Additionally, people learn from one another when in the observer position and draw on energy from their audience when performing in front of others.

While useful as an adjunctive technique across different types of group work, RfG lends itself well to achieving two distinct goals in therapy groups: (1) learning to explore different sides of oneself (for personal growth and self-discovery, where the objectives are diffuse); and (2) improving social functioning (theme-directed therapy where improv can be the main tool for confronting fear-based limitations by practicing a form of collective implosive therapy [Again, "Face Fear Through Fun" is our motto]). Improvising theatrical performance not only cultivates several important relationship skills, but is itself paradoxically risky: On the one hand, it is a socially stressful activity, since the player is performing publically, is accountable for meeting performance criteria that are known to the audience, is operating under conditions that make knowing or controlling the future impossible, and is highly dependent upon other, equally stressed players; on the other hand, improvising takes place in an atmosphere of playfulness, experimentation, distancing use of fantasy, and cooperation with others who are in the same condition. As a result, participants find frequent relief from the rigors of performing in laughter which is joining, cathartic, and healing all at once; they learn that one's social dignity is not so essentially precious, after all, and they bond affectionately with other improvisers and frequently overcome long-standing social inhibitions. It should be understood that the above-mentioned beneficial results are attained just by involvement in the activity of RfG while additional, specific therapeutic benefits result from the selective use of particular games and exercises.

Group therapy practice over the past 25 years has moved from several divergent approaches increasingly toward integration and eclecticism. Still, although improv may be applied broadly to many clinical and growth-oriented endeavors, the inclusion of RfG techniques in group therapy has certain implications for the character of group interaction and would be inconsistent with the tone, or contrary to the rationale of, say, purely psychodynamic group psychotherapy while being relatively congenial to a Gestalt therapy workshop. The same would be true of the uses for RfG techniques in groups constituted to promote interpersonal skills and enhance the quality of relationships, although fewer restrictions might apply.

Shaffer and Galinsky (1974) identify four parameters for comparing and distinguishing between the various major group therapy and training models:

> (1) a focus on the group versus a focus on the individual, (2) psychotherapy goals versus growth goals, (3) gratification of needs versus frustration of needs, and (4) a relatively structured format versus a relatively loose format. (p. 266)

By treating RfG as a group model I shall attempt to characterize my approach according to these parameters. Regarding (1), the group/individual focus dimension, RfG aims to promote both a therapeutic experience for individual group members and an enhanced sense of relationship functioning. While the therapist need attend to the context of the group-as-a-whole, particularly to accessing playfulness, the group is the vehicle and not the entity in focus. On (2), psychotherapy versus growth, though RfG may be employed to achieve specific therapeutic goals (as illustrated by the clinical cases in this book), growth is the preeminent rationale. As for (3), gratification versus frustration of needs, while frustration may arise in the form of group members being challenged in ways that evoke fear of failure, clearly the primary emphasis is on gratification of the playful, imaginative, and adventurous side of participants. The issue of relative degree of structure, (4), permits two answers: Regarding the conduct of the group experience, it is rather unstructured, though under the clear initiative and guidance of the therapist/director as group leader; regarding the introduction of games and exercises and the subsequent coaching and use of these, it is highly structured. In fact, what may most clearly distinguish RfG from psychodramatic and drama therapy group-work (other than its application to relationships) is the use of improv exercises having a distinct form and embodying principles and objectives that clients are coached to use during enactments.

Shaffer and Galinsky also consider the differences among group approaches over the issue of group pressure, or the influence over the autonomy of its members (what they term the "tyranny of the group"). In the 20-plus years since their writing, systemic thinking has become more widespread in the mental health field with the consequence that it currently appears more evident that all human experience is context-specific and influenced by socially constructed realities. Nonetheless, there exists at least one related area of concern in the application of improv to group therapy: the demand that may arise for entertaining enactments by the observing group members and the consequent comparisons of improv ability among members.

The contract that I establish with the group at the outset includes the following elements: (1) members share a mutual obligation to respect the vulnerability of the players, both as participants and as audience; (2) play is always voluntary and members are not required to account for a decision to decline playing; (3) potential players are offered an informed choice of participating in an enactment; (4) members agree to accept the therapist/director's decision to end an enactment and to follow stage directions to the best of their ability during an improv scene (this frequently takes the form of asking a player to accept a blocked offer or to incorporate a suggestion that advances the action). There are times when, as therapist/director, I will coach the audience to refrain from expressing their reactions to a scene during its enactment or to become more involved by asking that they offer suggestions, come into the scene as a character or inanimate object, etc.

A Characteristic Improv Group Therapy Session

In the way I have developed RfG, improv group therapy is directed primarily to exploration and growth and secondarily toward improving social functioning. Ongoing improv group sessions are patterned loosely after the warm-up–action–sharing format used in psychodrama groups. They start with some brief social conversation and any necessary orienting announcements, which reestablishes the nonpretense social reality base for what follows. Then, the leader offers a movement or verbal warm-up exercise which moves participants to nonconventional interaction with others and mildly evokes pretense. A movement example:

> Walk around the room in some way that corresponds to how you feel at this moment. Keep your focus on your own walking and feeling. . . . Now, become aware of the way others are walking. . . . Pick up someone else's walk. . . . Allow yourself to let their walk influence your feeling . . .

A verbal example:

> (While sitting or standing in a circle) Tell the group three things about yourself that are any combination of lies or truths without indicating which they are.

Following a brief sharing about their experiences with the warm-up, an improv exercise is offered, such as a *Mirrors* (p. 69) exercise that begins with one partner and expands to encompass the whole group. The therapist/director participates in these preliminary exercises, establishing an atmosphere of safety and trust in the group. Following spontaneous verbal sharing about the exercise, the therapist/director invites exploration of emerging feeling and thinking states as well as of social comparisons by asking questions, such as, "Did you prefer being a leader or a follower?" Out of the responses and ensuing discussion, an individual issue or group theme generally emerges which leads to the staging of an improv scene. For example, if the group splits into preferred leaders and followers and members make inferences about leaders being high-status players, a series of brief *Master/Servant* scenes (p. 119) is staged with players trying on each of the roles and with the master being instructed to play low-status in some of them.

After the series, participating players and audience group members are led to share and discuss their discoveries and observations. Out of this process, perhaps one member becomes warmed up to his distress that is triggered by a job situation with an unfair, high-status–playing boss; the therapist/director invites the member to first describe, then enact a brief simulation of a typical encounter with her boss. Next, a new scene is improvised around his issues, meeting two conditions: (1) the setting and characters are displaced from the "reality" of the previous simulation (permitting greater freedom from constraining associations); (2) an improv game is adapted that facilitates exploration of alternative responses, such as a *Master/Servant* scene in which the member plays a high-status servant to a dim-witted, low-status master. Most often, the tone of this improv will be playful, in contrast to the real-life situation it is derived from. At the conclusion of the scene the player is "debriefed" (that is, reinducted back into the social reality of the group session) and verbal sharing among all members occurs. At this point, other members may have been stimulated by the enactment to become warmed up to their own issues and new improv enactments will be developed; at other times, the therapist/director chooses a game or exercise that is not directly related to any member's problem, offering roles to selected members (or asking for volunteers). The session ends with some brief group exercise, such as linking arms, closing eyes, and singing a musical chord, held or varied at will and ending by unspoken consensus.

Issues involving the group-as-a-whole occasionally may be approached using improv techniques. For example, in one improvisational therapy group, the group became embroiled in and split over a dispute arising from one member's objection that three others had gossiped about him in his absence during a week when he had not attended the group session. Apart from the dispute over what had actually been said, two of the accused members maintained that, although they had spoken about the absent member, nothing on that occasion was said that they were not willing to say to the objecting member's face, and that their conversation was therefore harmless. Stating that I saw a way to test the plausibility of this assertion, I told them that we could first pretend that we were a family discussing an absent relative (Uncle Bruce in *Family Story*, described on p. 97). After they had played for a few minutes, freely inventing colorful tales about the absent relative, I ended the game.

At this point, I introduced a variation in which the same game was played for a second time using a different fictional family member, "Aunt Emily." I selected one of the members who had defended the harmlessness of gossiping to take the role of Aunt Emily and seated her outside the "family circle" (but within earshot of the storytellers). The contrast between the first story, where players gossiped in an untrammelled fashion, and the second, where they were in the knowing presence of that character, was considerable; members clearly saw that they tended to be far more reserved and qualified in their offers during the second variation. At the end of perhaps two minutes (there seldom is natural closure to stories in this game) I ended it and instructed Aunt Emily to enter the group and address each family member as well as the entire family with a monologue that incorporated both the story information and her character's reactions (like *The Trial*, described on p. 99). The result was dramatic: Aunt Emily fairly blasted everyone for "damaging her reputation," even though (a) all characters, referred to or enacted, were fictional and (b) the player enacting her knew she was thereby undermining her out-of-role assertion that this practice was harmless. In the discussion that followed, the group became clear about the importance of the confidentiality rule, the problems occasioned by gossiping, and how the known presence of someone spoken about alters the speakers' accountability.

CASE 1   *The Tough-Guy Within*

The following case illustrates how the group setting became an important resource for the growth of Micky, a client who began with me in individual therapy and who joined my improvisational therapy group at my suggestion four months later. A gentle, depressed man with a perpetually downtrodden air about him, Micky attributed many of his life problems to the traumatizing effects of terrifying family violence and child abuse. His fragmentary memories of these events were always recounted in a strained, frightened voice. In one incident, from around five years of age, he remembered crouching, frightened, under the kitchen table while the screaming and blows of his battling parents and the wailing of his infant sister resounded around him. Except for the added detail of clinging to his mother's leg while still under the table, Micky was unable to evolve in the retelling of his story, regularly choking up when he began to describe the worst of the fighting.

During Micky's initial month within the therapy group he maintained a low profile characterized by a sad shyness. He seldom volunteered a comment directed at other members, although he was attentive to other members when they experienced emotional distress. He "sat out" many opportunities to participate in the improv exercises and the enactments of others; when he did participate he invariably played tentatively. Once, I had him be the translator in a *Poet's Corner* (p. 84) scene; in contrast to the poet character's impassioned gibberish and sweeping gestures, Micky's translation was restrained and emotionally muted. On two occasions I gave Micky the *Stories from Feelings* exercise (p. 95), once when he came to the group session brooding over an injustice received at work. He told the story of a dog, too old to hunt anymore, who saved his family from assailants at the cost of his own life, dying gloriously in the arms of his master. I did not inquire as to the parallels to Micky's experience at the time, although I noted the satisfaction he took in the sad but noble ending to his story. Recounting this story brought him into more immediate contact with the group; he was able to participate in that session with a greater range of emotional expressiveness than previously.

Some weeks later, in discussing another member's improv performance, Micky became very animated and appeared warmed-up to an enactment of his own. As I wished to offer him the opportunity to take more definite character and prevent him from fading again into a background role, I set up *The Trial* scene (p. 99), with Micky as the seated protagonist and three other group members standing on-stage around him. The group offered Micky the character name "Stefan" and told him he was a bank teller who had embezzled funds (group members seldom assign characters uneventful lives!). Then B addressed Stefan as his boyhood friend from 40 years ago, reminding him of how they'd played cops and robbers together; C spoke as his tearful wife, deprived of a husband and having been forced to raise their children unaided while he was in prison; and D played the judge who sentenced Stefan, referring to how Stefan had abused the trust of his employer. At this point I directed Stefan to do the monologue in which he got to tell his story in the course of responding to each of the other characters.

Slowly getting to his feet, Stefan paced the stage, head down, arms folded around himself. Then he spoke to B, developing a tough-guy voice, hands now on his hips: "Yeah, Benny, you always played the copper. Left me to be the robber, so what kinda role-model did I have, see? You'da done what I done if you wasn't so yeller!" By this time he was fully into the Hollywood gangster persona as he swaggered over to C: "Ahh, you was always naggin' me how the kids needed this or that, so what was I t'do fer dough? You dames . . . " When he got to D he was bellicose: "You think you can put me away and that's the end of it, eh? Let me tell you, Mister high-an'-mighty judge, I'm comin' lookin' fer you when I'm out of the joint, see?" Turning to address the group audience, Stefan raised both fist and voice: "And that goes for any of you what gets in my way, see? Nobody crosses Big Stefan!" As he folded his arms and turned his back to the audience, ending the scene, everyone applauded. It was a vivid performance from a man who had previously seemed incapable of raising his voice in anger.

In the sharing following this enactment Micky reported that he had felt an unfamiliar infusion of energy at the time he was taking on character in the improv. It was as though there was another person inside him who would not remain passive but fought back at being mistreated or dismissed. The group became quite aroused in supporting the development of this aspect of Micky (his "Stefan," as one member put it); it appeared to me that the group saw in this side of Micky a heroic part of self that all could identify with and that they were investing Micky with their own hopes for transformation.

At the next group session, when I asked for volunteers in a *Directed Story* scene (p. 102) two group members urged Micky to take part, which he then offered to do. I reminded everyone that, as did all group members, Micky had the right to decline to participate. My restatement of this fundamental and well-understood rule was inserted for these reasons: (1) it reminded Micky of his opportunity to make his own choice in the moment; (2) I positioned myself as the group leader who would function as a restraining counterforce to peer pressure; (3) as the group would be having considerable lattitude to shape the ensuing scene, I wished to remind them of their obligation to the players. Micky chose to participate.

The scene was set in a basement where a male homeowner (player A) and a plumber (Micky) were tracing a leak to its source. The homeowner's wife (player B) was upstairs in the house and could be heard occasionally as an off-stage voice. A routine had been established where A would impatiently demand that the plumber locate and fix the problem at once; the plumber stammered a vaguely technical answer that implied he was covering up his incompetence and that costly repairs were needed; B would call downstairs to ask how things were going and A would call back cheerfully with reassurances that everything was under control. At this point, using the format of *Directed Story*, I froze the action on-stage and asked the audience: "The plumber discovers something unusual about the main water pipe; what is it?" The suggestion that came back was: "There's a hole being plugged by a dwarf holding his fist in it!" (player D came out of the audience to play the dwarf.) The scene continued as A discovered that the dwarf was the previous homeowner who hadn't paid his plumbing bill. A began to look scared, backing away from the plumber (implying that he was worried about meeting the dwarf/previous homeowner's fate) yet continuing to reassure his wife that all was well. As A lost his self-assurance, Micky-as-plumber became confident (this is explained as a status transfer in Chapter 7). I froze the scene again and asked the audience: "The plumber gets something from his tool bag; what is it?" "A contract for transferring ownership of the house!" came the ingenious reply. The plumber now calmly mimed taking out a pen and the contract and offered A the choice of signing over the house, or . . . (here he pointed to the still-imprisoned dwarf who screamed, "Sign! Sign!"). As the off-stage B called out: "Is everything all right, dear?" I blacked out the scene, amidst general laughter and applause.

The group discussion at first was self-congratulatory (they had indeed cocreated a wonderful scene), but then focused on the in-role experiences of the players. Micky was elated; he had experienced the status transfer as connecting him to a powerful side of himself. Although he knew there was some correspondence between this powerful side and his experience of the "Stefan" persona, he was unable to articulate it at the time. Later, in an individual therapy session Micky was able to reconstruct his experiences in the two improvs and find a common, energizing theme of *fearsome wilfulness* which counteracted his depressive theme of *frightened and traumatized victim*. It was not that he approved morally of the actions of his improv characters, he explained, but that they had vitality and lived as they pleased. He contrasted this with his father, whom Micky saw as a victim who had became a bully to his family out of frustration at his ineffectual life-style.

After the group-session enactments described above, Micky began to retell his traumatic childhood stories in our individual therapy sessions in a transformative manner. He now remembered the aftermath to the family battles as more pleasant times when he and his mother would cling to one another for mutual solace while his father would be absent from their home. As he now recounted these events he included mention of how his mother would tell him that men were likely to do terrible things if they unleashed their tempers and that he must never allow his temper to get out of control. In hearing his own account of this message from his mother Micky readily connected it to the previously dominant feeling of stifling uneasiness whenever he had thought to express mere displeasure, let alone anger. I encouraged him to tell first-person fictional tales about characters with similar problems, an activity he soon grew fond of. His own character in these transformative tellings underwent several changes, from scared and helpless victim, to emotional comforter of others, to physical defender of victimized others, to victorious combatant and hero. Ten months following the emergence of his "Stefan" character Micky was functioning socially as an averagely outgoing, confident man.

The emergence of recognizable, enduring character features (mannerisms and styles of speech) across different improv scenes (as noted in Chapter 9) is often a forerunner to the emergence of a distinct character. Metaphorically, I view these characters as "scouts" who are sent ahead to test the reception by other people of previously unused or untried social selves. RfG provides a "school" for the training and support of scouts.

APPLICATIONS TO INDIVIDUAL THERAPY

Improv in therapy may, at a minimum, be conducted with the client as player and the therapist/director as either audience or as coplayer while also implicitly taking an audience role. While many techniques require more than two players, and others are of value only when enacted with the client's significant others, there remain quite a number of situations in which improv is useful in therapy sessions with individual clients.

As was stated in Chapter 1, the therapeutic venture is often likened to a hero's quest, while RfG prepares clients to perform heroically on the stage of life. To do so, it is helpful to get clients involved in narrating and enacting *winning* stories, which are narratives with a morally positive outcome for the protagonist. This does not necessarily mean a happy ending in terms of final circumstances, but rather that the protagonist has the satisfaction of knowing he or she acted in accordance with principles he or she endorses. Along the way the client may explore what may be generally labelled as "alternatives to principled behavior," with both therapist and client treating these as harmless yet valuable learning experiences.

On this latter point, in RfG presentations to therapists the question sometimes arises whether "bad behavior" in-role might encourage a transfer of that behavior to real life as readily as do characters who embody socially approved-of behavior. As already noted in Chapters 2 and 9, I am selective in which roles I offer or encourage exploration of, to whom I offer them, and that enactments take place in a setting that is both psychologically safe and where the pretense-reality boundary is clear. In my experience, clients engaged in intentional pretense always recognize and usually go out of their way to acknowledge the distinction between their stage and off-stage personae. I will clarify, however, that I have *not* introduced improv to the clients I have treated who show marked dissociative disorder features.

While there are numerous exceptions in practice, the general sequence of using improv in individual therapy is:

1. The client tells his or her story from which the therapist/director learns the issues, themes, obstacles and resources.
2. The therapist/director offers warm-up exercises that familiarize the client with taking a stage-role.
3. Improvs thematically linked (though not necessarily related in content) to the client's story are told and enacted.

4. The therapist/director works with the client's "performances," observing and identifying obstacles to winning (heroic) narrative.
5. The therapist/director coaches and occasionally directs clients in rehearsal enactments that overcome the obstacles.
6. The client, with minimal coaching, retells/reenacts the original story, transforming it in the process into a winning story.

This sequence need not focus initially on the client's main thematic life-story but should be in areas where the client feels he or she has something at stake in the resultant transformation. Along the way one or more characters may emerge that are named and may be evoked later during both enactments and verbal therapy.

CASE 2   *Getting the Mother You Want*

Kate felt tense and highly conflicted in encounters with her mother. At the beginning of therapy Kate had characterized her mother as cold, selfish, and competitive with her. Living 200 miles apart, their contact consisted of semiannual visits on holidays and one or two short telephone conversations per month. She frequently telephoned her older sister and younger brother, both of whom maintained more frequent contact with their mother and who shared a similar impression of their mother. Yet Kate was the sibling who was most perturbed by contact with their mother and most desirous of improving that relationship.

About two months into the therapy, after exploring Kate's position in her family of origin both historically and currently, I asked Kate to close her eyes and visualize what things would be like in her life and in the lives of her family members if she had a positive and uncomplicated relationship with her mother. This question, an adaptation of Erickson's crystal ball technique, is frequently used in solution-focused therapy (de Shazer, 1985) to prepare the client to achieve spontaneously a desired outcome. My purpose, although consistent with this aim, included developing an alternative reality that might be enacted. Kate said she saw herself getting together occasionally with her mother in a low-key, emotionally detached way, without feeling any loss, guilt, resentment, or attachment. This description resembled more or less Kate's perception of the present position of her siblings with their mother.

It appeared to me that her description of this "ideal" relationship made reference only to the absence of negative emotions and that it represented a "settling for" rather than a truly wonderful outcome. All of us frequently avoid freeing our imaginations to dare to hope for what we truly want, probably out of fear of disillusionment or frustration. Yet only when we dare to acknowledge what we really desire do we grasp the thread of purpose in our life's quest.

I next had her role-play an imaginary encounter with her mother in this ideal scenario with the "empty chair" technique used in Gestalt therapy and derived from psychodramatic technique. This involves placing two facing chairs at conversational distance; the client "plays the projection" by speaking from one of the chairs as one person/ego-state/part-of-self to another, projected person/ego-state/part of self that is experienced as seated in the opposite empty chair. When the client experiences a reply forming from the projected other she moves to the other chair, adjusting her expression to match the inwardly-experienced characterization, and replies back to the first person/ego-state/part-of-self, still seated in the first chair. Of course, from an RfG point of view, this amounts to having one player perform the roles of two characters interacting with one another.

I started by having Kate sit in one of the chairs with her eyes closed, repeating "everything is better between us now" several times before opening her eyes and "seeing" the character in the other chair. Instead of the expected future or alternative present, the characters that emerged in Kate's scenario were a soft-spoken, kindly older woman and a shy, hopeful girl who traded expressions of tendernness and affection for one another, pledging that they would always love and help one another. I then asked Kate, seated in the girl-chair, what her name was ("Kathy"), how old she was ("six"), where she was ("in our garden at home"), and what would happen in the future ("We'll always be close"). I asked Kate to switch chairs and asked her name ("Betty") how old she was ("45"), where she was ("in the garden with Kathy"), and what would happen in the future ("She'll grow up and move away. I'll be very lonely"). Kate-as-Betty started to cry; I asked whose tears were being shed and she replied "mine."

I had her leave the Betty-chair and stand alongside me, looking across the room at both empty chairs. Addressing her as Kate (to increase her emotional distance from both chair-roles) I asked her to visualize the Kathy-Betty dialogue as continuing or repeating and to describe to me what she saw happening. As her adult self, Kate described Kathy as a girl tied to her need for her mother's affection and Betty as a nurturant and tolerant mother only when her daughter was docile and dependent. When the real Kate was growing up and began to show a will of her own, her mother had fought her maturation by attacking Kate's self-confidence and withdrawing support from her daughter. I then invited Kate, still standing beside me across the room from both empty chairs, to speak to six-year-old Kathy with the wisdom she now posessed, adding that Betty couldn't hear what she said. Looking at the Kathy-chair, Kate said, with earnest compassion, "Growing up is hard, but you can do it without Mom's support. Don't be afraid—life gets better when you're grown up." I then asked her if she wanted to address Betty; with tears in her eyes, Kate shook her head "no."

After discussing the empty chair enactment I invited Kate to write a letter before our next session to Betty, writing as herself at age 19 (when she had left home and Betty had actually been 45). The letter she brought in, which I had her read out loud, showed both anger and regret at her mother's unwillingness to accept Kate's autonomy. I observed that there was still a lot of Kathy in that letter and asked whether Kate-at-present was willing to move beyond her position at age 19; she answered emotionally that she now felt so much love toward her mother that she had been unable to express earlier. I then made use of the *Mantra* exercise (p. 135) by having Kate as her present-age self talk to her mother in the empty chair while mentally repeating, "I forgive you." To get a result, I emphasized, it is more important to focus on the mantra than on what in particular you have to say. Though her voice trembled at first, what emerged was a serene, self-confident Kate, willing yet not needing to reconcile with her mother. I noted that Kate referred to her mother as "Betty," a change that marked a shift to more equal status between them.

In the final step of this process I coached Kate to employ the "I forgive you" mantra when she next telephoned her mother. Two weeks later, Kate reported that she had done so, and that the tone on both sides of their conversation had much more warmth than she had remembered ever having with her mother as an adult. This led to further restorying of Kate as heroine in our verbal therapy sessions for having forgiven the possessiveness without, as in her previous story, accepting guilt for displeasing her mother. Their next in-person visit took place three weeks later; Kate reported that she used the mantra a few times to hold onto her confident position through some shaky moments, and that her mother seemed quite accepting of the shift in their relationship. In consequence, Kate now planned more frequent visits, even inviting (for the first time) her mother to visit her home. What she now had, Kate agreed, was even better than she had thought of as ideal only two months earlier.

CASE 3   *The Heroic Stag*

Lester and Antonio, a gay couple who had lived together for eight months, came into couples therapy after having a second violent fight that left their apartment in shambles and their continuation as a couple in doubt. Lester, a 40-year-old professional with a settled, friend-filled lifestyle was aghast at the disruption both to his feelings and his ordered life; Antonio, the 28-year-old outcast son of a prominent South American family, was nursing hurt feelings and struggling with jealousy of Lester's friends, two of whom were Lester's former lovers. Antonio had recently begun a casual sexual affair which seemed motivated both by a need for self-reassurance of his desirability and an attempt to get Lester jealous. When Antonio had flaunted this affair the physical brawls were precipitated that frightened them both into seeking couples therapy.

After two sessions it became clear that Antonio was unwilling to work on the relationship; the second session was essentially a negotiation as to how to arrange the removal of Antonio's posessions (he was moving in with his new lover) and what restitution for damage to Lester's apartment was owed. Lester was devastated; yet another relationship had failed, this time more disasterously than ever. He contracted for six months of individual therapy.

Lester's description of himself and his adult life was told with dejection and self-blame. Antonio, on whom he had lavished such affection, had betrayed him, which was painful enough. But Lester displayed an almost hysterical, generalized self-loathing for himself: He was a failure at relationships, incapable of judging character or of deserving good treatment from others; he must be a sick, violent person to have been provoked so readily; he must be self-destructive to have consorted with a vindictive, immature, and promiscuous person through whom, he was half-convinced, he himself would (deservedly) contract AIDS. His story of his prior relationships was characterized by a similar pattern of high initial hopes, disillusionment, estrangement, and self-recrimination.

Explaining that I believed his distress stemmed less from what had happened than from how he explained it, I next used a technique based on couples choreography described by Papp (1982) in which clients use visual imagery to depict themselves and the struggles of their relationship in non-human form. Lester described himself as a stag, self-reliant but lonely, who had befriended a needy wolf (Antonio). The stag's friends tried to warn him that no good could come of getting involved with such a creature, but the stag scoffed at such warnings. At first, the wolf was grateful for the stag's help but later turned treacherous, intent on usurping the stag's position, talking ill of the stag to other animals and trying to steal his friends. Finally, they had a tremendous battle; both were wounded and the wolf left for good. The stag was very ashamed to let his friends see his wounds and learn what had happpened, so he hid out for a long while, feeling sad, lonely, and defeated.

This story was told in a mournful tone and obviously reevoked the painful feelings of his relationship with Antonio. I offered Lester the opportunity to retell his story with my participation, using the exercise *Cooperative Storytelling* (p. 94) with elements of *Narrative/Color* (p. 98), the rules of which I then gave. Sitting directly opposite Lester, I asked him to retell the story with me but to be open to allowing it to transform in the telling. I made the choice not to label this as a new story, since I wanted to make it easier for Lester eventually to choose to own this as an account of what had happened in his relationship with Antonio. Immediately after Lester had introduced the character of the stag into the story, before the wolf was introduced, I asked: "The stag had a problem; what was it?" "He

was lonely and couldn't really relax around his friends," Lester said (Lester
had grown up as an only child, surrounded by adults, with no peer play-
mates. Antonio had been someone who had introduced playfulness into
Lester's overly grown-up world). After the story had continued to the part
where the wolf was introduced I called "Color!" as a signal for Lester to
add descriptive detail. He now portrayed the wolf as lonely and isolated,
with a history of being a "lone wolf" who would antagonize others and then
move on. When I asked: "How did the stag think he could help the wolf?"
Lester replied, "He gave him a home and his friendship, so he thought the
wolf would learn to settle down and become a reliable companion," sound-
ing doubtful as he said it, realizing that the wolf's history made this outcome unlikely.

The story continued, punctuated by my questions and my calling out
"Color!" or "Narrative!" As noted in Chapter 6, this latter device alters the
storyteller's pacing and emotional distance by forstalling the tendency to
bog down in details at the expense of getting to what happens or, conversely, advance the action so rapidly that its emotional impact is avoided.
I used "Color!" to obtain more details (and hence focus greater attention)
on the wolf's character and the stag's reactions to learning of the wolf's
treachery. I used "Narrative!" to move the action forward at the point of
confrontation leading up to the fight and to focus on the stag's actions at
the end of the story. The *Cooperative Storytelling* technique allows for
questions with and without preceding statements, so that there is ample
scope for injecting new elements and meanings into the narrative. My questions were guided by a sense that there was a more heroic side to Lester's
character than he was accessing around the relationship with Antonio, yet I
was not deliberately steering the story to achieve my therapeutic goal of
offsetting Lester's self-blame; I was willing to have the story told differently, not necessarily "my way." At one point I asked: "So the stag fought
the wolf in order to keep his friends?" which clearly reframed Lester's
original rendition by offering a justifiable cause for the stag's use of force.
By re-presenting the stag as acting generously at first and combatting unfair
treatment later he was no longer the shameful creature of the original
version.

The version of the story which emerged in the second retelling went as
follows:

> Once there was a stag who lived near his other animal friends in the forest. He
> had a good life but wanted a special friend whom he could live with. One day, a
> wolf appeared who looked sad and said he was lost and hungry. The stag felt
> sorry for the wolf and helped him generously, hoping they would become
> friends. The stag's other friends, especially the horse, were upset that the stag
> was spending so much time with the wolf and not with them. The horse didn't
> like the wolf and told the stag that wolves made bad friends. The stag replied
> that wolves only needed kindness and then they would be loyal.

The stag went out of his way to have the wolf accepted by the other animals, but the horse had talked against the wolf, so they were afraid of him. Then the wolf went to some of the other animals and gossiped about the stag's private life; the horse heard about this and told the stag this was happening. The stag confronted the wolf, who claimed this was a rumor started by the horse out of jealousy. The stag then checked with others and found it was true. The wolf admitted he had lied because he didn't want to be kicked out, as had happened to him before. The stag told the wolf that he expected honesty from his friends, which the wolf pledged in future.

However, the wolf continued to lie to the stag and tried to become best friends with the raccoon. Finally, the stag told the wolf he had to choose between being best friends with the raccoon and continuing to live with him. The wolf attacked him and they fought; although the stag defended himself well against this ingratitude and treachery, both he and the wolf were wounded by the fighting. The stag now knew the relationship was over yet felt at first embarrassed to let his friends, especially the horse, know about the fight. But he knew his friends would understand he had made a mistake, so he told them; they were sympathetic and glad the wolf was gone. The stag's life was really not so bad, although he still wished for a special friend. He had learned from what had happened with the wolf that both animals had to try to make a good friendship. So he continued his life as before, confident that he would eventually meet and make a new special friend.

Although Lester's telling of this story obviously differed in content, his performance as storyteller was now quite transformed. The story was told with pride and even some enjoyment in how the stag had survived the destructive treachery of the wolf and had learned a valuable lession. It now became possible for Lester to see how his pattern of operating overresponsibly in other relationships had led to disfunction and that only a more mutually responsible relationship could work. Moreover, his self-blame at the failure of these relationships now appeared to him exaggerated and a further manifestation of overresponsibility. At this point, with Lester having achieved a more emotionally-distanced perspective, I invited him to try the *Emotional Short-Circuit* exercise (p. 81) in which he was to think of the most painful moment in his relationship with Antonio and simultaneously to laugh heartily. Lester worked up to this by first practicing laughing at/with less painful memories but soon was able to "take on the Big One," as he put it. Immediately following his recuperation (this exercise is emotionally and even physically exhausting for many people) Lester reported feeling a new confidence in himself and that he was stronger for having gone through this relationship ordeal. This stronger, self-confident side of Lester was evident throughout the remainder of our work together; thereafter I felt I was in the presence of a person with far higher self-esteem. Therapy ended on schedule; at last report, Lester was not living with anyone but seemed quite happy with his active social life.

So often in therapy, we attempt to alter the course of the family drama. Typically, however, the more serious the family is about the drama, the harder it is to induce the possibility of change. It is in an atmosphere of play, rather than intense seriousness, that such shifts are likely to take place.

—Edward Friedman (1984, p. 26)

CHAPTER 11

Applications to Couples and Family Therapy

T HE APPLICATION OF RfG techniques to both couples and family therapy is guided by the rationale of playfully cocreating alternatives to entrenched, recurrent patterns of interaction between members. One significant difference between clinical work with couples and families is that the role inequality inherent in family organization is itself altered by the activity of play. That is, the activity of mutual play across generations accomplishes change in the way family members experience themselves and their family relationships.

In both couples and family therapy we observe how the established relationships between family members so limit spontaneity that predictable sequences of emotional exchanges are the rule. For example, A's anger is regularly met by B's fearful attempt to placate, leading to A's magnanimous soothing of B, followed by B's offer of humor or affection, etc. Therapists familiar with the concepts of Eric Berne's transactional analysis, Harville Hendrick's imago therapy, or Jay Haley's early work on strategic family therapy will recognize this phenomenon when described in different language. What is equally significant is the narrowed range of intensity of expressed emotion in these exchanges.

Consequently, improv exercises are indicated as a playful and effective means to alter these predictable sequences in order to open up new possibilities for the relationship. Frequently, it is a revelation for adult family members to discover that when they play with other family members outside of their usual character boundaries they can obtain consequences that are unexpected and different from those experienced in their families of origin.

APPLICATIONS TO COUPLES THERAPY

As the relationship itself is the primary focus of couples therapy RfG lends itself well to working on relationship features such as role flexibility, status, range of emotional expressiveness, cooperation/competitiveness, mutuality, intimacy, and capacity for play. Many of the clinical applications of improv were first developed in my work with couples and it remains the modality for which I continue to find the most new applications. Also, a majority of stage improv games and exercises are intended for two players, although it is not difficult to modify them for a greater number.

Four Clinical Concepts

In my RfG work I have found four broad clinical concepts particularly useful to my conduct of therapy, particularly with couples: stories, rules, intimacy/expressiveness, and status and gender. These concepts are not "pure" or even accurate representations of the original ideas that I adapted. Also, my use of these four concepts hardly implies that I ignore all others, or that other therapists might not find other concepts to be of equal or greater utility. Nor am I offering any kind of unifying theory or even attempting an integration at this time. RfG techniques can be applied with benefit across a broad diversity of theoretical stances and it is not necessary to adhere to my viewpoint to employ these profitably. I present my versions of these concepts in order to make the case examples that follow clearer. My alternating use of each of these four concepts, or descriptive lenses, generally enables me to stay unstuck and offer couples new experiences via improv techniques.

1. Stories A voluntary, enduring, dyadic interpersonal relationship is a construction of many factors operating at a number of complex and intertwining levels. Just as people's individual lives are understood as stories, relationships are stories that are collectively cocreated and shared. In marriage the understanding and experience of each spouse develops out of the intersecting of two individual narratives (each of which can be traced to family of origin themes) and develops as a common story (e.g., the story of "How We Met"). This narrative develops in stages, with continual restorying. In the beginning of a romance, two persons are each operating as separate storytellers who cultivate the illusion that their beloved is the person fitting perfectly into the role of hoped-for and needed mate. It's as though each is a playwright/director who has a part to cast and believes that they have found the right actor or actress to play that role. As they have strong and specific (though not necessarily conscious) expectations, they ignore, downplay, and misinterpret discrepancies between their expectations and the partner's actual attributes and behaviors. Moreover, their expectations extend to the way being in love or being married is supposed to be; to how others should regard them as a couple; and to themselves as fulfilled in love.

While lovers may be aware of their partners' idealized expectations and strive to fulfill them, this cannot be done to the full satisfaction of the partner or maintained indefinitely. At some later point, disillusionment sets in when each realizes the unreality of their projected expectations of one other, complicated by the fact that their disillusionment rarely happens simultaneously. Disillusionment, though disagreeable, is a necessary stage, since it forces the disillusioned partner to accommodate (i.e., to restory, or rescript) their narrative to recognize and incorporate changes in their expectations of the partner.* Unfortunately, encouraged both by cultural beliefs that equate accommodation with the renunciation of success and tenaciously (most often unconsciously) clinging to family of origin themes, contemporary spouses in Western cultures are apt to abandon the relationship in the belief that disillusionment is proof of a mistaken choice of partner.

If both spouses endure the disillusionment stage and begin to accept the differences from self-expectations that the partner contributes to the marriage, a new narrative may be cocreated, one based not upon the themes of resignation or defeat but on a positive valuing of their partner's differences and choices as contributions to the relationship and to their own growth. Put another way, they are freer to see the differences that they have as an assets, rather than to focus on the unity that they don't have as a liability.

---

*A more drastic, rare, and psychotic solution is the formation of a *folie à deux*, in which the partners give up separate identities, cut themselves off from any intimate connection with the outside world, and attempt to live a unitary reality at all cost.

2. Rules   Fundamental to the operation of a committed relationship are two mutual agreements: to continue the relationship and to operate within certain rules. Each couple is unique not merely because it is composed of two singular individuals but also because the partners have cocreated a relational reality that uniquely defines those aspects of self-identity and functioning that will be validated or invalidated within that relationship. Rules are procedures for deciding whether an event fits that relational reality.

The rules a couple operates by are never fully explicit and include features that may be judged as impossible or unworkable to an outsider (including their therapist) but it is axiomatic that, if a relationship is voluntary and enduring, both partners are contributing to maintaining it by adhering to its implicit rules. Seen in this way, the couple is actively creating and maintaining patterns that are, by inference, homeostatic, predictable, and that support the long-term continuation of that relationship. When agreement over keeping or interpreting the rules breaks down, a process that can occur suddenly or gradually, the relationship is in trouble; when a disagreement over meta-rules (rules about forming and interpreting rules) occurs, the relationship snaps. At any point where there is divergence in agreement regarding the rules, the partners are living different realities, a phenomenon that may be patched over by the formation of a meta-rule that forbids attending to the discrepancy, or by secrecy that misleads one partner into believing that both share the same reality while the other knows they do not.

This sketchy description of rules and meta-rules leaves out much of the complexity (and some of the sinister implications) of rules noted by early family communication theorists (Watzlawick, Bavelas, & Jackson, 1967; Laing, 1972). What Laing (1972) started from was the observation that the construct of family is maintained by the mutual collusion of its members (in itself a social constructivist viewpoint). However, there are layers of pretense embedded in the rules of family communication ("knots") that act to mystify and double-bind its members to deny or falsify experience (indeed, even to blind members to the existence of such denial or falsification) in the name of normality, loyalty, or love.

One such tangle arises when the boundary between pretense and reality is deliberately made ambiguous. The blurring or stretching of this boundary itself then becomes a meta-rule of play, but what makes matters more interesting still is the uncertainty and danger attendant upon losing control of one's own capacity to shape the context. In these cases, evaluating the context as playful or serious and choosing how to enact one's role assumes paramount importance. The prototype for such meta-play is tickling (discussed in Chapter 1), where aggression and enjoyment are playfully fused. A vivid dramatic example occurs in a scene from the film *Goodfellas* where

Henry (played by Ray Liotta) is challenged by Tommy (Joe Peschi) as to what he means by calling Tommy "funny." Tommy has a well-deserved reputation for having a lethally violent temper and Henry is on the spot, not knowing if Tommy is testing him playfully or is truly offended.

Another, more complex, example is central to the structure of Edward Albee's play *Who's Afraid of Virginia Woolf?* where several intersecting layers of pretense and reality are presented. The main characters, George and Martha, have a disfunctional marriage in which their maneuvers to hurt one another are presented as an art form that they enjoy playing out, especially in front of others. The audience is left uncertain as to how much of each's destructiveness is intended to win admiration from the partner, rather than be taken as punishment of the other; how much control each of them has over adhering to their rules in the face of escalating provocation; whether they have descended into warfare without rules by the end of the play or whether the meta-rules of their marriage *require* that they escalate in order to maintain the relationship; and whether their incessant drinking facilitates the ambiguity of intentions and judgments that George and Martha have of one another. George and Martha have cocreated an imaginary son who is triangled into their struggles; their rules around this constructed fiction include the familiar improv rule of "accepting all offers" such that whatever one of them adds to the son's biography is now true. When George, near the end of the play, kills off the son, Martha is anguished but bound by the rules to accept this "tragedy"; yet it is unclear as to how they can continue their relationship without their constructed son.

3. Intimacy/expressiveness   In addition to the domain of rules is the domain of intimacy. Some couples appear to settle for a "just-enough" style of connection to take the edge off their loneliness without risking the complicating and vulnerability-inducing effects of deeper intimacy. Others seem to strive for much greater mutual involvement, where far more is at stake in their coadventuring. In this more involved and involving relationship style, dramatic developments and dramatic reactions are predictable features. Extreme expressed emotionality is not necessarily a sign of great involvement nor is the absence of expressiveness proof of minimal involvement. I assess the degree of a couple's intimacy more by their capacity for cocreating adventures in which they rely completely on one another and in which they explore the terrors and delights of novel circumstances (see Chapter 6).

Many couples are experienced at creating a world of privacy that encompasses their intimacy, particularly their sex-life. This may take the form of baby-talk, pet-names for one another or parts of their bodies, cryptic references to shared experiences that are unintelligible to outsiders, etc. Its boundaries are demarcated by a (usually) tacit agreement to exclude everyone else from knowledge of their private world and are signalled by changed vocal inflection and/or specific gestures. Although I will inquire as to the existence of a private world I adhere to the belief that even a therapist should not intrude in that domain. In some cases, I even restrain conflictual clients who would divulge their private language as a way of embarrassing their partners. In the above-mentioned pathological relationship offered in *Who's Afraid of Virginia Woolf?* George and Martha repeatedly and hurtfully disrespect that boundary, with disastrous consequences. Couples who play improv games regularly report that doing so facilitates and enriches this existing private life. However, I have not been generally successful in getting couples to create a private world if they have entered therapy without one.

Marital and family therapists know that couples develop reciprocal functioning, such that each member specializes in certain tasks or functions and has the partner specialize in others. Complementarity is also evident in cognitive styles. What is not as apparent is that couples also develop reciprocal *emoting*, such that they each have specialized emotional responses and rarely share simultaneously the same emotional state or degree of emotive intensity. When one, for example, gets upset/excited/overinvolved in a situation, the other will become calm/rational/"grown-up"/overdistanced. In a way, then, the couple as a unit maintains control by having one member "on duty" while the partner is freer to be less functional and more expressive (the same dynamic prevails for families, groups, and larger social systems, of course). While normal and adaptive, this pattern is limiting if (a) the emotional positions are fixed (the same member is always "grown-up" while the other perennially "gets to be the kid") or (b) the partners never join in the same emotion or get to be expressive at an equivalent level of intensity (which is how they could adventure together).

4. Status and gender   Status transactions play an important part in codefining the relationship's roles. As in interpersonal conflict in general, during marital strife there is a status battle in which each partner disqualifies the attempts of the other to lower one's own status, and often makes an attempt to elevate one's own status that is rejected by the partner. Compared with conflict between nonintimates, marital strife is more painful for the partners and more difficult to become detached from for three reasons: (1) the intimacy of marriage permits each partner to know the vulnerabilities of the other in considerable detail, which increases the opportunity to have an impact by "hitting below the belt"; (2) the complexity of their marital rules means that the cause of any felt sense of wrongness can be projected onto the spouse with some reference to a past or present violation of some rule; (3) more is at stake in that each partner expects that his or her own worthiness will be upheld and supported by the other. The most damaging consequence of repeated conflictual encounters between spouses is the demoralizing effect of recognized failure in getting beyond the fruitless and hurtful repetitive patterns of conflict.

These conflicts are complicated in heterosexual relationships by gender differences, both in expectations and styles of defending one's self-esteem. Typically, a husband will operate from a position that equates his wife's expressed dissatisfaction with general criticism that challenges his entitlement to high or equal status. Thus husbands will try to silence the complaint by (1) finding an instrumental solution to the problem that they suppose caused their wives' complaint; (2) denigrating their wives as being unjustified in complaining; and/or (3) ignoring or absenting themselves from receiving the criticism. What appears particularly important to many men is to avoid, at all costs, accepting an account of the situation that makes them look bad — as foolish, incompetent, or as a failure. Significantly, being seen as uncaring is not necessarily status-deflating for such husbands and the wife's accusation of insensitivity will then, to her further frustration, be ineffectual. Moreover, men often interpret the unhappiness of their wives as a test of whether they can give what is perceived as asked for; if any attempt to satisfy is not appreciated they may take the resulting lack of the wife's satisfaction as a proof of failure, leading to blame or avoidance in future similar circumstances. Finally, criticism may signal men to treat the situation as a win-lose struggle in which winning (or not-losing) in the moment assumes greater importance than the long-term benefits of reconciliation, cooperation, and harmony.

Since women frequently regard their relationship's success as their sole responsibility, discord is equated with personal failure, resulting in the lowering of their own status. Even where a wife is looking solely for material assistance from her husband, his indication of shared responsibility, sensitivity to her point of view, and affectionate reassurance of her importance to him is frequently needed in order to resolve the strife. While women often signal a lower status position around men in social settings (by use of space, body posture, eye contact, vocal inflection, allowance of interruption, and use of verbal qualifiers) couples therapy frequently serves as a context to embolden women and put men on the defensive. Although this shift may seemingly offset the status inequality of gender, it often intensifies the woman-as-emotional-pursuer/man-as-distancer positions and brands therapy as a "woman's thing" in the eyes of husbands, resulting in unfavorable treatment outcomes.

CASE 4   *Setting the Mood*

Ellie, a wealthy socialite in her mid-fifties, had been treated pharmacologically for depression intermittently throughout her adult life. She came into individual therapy in order to deal with three seemingly unrelated problems: her worries for her 32-year-old son from a previous marriage, adrift following his recently-quit "solid management position"; her distress over her 14-year-old step-daughter Jill's lying and impudence; and her frustration with her fourth and present husband, Gordon, eight years her junior, who worked for a living and was, for that reason, insufficiently available to travel with and escort Ellie to her numerous social and charitable events. In the third month of therapy I persuaded Ellie to invite Gordon for a consultation session; subsequently, I worked with them conjointly over the next 15-month period. Jill was present for three of the sessions.

Ellie, an only child, had grown up in the shadow of her posessive, near-abusive father, whom she revered but feared. He had been fiercely protective of her to the point of undermining any confidence in her own judgment, drove away some of her suitors, and was instrumental in her decision to end her first marriage of eight years. After his death she remarried three times, ending each of her prior three marriages by judging her husbands as out to take advantage of her.

Gordon had been raised as the favored younger son of a perfectionistic mother from whom he had had difficulty separating emotionally. His one prior marriage, of eleven years, had been to Jill's mother, a woman whom he described as "willful and selfish." From his work as a free-lance management consultant, Gordon derived an irregular income which, though adequate for a middle-class standard of living, came nowhere near to meeting an equal share of the luxurious life-style he and Ellie enjoyed. In consequence, Gordon paid over his entire income to the joint checking account used to pay the household bills without ever feeling that his contribution was sufficient; on a number of occasions, he had passed up opportunities to build his business and increase his income, reasoning that he could never make enough money to alter his economic position relative to Ellie.

Jill, a spirited, pretty teenager, lived primarily with Gordon and Ellie, staying with her mother on alternate weekends. Her difficulties appeared to center on her lacking a sense of belonging to the world of economic privilege that her private-school classmates took for granted. Although liking Ellie, she found her stepmother rigid and clashed with her frequently over Ellie's attempts to dictate rules and standards. Jill's relationship with Gordon was easygoing by comparison; her father seldom made demands or challenged her explanations or excuses.

While Ellie was not at the point of divorcing Gordon, their six-year marriage had soured of late. Gordon's main complaint was that Ellie placed him in an unfair bind: He could either give up his independence in order to be a "kept man" and escort to her (in which case he would be both economically vulnerable and giving her grounds for her suspicions of being exploited) or he could continue to earn his own livelihood (in which case he could not be so available for Ellie and would still be incapable financially of matching her life-style). He also mentioned Ellie's use of her moodiness (she was not currently on antidepressant medication) to demand attention and stated that she was looking to find fault with Jill.

Ellie insisted that she supported Gordon's career but complained that he "hid behind work" out of indifference to her and countered with accusations of his siding with Jill against her. As real as their quarrelling was, it lacked the tension and passion that characterizes marital stife when the spouses believe that matters might get out of hand. Indeed, from their answers to my inquiries about their history, their fighting had never resulted in anything more significant than an afternoon's sulk in another room. I hypothesized that their rules included a collusive arrangement whereby Gordon would either withdraw from her demands but become emotionally and sexually more attentive whenever Ellie's moodiness turned to sadness, curtailing any outbursts or wide swings in their relationship intensity but also undermining any serious attempt to resolve their basic life-style dilemma. Additionally, in a classic triangulation pattern, Ellie's complaints about Jill brought Gordon more actively into the picture in order to deal with their conflict, while Jill became the proxy for Gordon's unstated resentment of Ellie's power due to her privileged financial position.

As I occasionally do when working with couples, I introduced improv to Ellie and Gordon by first asking for descriptions of times when their relationship was at its best, a time when it was easier for them to be relaxed, humorous, and playful. Both of them reported that their tenderness and good-will seemed to flourish when they were on trips out of town. I then had them describe, in alternate sentences, such a recent trip, which they did with good cooperation and evident enjoyment. Over the next two sessions I gave them *Yes, And*, *Presents* (p. 105), *Mirrors*, and *Poet's Corner* (p. 84) to play; while initially reluctant to engage in improv, Ellie quickly grew confident, even eager. These games appreciably lightened the atmosphere in the sessions and brought out an animated side in Ellie and a penchant for mischievousness in Gordon. My general aim in taking them through these improv experiences, which promoted mutuality, generosity, and cooperation, was to facilitate greater trust and pave the way for more painful and risky work.

During the middle phase of therapy Ellie and Gordon would regularly bring in stories about strife between them during the previous week; the recounting of these episodes during the session would routinely touch off further conflict. Whichever was telling the story first would assume a reasonable, "objective" tone in describing their own responses while playing up the undesirability or inappropriateness of the other's. Invariably, this would soon provoke a rebuttal of some detail, or a parallel narrative with a different meaning from the other, and a quarrel would ensue. As this is commonplace in couples therapy, it was some time before I noticed that the degree of upset shown by the listener was not closely related to the negativity of the teller's characterization. Instead, as I came to deduce, each was sensitive to being portrayed in a manner inconsistent with the self-image that the spouse was supposed to validate. In Ellie's case, she did not became reactive to Gordon's stories in which he characterized her as demanding, cold, or strident (clearly, traits he objected to), yet would become reactive to any suggestion that she was manipulative or lacking graciousness. In Gordon's case, being reproached for physical unavailability (Ellie's main peeve) did not greatly perturb him, yet any insinuation that he was selfish and inflexible was sufficiently provocative to bring on a hurt or angry response.

It appeared that the rules of their marriage required Ellie to validate Gordon for being flexible and generous, traits that assured him he was not like his mother; correspondingly, Gordon was expected to validate Ellie for being straightforward and well-mannered (for which, by her account, her father had given her approval). When unhappy with one another each would color his or her accounts of events with shades of meaning that threatened to invalidate the picture of the other as posessing those cherished traits. In this way both of them became highly involved in the moment in raising the emotional stakes of their marriage (an effective, if dysfunctional, way of increasing emotional intensity). Menacing one's partner by threatening to break or alter the rules of the relationship, especially rules concerning the validation of the other's identity, will reliably get his or her attention by activating vulnerability but will also evoke defensiveness and retaliation (as the above-mentioned description of George and Martha depicts).

After doing some conventional verbal therapy which effectively detriangulated Jill from the problems of their marital relationship, I focused on the conflicts occasioned by their misinterpreting the motives and behaviors of one another. I first had one of them stage-direct an enactment of one of the episodes over which they were quarreling (I stood in for the one directing) and then had the other stage-direct the same scene to bring home the differences in their versions.* Ellie directed a scene in which she politely invited Gordon to attend a charitable fund-raising dinner the following week, only to be snarled at for daring to propose an alternative to his unspecified plans to be with Jill that particular evening. In Gordon's version, Ellie planted herself in front of him, interrupting his business reading and demanding that he agree to accompany her to this function. When Gordon calmly brought up that he had a prior obligation to take Jill and her friend to an ice-skating rink, Ellie threw a fit, wailing that he never

---

*In couples group therapy, this technique has a number of additional benefits for the other couples and is easier to accomplish, since both the therapist and the couple whose episode is being staged can observe other players perform the enactment.

cared about making her happy. Even though the dialogue consisted of only 10 or 12 lines in each scene, the process of staging both versions took up nearly the entire first therapy hour (I worked with them in two-hour sessions).

So different were the characters between the versions of these dramas that Ellie and Gordon both expressed amazement at how divergent their realities were. I asked Ellie what qualities her own character posessed in her drama and what she saw as the qualities of the "Ellie" in Gordon's scene; I then had her list the qualities of the two versions of the "Gordon" character. I repeated the same process with Gordon. As they gave their answers I wrote them down on the chart reproduced below.

I gave them a copy of the chart and asked them to discuss the differences between their characters, first comparing the character of "Ellie" within Ellie's scene [(1) with (3)] and then across different stagings [(1) with (2)], etc. They were now better able to grasp how their characterization of one another was shaped by positively connoting one's own behavior and negatively connoting one's partner's. They also were beginning to see how unlikely it would be for agreement to result solely from their attempts to reconstruct events.

At our next session I brought out the charts again and selected the two contrasting characterizations of each of them that represented (a) their own view of their own character [(1) and (8)] and (b) their spouse's view of their character [(4) and (5)] for the purpose of enacting a version of *Behavioral Lists* (p. 137). Explaining that we were about to enact a new, fictional scene I then had them collaborate in drawing up a list of behaviors, each "To Be Thought ____" for: (1) "polite" (for Ellie's character, now named "Emma") and (4) "demanding and shrill" (for Ellie's character, now named "Esther");

CHARACTER OF "ELLIE"

	In Ellie's Scene		In Gordon's Scene	
According to Ellie	polite	(1)	hysterical, insecure	(2)
According to Gordon	meek	(3)	demanding, shrill	(4)

CHARACTER OF "GORDON"

	In Ellie's Scene		In Gordon's Scene	
According to Ellie	rude, insensitive	(5)	insincere, controlling	(6)
According to Gordon	snarling, impatient	(7)	reasonable, calm	(8)

(5) "rude or insensitive" (for Gordon's character, now named "Glen") and (8) "reasonable/calm" (for Gordon's character, now named "Gabe"). For example, the list for "Glen" ("To Be Thought Rude or Insensitive") contained:

- interrupt others when they're speaking
- laugh at others' misfortune
- say "no" to all, even reasonable requests
- demand a favor and don't thank the other person
- bump into others without apologizing
- yawn in the face of someone while they're speaking to you
- insult the other person
- agree sarcastically while rolling your eyes

while the list for "Esther" ("To Be Thought Demanding and Shrill") contained:

- raise your voice to drown out others
- angrily insist on being agreed with
- become offended by anything others do
- blame others for your not being happy
- tell others they must do something for you right away
- yell in the other person's face

Once we had the four lists I wrote the character's name at the top of the list and said:

> I'd like you to first try a scene in which you each get to play characters who are considered as "bad" in the ways described on your list. Use as many of the behaviors on your list as you can work into the scene realistically to get your character's nature across.

I then handed Gordon the "Glen"/"To Be Thought Rude or Insensitive" list and Ellie the "Esther"/"To Be Thought Demanding and Shrill" list. Gordon raised the question of how it would help them to play such negative characters. I replied that they were only attempting to fit the perceptions that they had already voiced about one another the previous week and reminded them that, as actors cast in their roles, they were only to play the parts assigned. I set the scene as between college classmates in a dorm room the night before final exams and turned it over to them.

The scene that resulted was farcical conflict, as each of them played up to the extreme those behaviors on their list. After both had done two or three things from their lists they began to break character, first giggling and then laughing openly, the scene collapsing in about 45 seconds. I asked them in turn what they found so funny. Gordon said that he had felt free to be as "bad" as he knew how and that it was funny to see Ellie throwing restraint to the winds and getting into the same spirit. Ellie, still laughing, didn't know what was so funny, but found relief in recognizing that real life wasn't nearly as conflictual as the scene they had just enacted. As I saw it, playing a caricature of one another's negative characterizations had had a paradoxical effect, both in overcoming resentment at feeling unfairly labelled and in giving permission to play fully the negative projections of each. It also allowed them to be intense and dramatically playful so that they could have emotional intensity (and a cathartic adventure) without full vulnerability.

Deciding that playing another *Behavioral Lists* scene with the positive characterizations would be anticlimactic, I saw another possibility. Explaining that it would be helpful for them to experience how changes in the emotional climate of their interaction could be controlled, I set up a *Wallpaper Drama* (p. 134). I began by having them assume the characters of "Emma" ("To Be Thought Polite") and "Gabe" ("To Be Thought Reasonable and Calm"), instructing them that their characters could alter during the scene. I told them that I would be coaching them both to make small, even subtle, shifts in the emotional climate (starting from emotionally neutral) and to keep the scene realistic. I set the scene in a bakery, with Gabe ordering a birthday cake from Emma for his six-year-old son.

I took them through a three-minute scene in which I changed the instructions from "Neutral!" to "Positive!" back to "Neutral!" to "Negative!" back to "Neutral!" about every 30 seconds, long enough to establish the emotional climate without losing sight of the climate as being temporary. With only two minor exceptions, Ellie and Gordon were able to make the transitions for their characters smoothly and convincingly. During the positive part of the scene the characters were generous, even flirtatious; in the negative part Emma was snippy and a bit sarcastic, while Gabe subtly implied that Emma could neither ice the birthday cake neatly nor be trusted to spell his son's name properly. When I asked them afterward about their experience of the enactment Ellie exclaimed that she could now see how a small difference in attitude resulted in a very noticeable change in mood. Both also commented on how easy it was to find a matching response to any shift in mood by one's partner, which led to a conversation in which they productively analyzed the effect of their partner's mood on themselves. Gordon aptly and poetically said that "Emma" in the just-enacted scene had been like the sun on a fall day, quickly coming out to warm the air and then gradually disappearing behind the clouds, putting a chill into him. This observation led to an inconclusive discussion of whether Ellie could turn her charm on and off at will or whether her moods were outside her control. However, Gordon realized that, in either case, *he* had a choice of withdrawing or remaining in emotional contact when Ellie became moody.

Over the next two weeks Ellie and Gordon reported a considerable improvement in the emotional climate of their relationship; Ellie explained that she had become less fearful about her capacity to handle her mood swings, and Gordon described a few successful incidents where he had chosen to shift positively the emotional climate. Also, they reported having fought far less frequently.

CASE 5 *Serving One Another Right*

In a case I have described in detail elsewhere (Wiener, 1991), a marital couple (Rose and Alan) were locked in a struggle over Alan's inaction in seeking steady employment. As is commonly seen in marital therapy, each denigrated the other for being critical while justifying one's own criticism. Since they appeared equivalent in their ability and readiness to denigrate one another it might have been supposed that they functioned as status equals. However, the distinction between *playing* status and *having* status (noted in Chapter 7) applied to this couple, for although Rose played high status to Alan in our sessions, she lacked the power to elevate her real-life status outside of therapy. Rose and Alan presented with a typical belief system that located the power to solve the problem in the husband; Alan, though affected by Rose's criticism, was perceived by both as having the power to change or not, while Rose could only withhold or grant approval for Alan's choice.

After I used *Tug-of-War* (p. 121) to get them to experience yielding to one another, I directed this couple through a total of eight *Master/Servant Games* (p. 119), during which each of them got to play high and low status within each role. In the course of these scenes, each experienced being high status without lowering the other, and supporting the other's high status without being lowered thereby. My directing of their scenes had been focused mainly on Alan, thus making use of the couple's belief that Alan had the power to change. These enactments had offered Rose and Alan a safe opportunity to explore different positions in ways that would have been too threatening in reality and that also made their status struggles transparent to them, something that verbal methods alone would have been unlikely to achieve. With their struggle unmasked and alternatives rehearsed, Rose and Alan were successful in reestablishing a partnership of mutual esteem and playful intimacy.

CASE 6 *Becoming Again as Little Children*

Sharon and John, a childless couple who owned and operated a convenience store, came to therapy for help with their bickering and to resolve differences arising in virtually every area of their lives except business. Sharon, now 36, had been raised by an eccentric, fearful grandmother after being removed from her psychotic mother at age 18 months. After her grandmother's death at age 14 she lived with her aunt and uncle, functioning as the eldest sibling to her nephews. John grew up as the only child of an overprotective, dominant mother and a warm but passive father. Sharon complained that she never got to "be the child" in their marriage and always had to "be the mom." John insisted he was willing to function as the parent, but Sharon wouldn't accept the child role. When Sharon offered to be the child and leave things up to John, he typically would refuse to make the decision, instead asking what she wanted: "Do you want to walk or take a cab?" when he wanted to walk. Whenever Sharon saw John making a choice that was not to her liking (and she apparently needed to feel in control nearly all the time), she became critically parental. It was difficult for her to subside and accept the passive position.

When I coached them in improvs, Sharon would invariably take the position of overseeing John's performance, critiquing the way and extent to which he heeded the instructions, thereby lowering his status and assuming once again the overseeing parental role. John would become silly or argumentative, sometimes turning to me to declare that he couldn't win.

In order to instill mutuality and cooperativeness I gave them *Presents* (p. 105), which they did quite well with. Each was pleased with the present given by the other and each was generous in expressing gratitude. Then, to test their capacity for pattern reversal, I devised a scenario in which Sharon was a lost, fearful child and John a benevolent policeman. It was hard for them to stay in character; John kept joking around, becoming a dirty old man, thereby successfully provoking Sharon to break character and then get angry with him for "violating the rules." Both were stretched to play the scene authentically. John's provocation was clearly a "homeostatic solution" to bring them back to their familiar status positions and Sharon readily colluded with him. I drew the conclusion that they were not ready to challenge this pattern and therapy continued along more conventional lines (improving communication skills and detriangulating John's mother from their marriage).

Interestingly, four months into treatment Sharon became pregnant and began sneaking off to the laundry room to smoke an occasional cigarette. In a reversal of their usual pattern John now became the parent-detective, catching Sharon smoking and sternly lecturing her on the harm she might be inflicting on their unborn child. Sharon giggled at his demeanor and continued to smoke surreptitiously. However, she was not really trying to keep her smoking undetected from John and appeared to derive some enjoyment from his indignant attention. For his part, John appeared genuinely upset at her smoking, yet seemed to obtain some "secondary gain" from his policing function. John did not recognize this "childish irresponsibility" as an authentic part of Sharon, attributing it to "female hormones," a temporary aberration. In my experience, relationships often consist of child-parent transactions, with the child role allowing the player to explore dependent, needy, even bratty sides of self. What appeared atypical in John and Sharon's relationship was not that both could behave "out of character" but that such reversals were so infrequent and viewed as aberrant.

Such exceptions to habitual patterning are, however, clinically impor- tant, since they reveal to the therapist which of the less-frequently utilized character choices available to the relationship can be mobilized for redefin- ing and enhancing the couple's interaction. As is regularly done in brief systemic therapy, pointing out exceptions to clients helps the therapist con- vince them that they have unrecognized resourcefulness and are capable of adventuring beyond the status quo.

During one of their in-session spats featuring the familiar Sharon-as- reproving-parent and John-as-defensive-child, it dawned on me that I was being subjected to a performance that the actors were sleepwalking their way through; there was nothing immediate, novel, or even particularly conscious in their arguing. I began to listen as a musician might, tracking the tonal cadences and volume dynamics. What I heard, and was able to compare as similar to previous hearings, was at first Sharon's voice being fairly soft and neutral, but with a growing edge of disparagement. At the same time, responsively, John's voice became more hurt, louder in protest, and yet despairing. Sharon's voice now would get more emphatic, her dis- missive tone more pronounced, louder, and more intense. Correspondingly, John was becoming less confident and more constricted; it sounded as though his voice was being driven back down into himself. In that moment I decided to experiment with a metaphorical role for myself as a musical conductor with the aim of finding a new vocal style for this duet.

Rather than being induced into accepting their performance, I inter- rupted them to state that they were not doing such a good job anymore of convincing me that this quarreling reflected the true state of their relation- ship. I next taught them the variation of *Volume Control* (p. 129) in which I called out the five-point-scale volume instruction at the start of each player's turn and combined it with *Yes, But* (p. 64) which they already knew and had been doing a credible job of playing at the time of my interruption. Probably because of my offering their interaction as an im- prov exercise they were more alert, less sure of themselves. The volume cadence I had previously noted I now directed them to repeat; they were tracking my instructions exactly. I began to switch the pattern, matching Sharon's getting softer to John's getting louder instead of their familiar way. John became angrier as he got louder; his body posture was more forward, intruding into her space. As Sharon got softer she lost some of her self-confidence; she began to avoid eye contact, even closing her eyes altogether. A totally different set of status transactions was unfolding.

In the discussion following this exercise both John and Sharon were impressed by how different it had felt to vary their volume pattern. John reported that he felt validated by Sharon in expressing his anger, something he never experienced in their relationship and that it made him feel more generous, even appreciative toward her. Hearing this came as a surprise to Sharon, who had supposed John's increasing anger betokened some vengefulness. After pointing out that Sharon had the power to make John look powerful I asked Sharon what her experience had been during the exercise. She reported that she had felt a sense of being with her "crazy grandma" as a young child around whom she felt confused and lost. She often lost her voice when with her grandma, retreating into herself for hours at a time. Her near-constant exercise of control as an adult, she now recognized, kept her from feeling lost, like the child she had been.

As they appeared eager to continue, I next had them try *Gibberish Emotions* (p. 128), giving each a short phrase in gibberish that they could repeat (this was to keep them from getting distracted by having to invent new gibberish at each turn) and suggesting that they intend, through a dialogue, the following four scenes:

1. Grown-up Sharon ordering child-John to clean up his room (their habitual pattern)
2. Grown-up Sharon apologetic toward angry child-John (an intended approximation of what had occurred in their *Volume Control* exercise)
3. The same as (1), but with Sharon reversing roles with John
4. A repeat of (2) with roles reversed

Each of these lasted less than 20 seconds — just long enough to establish the inflectional pattern. Except for checking briefly that they had gotten a sense of the pattern of the just-played scene and giving them the instructions for the next, I directed them to play these scenes in order and without interruption.

In (1), both readily adopted the familiar cadences played out around many issues. In (2) John again sounded louder and angrier, although Sharon did not become lost, just monotonic. In (3) Sharon's child protested in a playful way that surprised her; she later reported that she had enjoyed the feeling of playfulness as though for the first time. Scene (4) gave Sharon a sense of freedom to express anger without adult-style verbal justification ("So that's what anger sounds like!" was her later comment); John reported liking soothing Sharon from the grown-up position, making the connection to his affinity for policing her smoking. By screening out the words and focussing on the "music," both had gained a greater understanding of their present and potential emotional dynamics.

In subsequent sessions we gave names to the different voice characterizations available to each; they were successful at using these *Gibberish*

Emotions exercises at home to playfully alter their habitual patterning. I also used *Status Conflict* (p. 116) to teach them about how their vocal tone reflected status positioning, and gave them two *Status Transfer* (p. 116) scenes to enact to show them how status positions can be shifted, even reversed. By the end of our therapy work, eight months and twenty-six sessions later, Sharon and John had almost entirely eliminated their bickering and were viewed by their extended families as a couple who had "settled into" marriage beautifully. Of course, credit for the change was given to the impending arrival of their child and the wise counsel of their relatives. At our final session I counselled them to keep their playfulness as a private, special resource that they could let the baby in on in later years. I got a birth announcement and a note of thanks from them three months later; as of that time, they were doing fine.

APPLICATIONS TO FAMILY THERAPY

Apart from the specific applications discussed below, families benefit by participating in improv in a variety of ways. Frequently, families who play together come to see other potentialities in their relationships and new qualities in self and other family members, including the discovery that they are a pretty interesting bunch and don't require a turned-on television set to bear one another's company. During play they may experience something of the arbitrariness of family rules and their habitual patterns, as well as other possibilities for future interaction. As with pretend techniques, improv allows the experience of change without real consequences. Competence can be de-emphasized in favor of play; competitiveness is set aside for exploring cooperation and its benefits. Family members learn to "be there" for one another and to take responsibility for the larger enterprise, not just for themselves. Indeed, the experience of exploring the creative moment with other family members opens up interactive possibilities in their relationships comparable to that obtained by embarking upon shared outward adventures.

As with other action techniques, improv puts children, especially younger ones, on a more equal footing with their parents since therapy need not be restricted to tracking verbal information and sitting still for long stretches of time. Especially when introducing play based on fantasy, as opposed to rule-governed games, I find that younger children are generally the initiators and parents the unsure followers. This creates a tactical problem in families with both younger and older children (especially adolescents), since the older ones may be most reluctant to participate on a peer level with their younger siblings, especially when the parents are present. This situation can be handled in one of a number of ways: structure the play as turns-taking, with each member leading at different times; use games and exercises that assign roles and functions at different developmental levels; give "commentator" roles (explained in Chapter 6) to older children and adolescents.

Introducing improv to families can be facilitated by mentioning how little time the average family spends together, how "the family that plays together stays together" and how they each have unsuspected talents to be discovered. In a few cases (mainly when faced with overintellectualizing adults in a child-centered family) I will refer to research of the sort cited in Chapter 3 that has demonstrated the value of increasing playful parent-child interaction. I also find it useful to point out that becoming empowered to be playful, particularly in circumstances associated with unhappiness, is a valuable resource in life.

It is typically the case that one or more family members will be reluctant to participate. I take the position that when members are unwilling to play I will respect that, provided that they are making their own decision, not deciding for others or letting others decide for them. When the therapist fully accepts the refusal the reluctant members usually end up playing.

Since most of the games and exercises described in this book work best when promoting cooperative effort, it might be supposed that improv is only useful in working with disengaged families. However, not only do these games work well with enmeshed families, there are also games that emphasize individual contribution and narrative structure; moreover, the therapist can always modify or create rules and conditions that offer alternatives to any tendency or pattern of the family.

CASE 7   *The Gift of Play*

In a case I supervised at a social agency, the therapist, Inez, was working toward returning William, age nine and living for the past seven months in a residential treatment facility, to the custody and home of his biological mother, Mrs. Porter, age 29. William had been removed from Mrs. Porter following a state agency investigation that led to a court finding of parental neglect. Such cases are complicated by the quasi-coercive context in which therapy is offered. On the one hand, the therapist is a helper, working toward a goal most often desired by the clients (reuniting parent and child); on the other hand, the therapist is an investigator, accountable to the system that ordered the initial separation. Consequently, clients do not readily extend trust to their therapists and are reluctant to disclose information or react in a way that might make them look bad to the therapist.

At the time I began supervision with Inez, she had been working with Mrs. Porter and William for nine sessions, during which they had displayed poor functioning as a mother-son dyad. William, who was fairly obedient and attentive to the staff of his residence, behaved distracted and indifferent to Mrs. Porter during sessions. Mrs. Porter, feeling under pressure to appear competent as a mother, would issue sharp commands to William whenever he would fidget or appear inattentive to Inez. Typically, William would then ignore Mrs. Porter, at which point she would turn to Inez and offer, in a matter-of-fact voice, anecdotes to show how difficult a child William was. These stories would slide into accounts of how difficult Mrs. Porter's life was, which were narrated in a plaintive tone.

Parental skills training is often utilized by family therapists in such situations and is generally preferable to having the therapist take charge of discipline, which further disempowers the parent. In the present case, more than ineffectual discipline was involved, as Mrs. Porter and William appeared extremely disconnected with little intensity in any of their interaction. What intensity there was, moreover, appeared to be oppositional in character and around parental discipline issues. Noticing this, Inez had become more tentative in recommending family reunification for Mrs. Porter and William in her treatment team reports. What she hadn't noticed, and what came as a surprise to her when I pointed it out in video feedback, was that after the first ten minutes or so of a session she would lapse into a low-intensity affective vocal and gestural mode similar to Mrs. Porter. When the therapist is inducted into the problem mode of the family system, it is time to try something else.

Functioning more as an active cotherapist than a noninterventive supervisor, I sat in on six sessions with Inez, Mrs. Porter, and William. My goal was to support Inez so that she could establish a trusting, playful atmosphere in which a new, more nurturant relational reality could emerge. As Inez had previously experienced some improv as part of her family therapy training with me and was open to improv, I took the initiative in introducing games and exercises into these sessions.

After introducing myself and establishing rapport with both Mrs. Porter and William, I asked what they did for fun when William came on weekends for home visits. Other than watching some TV programs they had no answer to this question. I then stated that I knew some games that could be fun and asked if they were interested. Hesitantly, they agreed to try.

I began with *You Will/I Won't* (p. 129) for the following reasons: (a) the instructions are simple, (b) the blocking premise is similar to what they were already manifesting, and (c) the exercise encourages emotional intensity. After Inez and I demonstrated the exercise (both in order to model it and to show them that we weren't asking them to put themselves in a position that we wouldn't take ourselves), Mrs. Porter and William played it twice, exchanging parts the second time. While Mrs. Porter added verbal justifications for her position a few times and had to be coached to stick with the minimal dialogue of this exercise, both of them seemed to enjoy the emotional variety and heightened intensity.

In the next session the atmosphere was distinctly more lively from the outset and William appeared quite eager to play more games. When Inez inquired about the latest weekend home visit Mrs. Porter mentioned that they had played the game twice, once around an actual confrontation they were having, with the result that they were able to have a constructive discussion that ended in a compromise. As we had not even asked them to use the game at home, this was a totally unexpected yet welcome outcome! During our discussion of the confrontation in which they used the game, I realized that the impression both mother and son had gotten from the previous session was that I had recommended the game as an enjoyable way to argue (Afterward, in postsession analysis with Inez, she thought I had charmed them into compliance).

I decided that we were in a good position to move to a more advanced game; after briefly conferring with Inez in front of mother and son, I described *Couples with Contrasting Emotions* (p. 131). My rationale for selecting this game was twofold: (1) the game encourages teamwork, both in supporting one's partner and in presenting self as part of a team to others, something Mrs. Porter and William had little experience with; (2) players need to justify a particular emotion, which trains them to create and sustain emotional expressiveness, a skill I wanted to increase in both of them. I selected "The Complainers" meeting "The Cheerfuls" and chose the scene of mother and son meeting an adult couple who lived in their building in a neighborhood fast-food restaurant. It seemed important to keep the roles and setting familiar to their experience; had I chosen another parent-child dyad as roles for Inez and myself, or chosen an unfamiliar location, the incongruity would probably have proved too distracting for them to have played the scene. Also, both emotions chosen have the advantages of being relatively easy to justify and being complementary, such that offers by one couple readily spark contrasting responses on the same topic.

I had William direct the rearrangement of the furniture to simulate the fast-food restaurant and then coached Mrs. Porter and William to assume different names (important to do, since a character name marks the play-context for self and others) and take the complainer position in-role while waiting in the restaurant before the other couple arrived. Although this game can be played with the characters complaining about one another, I instructed them to find other things and people to complain about, as it would not have been consistent with my purpose to have them denigrate one another, even in character. Once they had done so, I asked them to continue in character on their own while I went off to another room to practice cheerfulness with Inez for a few minutes (she was not so experienced an improviser that I could have proceeded directly to the four-person scene). Inez and I reentered in character and we played a three-minute scene in which the characters of Mrs. Porter and William animatedly criticized the unsafe and unsanitary condition of their building (probably quite accurately to their actual living conditions) while Inez and I played characters who fancifully made a virtue out of the building's faults (it crossed my mind during the enactment that staying on this topic in the reversed mood positions might prove quite cognitively dissonant for them).

During the scene I stopped the action briefly, assuming the director role to point out that their characters might be offended at our character's cheerfulness and complain about that as well. When we continued the scene they were hesitant at first, but soon became quite supportive of one another's criticisms that were directed toward our characters' unacknowledging attitude. Mrs. Porter proved quite eloquent in this criticizing, and William appeared happy to take her lead. This was valuable not only for their team effort but also expanded their repertoires to expressing anger more directly yet safely toward those who invalidated their expressed unhappiness, something not readily available to agency clients. Agency practice often pays lip service to empowerment as an abstraction, but discourages clients from expressiveness in practice.

Time did not permit the intended team mood reversal for a second scene, nor did we complete the exercise. However, the discussion and debriefing were quite fruitful, as they established one way in which mother and son could bond emotively in a social setting. Mrs. Porter seemed a changed woman; she spoke expressively to us and connected with both nurturance and authority to William for the first time. Discipline at home had greatly improved, while Inez later reported that Mrs. Porter thereafter assumed a more active role in the agency's Mothers' Support Group as well.

The final use of improv in this case occurred two sessions later when a problem arose during the approaching Christmas season. For a variety of reasons, Christmas is a stressful time at a residential treatment agency; for one thing, the low-income parents are financially incapable of meeting their children's expectations of presents, which are further fueled by the often unsubstantiated boasting of other children. Having already committed himself to announcing that he was getting a certain video game set, William had begun to pressure his mother to keep him from looking bad in the eyes of his peers. Rather than move directly into a process to handle this situation I proposed that we first play *Presents* (p. 105).

I began by having William hold out his empty hands to Mrs. Porter, reminding him that he did not know what he was offering, only that the present was desirable to her. There were tears in her eyes as she slowly took, and mimed putting on, what she later described as an expensive pair of fleece-lined boots. Mrs. Porter then embraced William emotionally and thanked him for such a wonderful present. Although embarrassed by her display of affection, William was pleased at "his" generosity and announced that he was going to get these boots for her in reality. I then had Mrs. Porter hold her hands out to William. As expected, William's imagination supplied the wanted video game set and he joyously exclaimed, "Great! Thanks, Mom!" Mrs. Porter's eyes welled up again as she appeared in pain at not being able to gratify her son's wish in reality, yet she smiled at his evident pleasure.

I then had William stand in front of his mother and declare, "I want you to have those boots," to which she spontaneously replied, "Honey, I know you do, and that makes me feel real good." Next, I asked Mrs. Porter to stand in front of William and say, "I want you to have the video game," which she did in a soft, almost shy voice. William looked down at his feet and didn't answer right away, then quietly said, "I know." I now led a discussion concerning the importance of intentions, pointing out how much happiness each of them took from imagining that the other was giving a desired present. I also congratulated both of them for seeing the other as a source of such a wonderful present (contrasted with their likely reaction to being offered an imaginary present by someone they disliked) as this showed that each expected to be treated well by the other. While they both appreciated these points, William was understandably confused by the concurrent unhappy feelings stemming from not getting the actual, desired present. I acknowledged that he really wanted these presents and that not getting what you want is frustrating, yet there was some happiness in knowing that the other person wanted you to be happy. The real point of giving a present, I said, was making the receiver happy, which they had both already accomplished in the game.

From here, it was relatively easy for Inez to assist them in negotiating a way around the impasse of William's boast to his peers; he agreed to tell them that he had withdrawn his request, since he knew that was putting a lot of pressure on her. This made him appear mature and yet powerful, since the implication was that he had made the decision to forgo the video game set.

During my final consultation session, I played *Presents* with each of them, receiving a sports-car from William, who received a mountain bike from me. Mrs. Porter gave me a new sports jacket and I gave her a fur coat. All these presents were received with great appreciation and good humor. Three months later, William was returned to Mrs. Porter's custody; follow-up visits at three-month intervals up to one year afterward showed that things were still going satisfactorily.

CASE 8   *The Importance of Importance*

Steven, age 61, was convinced he was no longer attractive to Faith, his 43-year-old wife of 11 years. Forced into retirement six months earlier from his own corporate career, he had recently begun to work in her fashion business as its general manager. Their adjustment to this change in their until-then separate work lives had scarcely begun when 20-year-old Andrew, Faith's son from a previous marriage, dropped out of college and returned to live at home.

Their problems had been confined previously to adjusting their occupational roles to reflect a shift in both roles and status. Faith was now publicly Steven's boss and both had to maintain that position in front of other employees and customers, yet Steven had considerably more expertise in finance and had supervised a larger number of employees than Faith's business employed. In addition, they differed stylistically in their ways of managing subordinates, something that had become a source of increasing conflict that was being further aggravated by one of Faith's employees. It had also become more difficult to keep their family and social lives separate from their business relationship. On top of it all, Andrew was once again living with them, staying out all night, taking one of the family cars without permission and acquiring numerous parking tickets, refusing to do anything useful around the house, sulking when addressed by Faith, and getting into loud arguments with Steven.

Although their relationship had never been close during the eight years they lived together as stepfather and stepson, Steven felt certain that he could successfully discipline Andrew and serve as a needed role model to this spoiled young man who was, he felt sure, headed for a totally self-indulgent and parasitic life. Steven, believing that Faith was paralyzed by guilt and allowing herself to be taken advantage of and disrespected by this loutish youth, could scarcely contain his anger at this disfunctional state of affairs. However, whenever he objected, much to his dismay, Faith would intervene to side with Andrew against him, leading him to conclude that she no longer cared about him and had transferred all patience, tolerance, and nurturance from him to her son. In my way of thinking, Steven's jealousy of Andrew stemmed from believing Andrew to be more important to Faith than he was (because of her seemingly unconditional deference to Andrew's wishes in contrast to his having to earn Faith's approval). To be treated in a less favored manner than another person by someone you love results in your status being lowered against your wishes and gives you an incentive to lower the status of the favored other.

While Faith could agree with Steven's description of her son's behavior as ungracious, surly, and quarrelsome, she perceived Steven as motivated by a need to dominate Andrew and was turned off by what she described as his harshness, impatience, and insensitivity. She also was unhappy that Steven made life more difficult by putting her in the middle of the quarrels that frequently erupted between him and Andrew. If Steven truly loved her, she reasoned, he would exercise forebearance and join with her in permitting Andrew to get his bearings before venturing forth in the larger world again. It was clear that each spouse was becoming entrenched in a previously held negative perception of the other that had resurfaced around recent family interaction. Until I pointed it out, neither Steven nor Faith was initially aware of the distinct isomorphism between their family- and work-life patterns (Steven entering an established system intent on making a contribution in his own way; a third party exacerbating tensions between Faith and Steven; the couple having difficulty separating their private dyadic relationship from the demands of a larger system).

Andrew, whom I had met with twice individually, was fairly self-absorbed with his own life problems. While unclear as to the source of his own difficulties he was aware that he lacked self-confidence, something he privately admitted he envied Steven for. At the same time, however, he felt resentful toward Steven's criticism of his present lifestyle and was defensive whenever he detected disapproval. It was clear to me that Andrew *thought* himself entitled to do as he pleased, and *played* high status in his quarrels with his stepfather, yet he actually *had* a low-struggling-to-become-high status position in that relationship. With his mother, by contrast, Andrew felt secure in his high-status position. To round out the picture, Andrew thought he was helping his mother by standing up to Steven and thereby supporting her struggle not to let Steven dominate her. This attempt to reverse their relative status represented Andrew's triangulation of himself into Faith and Steven's relationship.

It was significant to observe that the fighting between Andrew and Steven did not always begin at Steven's initiative; Andrew often acted provocatively to initiate conflict, usually when Faith was around. This gave Faith her cue to side with Andrew over Steven and set up a competition between them for her support, thereby raising her status. It also illustrates how there can be advantages in taking the lowest status position, since you will be courted and never attacked so long as the others do not need to join one another by lowering your status.

As is often the case, this family exhibited internal conflict regarding what the causes of their problems were, who was or who "contained" the problems, and who had the optimal solution to their problems. I have observed that for many people, including members of this family, it is more important to be right than happy. All were genuinely motivated to be helpful to the family and had come to believe that only their own problem descriptions were valid and only their own offered solution could solve the family problem. The real mischief was not that disagreements existed over who had the problem and whose solution could best fix it, but because (a) the designation of who had the problem led to raising one's own status while denigrating the status of other members (in other words, "You have the problem which is causing the rest of us problems, so I will [nobly] help you out, for which you should be cooperative and grateful"; and (b) members were reactive to the rejection of their solutions as indicative of their status being lowered by the rejecter (in other words, "You don't agree with/support my solution, so you must not value me very much.") This is consistent with the MRI dictum: "The solution is the problem."

My analysis of their interaction led me to diagram the dominant pattern (i.e., the pattern that they gravitated toward) of played family status relationships; see Table 1. The numbers represent the status ranking relative to the other members.

TABLE 1 Perceived status rank

Person Attributing Rank	Faith	Steven	Andrew
Faith	3	2	1
Steven	2	1	3
Andrew	2	3	1

Reasoning that the family problems could be lessened through experiencing greater status flexibility and separating self-esteem from the choice of status position, I set out to teach them how to shift status. After familiarizing the family with the theme of "importance" through status exercises (using status cues and *Imposing Status* (p. 115), I set up a three-person *Unknown Status* scene (p. 117) for a fictional family (all members playing their own family position, although ten years younger than their actual ages) who was planning a vacation over the dinnertable. Using a variation I ordinarily choose for training therapists (see Chapter 14), I assigned each the status positions for the family on slips of paper that I had written out in advance, asking all of them to keep these instructions private for the time being. Table 2 shows what I gave them:

TABLE 2 Assigned status rank

Person (Role)	Faith	Steven	Andrew
Faith (Mother)	1	2	3
Steven (Father)	1	3	2
Andrew (Son)	2	1	3

What I intended was to alter their habitual experience of family status transactions in the following ways:

1. Faith and Steven would now be in agreement regarding Faith's greater importance than Steven.
2. Steven and Andrew would now shift from high-high to low-low status conflict, a change that alters the character of a power struggle for importance from attacking the esteem of the other to enhancing it.
3. Andrew and Faith would now be in agreement about Andrew's lesser importance relative to the marital dyad.
4. Andrew and Faith would now be in agreement regarding Steven's, rather than Faith's, greater importance.

To understand what followed, it is important to keep in mind that each of the players was initially unaware of the status assignments given to the other players.

FATHER [to Son] I think your mother has some good ideas we ought to listen to now. [raising Mother, yet still taking a higher position than Son, contrary to his assigned positions]

SON Yeah, Dad, I guess, but I like your ideas even better. [partially blocking Father in order to raise him relative to Mother]

MOTHER It's time we took a trip across country. Lots to see, all those places we read about to visit . . . [by offering reasons, weakening her own high-status position somewhat]

FATHER Great! [to Son] And you can bring your skateboard to use all over, whenever we stop. [raising both others]

SON [to Father] But would it be fun for you, Dad to do all that driving? [as before, partially blocking Father in order to raise him relative to Mother]

MOTHER [to Father] Junior seems to worry an awful lot, nowadays. [including both self and Father as distinct from, and above Son in status]

FATHER As long as *you're* happy with the decision, pet, I'm sure we can work out the details later. [to Son] I only brought up this thing about the skateboard 'cause it's your vacation too. [raising both Mother and Son by his deference]

The dialogue continued for a few more exchanges, repeating the bracketed status positioning moves. I stopped the scene and asked each of them to say what they noticed: first, about the feeling of playing the scene and, second, of the status positions held by the others. All agreed that this scene had an unreal quality of cooperation and politeness; each felt some awkwardness in the way she or he was treated by the others. Faith reported that she felt like a boss who was being handled with great caution by her employees; she noticed her tension at expecting conflict between the other two which never materialized, and was aware of a sweetness in Steven which she had forgotten existed. Both Steven and Andrew reported that Faith didn't seem comfortable in being deferred to and were surprised she was playing her role as top status. Andrew reported that he felt some power in being able to raise Steven's status and added that he didn't mind playing lowest status when Steven was being so thoughtful toward his character.

Steven chimed in to agree that his character, too, was well-treated when he was playing lowest status. Faith and Andrew quickly countered that Steven seemed to take charge even though he thought of his character as lowest-status, overlooking that their characters were elevating his status. All agreed it had been an interesting experience.

At the end of that session I left them with the following homework assignment: (1) During the next week, each member was to select two occasions on which everyone was present to choose a status position for oneself and for each of the other two and play out the status choices without letting the others know; (2) the choices on the second occasion had to differ from those of the first; (3) no one was to ask or answer questions about what the choices were or whether another was deliberately making status choices on a given occasion.

In the following session they came in quite eager to discuss their experiences with the assignment, which had been novel and enjoyably unpredictable. Each had been conscious of his or her own status position and vigilant about being manipulated by the others; Faith described it as remeniscent of that benign conspiracy when everyone would be surreptitiously smuggling presents into the house and wrapping them just before Christmas. Among the unprecedented behaviors, Andrew had cleared the dinner dishes from the table, Steven had asked Faith's advice, and Faith had told Andrew to wear a shirt at dinner (even having had dinner together was a rarity). In a somewhat shy, stumbling manner I told the family that I never expected they would have done so well with the assignment and hesitantly asked Andrew if he could explain to me why this week's events had been so different. Andrew was two sentences into an earnest explanation before Faith's and Steven's tittering alerted him to my playful status manipulation.

While the above-described status work was the main RfG intervention in working with this family, I later used two other games as well: *Insults* (p. 132) to have Steven and Andrew playfully detoxify their high-status-conflict quarreling while simultaneously desensitizing Faith to maintain herself in the observer (and nonintervener) position; and *Excuses* (p. 97) with Faith and Steven joined as the naughty-yet-imaginative children having to convince parental Andrew that they should be let off without punishment (to shift the habitual Faith-Andrew coalition, to give Steven and Faith an enjoyable experience in supporting one another, and to offer Andrew a high-status outside role). Both of these games were well-played and appeared to contribute to the changes already set in motion by the status work.

The subsequent work on Andrew's floundering, Andrew and Steven's fighting, and Steven and Faith's marital adjustment was conducted along structural family therapy lines. The family's mood and attitude was highly cooperative (due to the playful experiences of the improv work, no doubt) with the result that the above-mentioned objectives were achieved without much difficulty. When therapy terminated five months later, Andrew was considerably more self-confident, having begun to work for a year before attempting to resume college; Steven and Andrew were getting along; and the marital partnership of Faith and Steven, both domestically and in business, was operating smoothly.

If you have made mistakes . . . there is always another chance for you . . . you may have a fresh start any moment you choose, for this thing we call "failure" is not the falling down, but the staying down.

—Mary Pickford (cited in Anonymous, 1989, p. 24)

CHAPTER 12

Instructive Failures

T HERE IS CONSIDERABLE anecdotal evidence that play and dramatic enactment are not accessible to certain clinical populations. Landy (1991) notes:

> For most neurotic clients, the act of transcendence through role is a liberating one. But they know how to play, at least theoretically. For many crack addicts, alcoholics, and those with severe eating disorders, play is not even in the realm of possibility. Their addiction is to extinction and denial; they become Beckett characters without the poetry and comedy. The possibilities of being more than one thing, of creating a diversity of roles and an imaginative life need to be extinguished. (p. 36)

Johnson (1981) notes the problem of reaching psychotics with dramatic techniques:

> The issue is that the person simply cannot personify roles, either because he is no longer able to represent other people as having any solidity or reality, or because by becoming another personality, even in play, he would no longer know who he was: that is, he fears his sense of self would be lost forever. (p. 26)

213

Grainger (1992) views the capacity to enter and leave the stage-world of the "as-if" as contingent upon the faculty of giving structure to the way one construes the world, a faculty lacking in schizophrenic thought. For a person with such a thought disorder there is difficulty in recognizing in other persons or roles *someone else who might be me* and difficulty in shifting from *it is* to *it is as if*. As drama "consists in acting as if I were someone else and knowing that I am doing so" (p. 166), clients who have difficulty in maintaining this distinction will be incapable of participating in full improv scenes, although they may still benefit from some improv exercises that do not require interaction in role.

On the other hand, improv role-playing may not always be governed by the rationales advanced by the authors in the paragraphs above. B. Fritz (personal communication, 1994), a psychologist who has offered improvisation workshops to diverse populations, reports that adult alcoholics in an inpatient detox center opt for creating fantastic, extremely caricatured roles while normal adolescents make predominantly concrete, familiar role choices during improv scenes. He speculates that these role-type preferences are consistent with the preoccupations of each group: Chronic, institutionalized alcoholics find solace in escapist fantasy, while adolescents look outward to try out projected, realistic futures as adults. E. Nash and her colleagues, working with groups of adolescents and young adults in an acute schizophrenic inpatient unit, have been moderately successful in inducing playful and imaginative improvised scenes (personal communication, 1993).

Sonne (1973) has coined the term "metaphorolytic family" to refer to those families that allow experience to have only one level of meaning. As Keith (1987) observes, "this is the kind of family that does not know how to play, the kind of family that is cornered by its own normality" (p. 68). This description appeared to fit Chuck and Brenda, both former drug addicts who had been married for nine years, and came to see me over the recurrent crises that involved them and their four children. Each was the parent of two adolescents from their former marriages; three of the four had been in repeated and serious trouble in the schools, with the courts, and on the street. Their home life was punctuated by periodic violence; the work with their family went on for a few months before things stabilized enough to even consider using improv.

What was most noticeable about Chuck's interaction with both me and Brenda was his extreme egocentrism, a near-total inability to consider even the existence of a different point of view. When I attempted to have them use improv exercises I also discovered that Brenda had a severely constricted idea of play, never played any recreational games, and rarely manifested any humor. Once, I gave them a tennis ball, stood them facing each other six feet apart, and instructed them to make up and play a game.

Chuck took charge at once, explaining how they were going to bounce the ball to one another. Brenda seemed willing to go along with this offer, but after three or four turns stopped, saying she wasn't getting anything from continuing. Chuck tried to complicate the game to make it more interesting but Brenda was finished with what she saw as a pointless activity. While I was able to get her to try some improv exercises, Brenda never accessed a spirit of playfulness during our none-too-successful therapy over a total of 19 months.

INCOMPLETE INDUCTION INTO IMPROV

Examples of insufficient warm-up, or induction, are often recognized by noticing that a player insufficiently physicalizes his role. That is, his body posture and movement are not well-developed or congruent with the character in the context of the task or scene. A different problem occurs when a player's performance is emotionally deficient or otherwise inadequate for his role, as the following case example demonstrates.

CASE 9   *Cut Off from Anger*

Jane and Matthew, a professional couple married four years and both in their mid-thirties, came into therapy at the point where the decision over having a child had triggered a reassessment of their commitment to continuing their marriage. Despite a great fondness each professed for the other, Jane found herself doubting Matthew's emotional strength and maturity while for his part Matthew had become increasingly unsure of Jane's loyalty to his long-range plans for their financial security. It appeared to me that they both were fearful of meeting the demands that embarking on this greater adventure would bring and were seeking reassurance of the commitment and capability of their partner in order to proceed. In the course of testing each other they colluded in heightening their partner's insecurities, leading to closer scrutiny and further defensiveness.

When we began to explore the day-to-day specifics of their interaction, it developed that Jane was frustrated with Matthew's emotional withdrawal and occasional sexual unavailability. For Jane, who had been raised to be a "good girl" who did not make demands, particularly those of a sexual nature, matters were not only unsatisfactory but unsolvable. By avoiding her Matthew knew he was making matters worse, but he claimed to be tired from the intense and long hours he devoted to his job, the life area where he derived his major satisfaction and which he refused to limit on behalf of their relationship.

They also fought, although teasingly, about who spent more time in the bathroom; Matthew would charge her with primping endlessly while Jane would counter with accusations that he would get lost in reading while sitting on the toilet. At times there was joking and sexual innuendo in their references as to what went on behind the locked bathroom door.

Observing the element of playfulness within the combativeness of their verbal exchanges over the bathroom, I invited them to try an improv exercise I call *Own Without Touching*.* In this exercise, an object (I used a small book) is placed midway between the two players (who are standing at least ten feet apart). At the signal "Go!" each tries to get the object—but touching it is not permitted. After also reminding them that they were not permitted to speak, I called "Go!" Jane took three quick steps and crouched over the book, surrounding it from all sides. Matthew, who had hesitated at first, looked uncertain; he walked around Jane twice and began tentatively to tickle her. Jane ignored him.

I set up the exercise again with the altered instruction that now they could talk. Once again, Jane got to the book first, crouching as before. Matthew paced in front of her, softly and earnestly talking on and on about how she had promised him the book, knew it was his, had to give it to him now, etc. Jane mostly ignored him, except once when she said, matter-of-factly, "It's mine."

In discussing this improv both Jane and Matthew agreed that Jane had owned the book both times. Matthew said that he didn't see what else he could have done once Jane had surrounded the book. I pointed out that he had actually weakened his case by talking so much and suggested one more round, this time starting with Matthew crouched around the book and Jane standing. Instead of cajoling him to change, Jane spoke to me, saying how well-trained Matthew was as a guard dog, that he was "on the job" right now, protecting this valuable and rare book of hers. Reaching down, she patted his head and sweetly said, "Now Matthew, only another hour and then you get your treat, Okay? Good boy!" Clearly, Jane had won again.

As I did not want Matthew to become discouraged about "losing" I had them play *One Word at a Time* (p. 65) at which both did quite well, creating three imaginative and coherent success adventures. In contrast to his uncertainty in the previous improv Matthew was verbally decisive and quick, delighting Jane with his wit.

At the next session, mindful of Jane's complaints of Matthew's emotional withdrawal and my observations of his reserved, intellectualized style, I suggested we play *Emotional Lists* (p. 131). I set the scene that they were a dating couple who had just arrived at the beach and gave them a number of successive emotions to play the scene in (joy, boredom, gratitude, grief, fear, envy, anger). What became quickly evident was that Jane could access the full gamut of strongly expressed emotions, while Matthew was unconvincing at all of the above-mentioned emotions except fear and

---

*I learned this exercise from Rebecca Rice.

gratitude. In contrast to Jane's emotionally intense character, Matthew's was, by turns, urbane, aloof, distantly sympathetic, or distracted.

When we got to the emotion anger, Jane's character immediately and strongly berated Matthew's that he hadn't brought the suntan lotion. Matthew, instead of also playing an angry character, began offering soothing excuses. When I interrupted the scene and asked Matthew to replay this segment of the scene with his character getting more angry he was only able to sound like someone mildly resentful; his anger lacked intensity and he appeared uncomfortable. I halted the improv and invited Matthew to share his experience. He knew his character's anger was inhibited and reported feeling nervous at the prospect of expressing strong anger, even though he knew it was just a game. Although he was not ashamed or worried concerning his limited expression of anger, Matthew stated that he would like to be more expressively capable. Jane shared that she had never seen Matthew truly angry; he would became reproachful and hurt, withdrawn, or complaining in a nonspecific way.

I asked Matthew to think of of something or someone that angered him. After some time he came up with a colleague (Ben) who repeatedly put him down at work. I set up a scene where Matthew role-played an encounter between himself and Ben, having him role-reverse to play Ben and having Jane stand in for himself. Matthew's portrayal of Ben was full of sarcasm and bordered on viciousness—the performance had an intensity lacking in anything he had displayed thus far. When I had him reverse back to himself the mask of inhibition was back instantly.

After trying unsuccessfully to coach Matthew to respond with anger to Ben (played by Jane) I had Matthew stand aside and took the role of Ben myself while having Jane play Matthew. Alternating between the roles of Ben and therapist/director, I had Matthew coach Jane-as-Matthew to get angry at Me-as-Ben, even having "Matthew" strike "Ben" (with a pillow). Matthew was able to coach Jane to say the words and make the gestures of anger, yet when I had him return to playing himself the inhibitions returned. Matthew was able to give voice to his anger so long as he remained safely distanced from enacting it; he could only enact anger by proxy. This was instructive to Jane (who now saw Matthew's withdrawal and aloofness as stemming from his limitations rather than as a result of any calculated choice), yet we had still not succeeded in overcoming Matthew's inhibition.

In a further attempt to bring out his anger I had Matthew play *Volume Control* (see p. 129) with Jane. I started with a scene in which Matthew was a student whose textbook was borrowed and lost by Jane's character just before final examinations. Given our experiences with improvs to date, I had Matthew contol both their character's volume by holding up between one and five fingers before each of their speaking turns. Matthew gave Jane the full range of volume levels but assigned himself only up to Four. I coached him to use dialogue that fiercely accused Jane's character of ruining his chances for a good grade in the course, his career plans, and even his entire life. At his level 3 (normal conversation) Matthew sounded more dignified than angry; at his level 4 (somewhat louder than average) his inflection had changed only to the extent that his character was speaking to someone hard of hearing or at a greater distance. I suggested that he shout his dialogue (level 5) but he appeared incapable of simultaneously shouting and accusing. I was able to get him to shout nonangry gibberish, to complain loudly how hurt he was, and to state accusations as a character in a normal tone, but that was as far as I could ever get him to expand his emotional range with regard to intense anger.

IMPROV ENACTMENTS THAT BREAK DOWN

A common yet clinically significant occurrence in improv scenes is the "breaking of character" that occurs whenever a player steps out of role during enactment. In effect, the player who breaks character is blocking the offer of everything that has been established in the scene to that point. This may have a number of causes:

1. The player may be insufficiently warmed up to taking the role.
2. The demands of the role are beyond the capacities of the player.
3. The stage reality at that moment may present a challenge that is too threatening for the player.
4. The conditions or instructions offered for playing the scene may evoke incongruity or confusion sufficient to distract the player from staying in role.

By observing a player's behavior across repeated improvs the therapist/ director may discover which specific causes are habitual to that player, information often of value in assessment (see Chapter 9).

While causes (1) and (2) are fairly easy to trace, establishing (3) or (4) is more complicated. Regarding (3), numerous breakdowns arise from the near-universal tendency to censor our imaginations, often outside of our awareness. An important instance of this is avoiding the danger of embarrassing or hazardous offers, which are experienced as threatening despite knowing that these would affect only the characters, not the players. The degree to which a player is invested in a character (meaning how strongly the player identifies with the character and refuses to accept offers that threaten to change or harm it) is an unknown factor that cannot be accurately predicted in advance of enactment; indeed, since improv characters are created on the spot, such investment or identification may not exist prior to the character's being defined by the hazardous offer in question.

Occasionally, some feature of a game or exercise triggers a strong emotional reaction for a player which interferes with him staying in character. The most frequent trigger is an offer by another character that is repugnant to the client in real life, such as a racist or sexist remark, or an offensive act (as was described in the case of Diane in Chapter 9). It may not be easy to clearly attribute such a reaction to challenge/threat (3) or to incongruity/ distraction (4). When a player encounters such an offer, an observer can often see the effects of the inner conflict aroused; the character vanishes and the player transforms into an emotionally reactive client. Humor and playfulness also evaporate as does the option of pretense; once something is experienced as offensive or even "not funny" by anyone involved, it loses its power to access that unself-conscious absorption necessary for play.

It seldom happens that the disrupted scene can be resumed; typically, these occasions become verbal-process therapy or conflict-resolution sessions. The one who is offended, distracted, threatened, or disgusted most often reports that to have "played along with" the offer would have felt like condoning the offensive value and thereby compromised oneself, or even "contaminated" one's morality or self-respect. I view this phenomenon as demonstrating how a "deep structural obligation" (see Chapter 3) may emerge to shift the context of one's experience; none of us is totally free to embrace all possibilities. Clinically, these occasions can be useful to help explore both the offending and offended clients' choices and boundaries (discussed in Chapter 1).

CASE 10   *A Conscientious Objector*

Consider what happened with Gretchen: As a member of my improvisational therapy group she was playing the interrogator role in *Boris* (p. 72) when she suddenly broke off playing the scene. Her voice was strained; she refused eye contact and appeared quite agitated. After choosing to sit by herself quietly for some time while the group continued a different activity, Gretchen was able to look at what had happened for her. She reported that she had suddenly felt strong anxiety and a sense of shame associated with being watched by her paternal grandmother, a woman who had told the young Gretchen vivid stories about the Nazi concentration camps. In that moment when she had broken off the game, she had seen herself as a torturer in the eyes of her grandmother and could not continue.

Experiencing my role as less of a director and more of a therapist, I saw that a number of choices were possible at this point. Since she was quite warmed up to an encounter with her grandmother I might have enlisted the group's support to have conducted a psychodramatic enactment at once, but instead invited Gretchen to explore her extreme reaction to this enactment with the group. They were puzzled because Gretchen had enacted a determined, but not sadistic, interrogator.

Placing two empty chairs facing the stage, I invited Gretchen to be my assistant as we replayed the game. When we got to the point in the scene where the interrogator first calls on Boris, I froze the action and had Gretchen replace, in turn, each of the characters on-stage (including the invisible Boris), giving that character's inner monologue. Her responses follow:

(AS INTERROGATOR) He won't stall me — I'll get to the truth!
(AS PRISONER) Uh-oh. What's that giant gonna do to me?
(AS BORIS) Ahh! Here's my chance to break some bones!

Then I labelled the two empty chairs facing the stage as Gretchen's chair and Grandmother's chair and invited Gretchen to sit in one of them and speak as that character. She chose Grandmother's chair; leaning forward with clenched fists she fairly shouted at Boris and the interrogator, "No! Hurting others is bad! Not allowed!" I motioned her to switch to the other chair; when she had done so I had her dialogue as herself with Grandmother in the now-empty chair, having her switch chairs and roles to construct the dialogue:

GRETCHEN Grandma, they're just playing! Nobody's getting hurt.
GRANDMOTHER It starts as a game and then, who knows? People forget.
GRETCHEN But if people are having fun and know it's a game they aren't going to really be mean.
GRANDMOTHER No. When people see how much fun this is they will forget that in real life they can be cruel and that others suffer from these acts.

As Grandmother in this dialogue, Gretchen showed great dignity and moral authority. Evidently, Gretchen respected and trusted that part of herself that spoke as Grandmother; the ethical repugnance to hurt others, even in pretense, remained intact and Gretchen endorsed her own refusal to play this game. This last empty-chair enactment also shifted the mood of the group, which now no longer wanted to play *Boris*.

An example of how incongruity may distract an improvisation occurred when I was conducting marital therapy with an overtly conflictual couple, Miguel and Eva. Eva had a disapproving attitude toward a number of Miguel's habits, including his hobby of collecting military replica toys, which she thought wasted money and cluttered up their home. Early on in their treatment I instructed them to play *Presents* (p. 105). First, Miguel offered a present which Eva received as a pair of pearl-drop earrings, much to her delight. Following the instructions, Eva then held out her open palms to Miguel. Miguel, with a smile, began to pick up his present when, with a frown, he suddenly dropped his hands to his sides. When I asked him what had happened, he replied that he had just gotten a much-prized toy German Leopard tank when he realized that Eva would never have given him a present that supported his detested-by-her hobby. At that point, the illusion of receiving the present vanished and he was left with a familiar hurt and resentful feeling.

Miguel's statement hit Eva hard. She became tearful and ashamed at seeing his pain, which she understood to have stemmed from her disapproval of his hobby. Her emotional state was, she reported, heightened by the context of the *Presents* exercise, in which she had first received a wonderful present from Miguel, only to "ruin his happiness." In the ensuing discussion, both readily saw the damaging consequences of their quarreling.

INAPPROPRIATE TIMING OR CHOICE OF IMPROVS

Contamination of the play-context may arise when play behavior is perceived by others as serving an ulterior, real-life motive. Often, engaging in "bad behavior" as a character becomes an opportunity to express concealed feelings toward other persons under the guise of exploring a "shadow" side of oneself or of following the logic of the character's personality. Yet it also happens frequently that players project motives onto their scene-partners that are not intended. This ambiguity arises more frequently in improv enactments where the players are involved in intimate relationships, since intimates invariably judge how familiar or characteristic of the player the performance of that player's character is. When the ambiguity of interpreting such play behavior is resolved by supposing that the behavior in question is malicious, the mental set of playfulness collapses and habitual defensive dynamics take over. Note the following example.

CASE 11   *When Play Evaporates*

I had been working with Ellie and Gordon, the couple described in the first case example in Chapter 11, for about five months when I attempted to work on changing the way each activated the other's vulnerabilities. My own reaction to working with them up to this point in the case was one of cautious optimism: On the one hand, they had done well together in improv exercises and in verbally exploring their vulnerabilities; on the other hand, things had not improved substantially in their domestic life and I was picking up an undercurrent of tension whenever these vulnerablities might be activated. As noted before, the improvs already used had opened the way for a less defensive examination of how each triggered the vulnerability of the other and what being vulnerable changed for them, individually and interpersonally. Gordon reported that his vulnerability was triggered by either a coldness or stridency in Ellie's tone of voice, both of which evoked a scared withdrawal into himself, reminiscent of his early reactions to his perfectionistic mother. Ellie stated that Gordon's leaving her presence in a hurried and impatient manner made her feel unloved and insignificant, akin to her fears of abandonment brought on by her father's frequent business trips in her childhood. Her impotent anger at being thus devalued appeared to mask considerable depression while Gordon's emotional withdrawal seemed associated with an increase in his drinking.

I then decided to introduce them to *Play the Monster* (p. 139), reasoning that their vulnerabilities would be lessened by sharing the playing of the same disagreeable attributes. Ellie went first, selecting arrogance, which Gordon accepted. I asked what it was about arrogance that was difficult for Ellie to accept in herself; she replied that she herself had always been careful not to misuse her wealth and social position to dismiss others, and that displaying arrogance represented a failure of her principles. I suggested we enact a scene between two arrogant bank robbers (attempting to offer them roles removed from their actual social ones), expecting a high-high *Status Conflict* (p. 116) scene to emerge. The scene that unfolded had each of their characters freely boasting about their exploits while sneering at the other's attempts to claim greater daring, cleverness, or skill. As they had not established a specific location for the scene, I decided to give myself the character of a prison guard who walked in to remind them that it was two minutes until lock-down. Suddenly, the scene was transformed into the futile boasting of two losers who were doing time in the big house. Gordon's character became sarcastic, as he derided Ellie's character for getting them imprisoned. Ellie's character, appearing stung by the accusation, archly shot back that she didn't intend to dignify his remarks with an answer. Gordon, to my surprise, angrily told Ellie that he wasn't going to tolerate her speaking to him that way. It was evident that Gordon had dropped out of character and that the scene was over.

At this point, I called a halt to the scene and had them return to their usual client seating (at opposite ends of a long sofa). I asked Gordon what had happened just then to make him so angry. Still upset, he tightly replied that Ellie had hid behind her character in order to be mean to him, just like she did in their real-life fights. I looked over at Ellie, pale and tense, and asked if she knew what was going on. Slowly, not looking at either one of us, she said that she had felt quite hurt by Gordon's sarcastic tone but plaintively insisted that her reply had "just came out of her character," not from her personally. It was clear that Gordon wasn't buying it.

I asked them to think over what had just occurred in order to locate the point for each when the improv ceased to be playful. For Gordon, it had occurred when he heard Ellie's cold scornfulness which reminded him of his mother's disapproving tone. Ellie had been shocked to hear Gordon's anger, which had scared her, but she thought of herself as still in character up to the point he dropped out. She could see how Gordon might have reacted to her character's tone, but still maintained that he wrongly accused her of hiding behind her character to put him down personally. Ellie remained upset for two weeks following this episode and came close to terminating therapy. By Gordon remaining angry and disbelieving she felt judged as devious, a major invalidation. Clearly, we were at an impasse and no further use of improv was made around this subject.

My conclusion was that my selection of *Play the Monster* was a blunder, since this particular game invites a player to explore an area of vulnerability in the presence of a partner who had already exhibited the power to activate it. Even so, things might have worked out well had I directed their scene so that their characters could have joined cooperatively in order to behave arrogantly toward some real or imagined third party; then the clients might have detoxified arrogance by successfully playing with it, without becoming defensive. By walking on as a high-status prison guard during the scene, I lowered both their status, unwittingly activating a low-status-avoiding conflict between them.

EXPLAINING (AWAY) SUCCESS

As with many other psychotherapeutic techniques, it is possible to attribute the successes of RfG to the placebo effect. That is, if clients are presumed to have been given leading suggestions that learning to play will resolve their problems, and then are induced to enact improvs (which are labelled as successful play experiences), any improvement could then be attributed to the alteration of their belief system, rather than to improvisation as an independent agent of change. However, this explanation supposes it to be possible to separate the activity of improvising from the meaning and purpose of doing so for the improviser. Any attempt to provide a laboratory atmosphere in which people were impersonally instructed to improvise would doubtless alter and probably "kill" the playfulness that is the soul of this approach. Moreover, for a social constructivist community of speakers, the construct of independent agent of change (which implies a belief in a knowable objective reality) would not even be meaningful.

Genius is not a gift, but rather the way one invents in desperate situations.

—Jean-Paul Sartre (cited in Heilbrun, 1988, p. 44)

Competence that loses a sense of its roots in the playful spirit becomes ensconced in rigid forms of professionalism.

—Stephen Nachmanovitch (1990, p. 67)

CHAPTER 13

Artistry: Improvising Clinical Scenarios

W HILE THERAPISTS NEED to be conversant with theory and skilled in the application of practical technique, the essence of therapy is not technical competence but artistry—the capacity to utilize all of oneself spontaneously in the service of a healing relationship. The RfG spirit of playfulness and willingness to experiment stand in healthy contrast to the cautious, overdistanced posture that is widely held up as the proper professional image.

To attain artistry as a therapist, as in any other endeavor, it is necessary at some point to leave one's grounding in technique and factual knowledge and soar aloft on the wings of imagination and daring. Aloff (1993) puts it this way:

> To embrace accuracy as the ultimate goal of truth, in any sphere, does appeal to the part of us that pleasures in mastery—in being able to color within the lines.

224

This mastery is crucial to human development on an intellectual as well as a physiological level, but it is not as freeing as the notion of playfulness—of improvisation—for which one has to throw away the coloring books and begin with a blank page, a ready hand, and an open mind. (pp. 88–89)

CREATING A PLAYFUL CONTEXT FOR ONESELF

Though it may seem too obvious to deserve mention, therapists provide the context for what may be developed in sessions. We can only share what we have; to assist clients to access their playfulness, their willingness to take risks, and their exploration of the unfamiliar, the therapist needs to be open to that same spirit of adventure. While each therapist will need to find his or her own best ways of accessing playfulness and adventuresome spirit, the therapists I train and myself regularly derive these qualities from our own improvising. Thus, in RfG improv is not merely a therapeutic technique applied to clients, but a means by which the therapist opens to her or his own courage, resourcefulness, and creativity. In addition to contributing to the therapist's capacity to use improv exercises with clients, improvising heightens the therapist's involvement in the present moment, increases tolerance for both ambiguity and risk of the unknown, and stimulates metaphorical connections, particularly nonverbal ones. Faking it (relying on mechanical technique) does not work well in RfG. In my repeated experience, the times I have been least effective in utilizing improv have occurred when I was too preoccupied with controlling the outcome of the exercise or session, or where, feeling withdrawn or self-protective, I tried to get the clients to supply the energy I lacked or was unwilling to expend. A related trap occurs whenever I attempt to shame myself into acting as nurturant because the client has a right to expect this from our social contract. As Carl Whitaker has noted, "do not feed the patient when he is crying that he is hungry, but only when you feel the milk overflowing from your own nipples" (cited in Kopp, 1972, p. 17).

TAKING SELF-INVENTORY

While I have often planfully used improvs as tools of assessment or as clinical interventions, I frequently also introduce an improv game or exercise on the spur of the moment, with no clear idea of why or how it relates to the case. In retrospect, I nearly always find that there was a plausible rationale or that one could be invented, yet a truer explanation is that I "improvise improvising" out of a gradually-acquired trust in the process of giving over to the flow in the moment. An example of this comes from my work with the couple Sharon and John, presented in Case 6 in Chapter 11. By spontaneously following the musical-conductor metaphor, I was able to open myself up to an entire realm of emotional and status transactions.

Since psychotherapy practice infrequently provides detailed or even unambiguous feedback regarding its effectiveness, it is important for therapists to seek frequently fresh and varied perspectives on what they believe
about therapy, what their strengths and weaknesses are as clinicians, and
how they approach the role of therapist. An innovative approach is offered
by Keeney (1991), who champions the therapist's use of self to be spontaneous and original, both to the development of his or her own unique approach
and to each case—even to each session. His book offers a 58-question self-
assessment to bring out personal resources and identify the uniqueness of
the therapist. Many of his questions are provocative and useful, such as: (a)
Fantasize directing a movie entitled, "The World's Most Successful Psycho-
therapist." Use a brief phrase to describe this therapist's work. (b) What are
the most outrageous things you've ever done in your therapeutic work? (c)
In one sentence, what is the most mysterious aspect of psychotherapy?
The answers to these questions constitute a comprehensive list of "resource
frames" which are to be sorted into two groupings: (1) beliefs and under-
standings and (2) therapeutic actions. The therapist can then identify the
patterns of his or her therapeutic style by attending to the orchestration and
sequencing of resource frames when conducting therapy. The advantages
of utilizing this process are: (a) it allows the therapist and/or supervisor to
draw upon the therapist's own natural resources; (b) new resource frames
may be identified, leading to the design of a new approach; (c) eventually,
the therapist may become resourceful enough to design a unique therapy
for each unique client.

While admiring Keeney's ingenuity and acknowledging the usefulness of
his self-assessment questionnaire, I nonetheless do not agree with his claim
that this method constitutes improvising. For one thing, the presented uni-
verse of therapeutic technique is the verbal; there is no mention of emotional expressiveness, movement, nor enacted fantasy. The techniques he
offers may be, at best, taken as a preparation or foundation for improvising
but they do not include the development of playfulness or spontaneity.

On one point I fully concur with Keeney: Therapists are better off
viewing themselves as improvising artists, being creative with what they
know, rather than impersonating devotees of other (eminent) therapists.
The absence of unambiguous evidence of one's own clinical competence
leads even experienced therapists to rely on comparisons of themselves with
other therapists to obtain some measure of uncertainty reduction as to
where they stand. While it is unquestionably useful to learn from others,
there is a danger that training or self-education will influence the therapist
to trust only the introjected style and voice of others, rather than developing his or her own ways and integrating new learning into his own repertoire. This reliance on comparisons with others rests on a fundamental
assumption: that there exist objectively valid methods for the achievement

of clinical results. It appears preferable to regard the practice of psychotherapy by the criteria of artistic performance than as the correct application of technique; from this viewpoint, the therapist's insecurities are not
an indication of ineptitude but constitute "stage fright." Of course, this is
not to deny that skill and knowledge are necessary in therapeutic practice,
only that a lack of confidence itself is no proof of lack of competence.

It should be remembered that verbal or written descriptions of cases
(including the ones in this book) are not objective data in the paradigmatic
mode, but are narrative mode constructions by the author/therapist that
condense, oversimplify, distort, and omit information, and are open to
divergent interpretation when seen from another's perspective. Videotaped
cases, when edited, are subject to the same biases as written case histories.
Observed live or unedited videotaped consultations by "master therapists,"
as are done at group and family therapy conferences, offer the learner alternative examples that are still performances, albeit less knowingly shaped
to prescribe the observer's conclusions. All of these are valuable learning
resources but they do not confer "truth." Keeney makes the point that
schools, orientations and models of psychotherapy are

> portraits, exteriorizations, or rationalizations for the people who invented them.
> They are simply examples of different people's ways of evolving a style that fully
> utilizes their own unique resources in a particular context. (1991, p. 3)

He then goes on to trace the progression of existing schools from their
"originating insight" through a written canon to the foundation of bureau-
cratic (and, I would add, even theocratic) institutions, and finally, to the
deification of "master therapists," all of which constitute a danger to the
freshness (and creative insecurity) of clinical artistry.

A point touched upon in Chapters 1 and 6 is that the therapist can be
viewed as a performer not only in the eyes of clients but also for an audience, physically present or not, of professional peers. As a result of considerable changes both in conventions of practice (group and family therapy,
live supervision and consultation) and technology (one-way mirrors and
video equipment), clinical practice, supervision, and training have become
far more public events than was the case 40 years ago. Therapists now live
in a professional community where clinical artistry may be *displayed* (in
both the senses of "for training others" and "for showing off oneself") as
well as merely *described* and where, as in society at large, no consensual
standards apply to the style of conveying the social role of "therapist" (by
contrast, almost every male psychoanalyst in the 1930s had a beard, I am
told). The need for inspiring performance models as professional heroes
as well as for great bards or storytellers (Where would Achilles have
been without Homer? Or Milton Erickson without Jay Haley?) are surely
no less important to the well-being of the tribe of psychotherapists than the

"better theories" or "more research" incessantly called for in professional journals.

OPENING TO METAPHORICAL AWARENESS

Psychological expansion and growth is gained not by being presented with a metaphor of expanded reality but rather by being liberated by metaphor to expand one's reality. (Atwood, 1992, p. 16)

Metaphor has a long and continuing history of use in psychotherapy. A metaphor functions as a bridge that connects different levels of description of experience; it makes the strange familiar and the familiar strange. From a social constructivist perspective, clients are actively engaged in the constant process of creating their world by interpreting their own experiences. The therapist participates in the client's creation by constructing a bridge from his own world to the client's; across this bridge, meaning travels in both directions. When metaphors are effective they generate alternative frames of reference and new possibilities for viewing overfamiliar problem descriptions, thus serving as a resource for change.

Therapeutic metaphor, like therapy itself, is predominantly verbal, a way of talking about experience. Improv offers a multichannel bridge or bandwidth for the expression of meaning that both therapist and client can benefit from utilizing. Compared with verbal metaphors that arise in therapeutic conversation, improv enactments have the further advantage of being cocreated outside the unilateral control of the offerer, with the frequent result that unique and unpredictable metaphors emerge.

CASE 12   *The Mind-Reader*

Jerome, a 31-year-old electrical engineer, and Ruth, a 34-year-old department store clothing buyer, had been living together for six years. In the initial telephone contact Ruth had stated that Jerome was incapable of having meaningful discussions with her, leading me to expect a routine emotional pursuer-distancer pattern. Indeed, in the first two sessions they displayed an extreme contrast in expressiveness: Jerome was muted, emotionally distant, socially passive; Ruth was vibrant, emotionally intense, emotionally in-charge to the point of consistently speaking for both of them. However, when discussing subjects like sports, finances, and technology Jerome came to life; on those occasions Ruth appeared to tune out, effectively trading functional roles. This told me that they were capable of far more symmetrical interaction than I had seen or that Ruth had described.

During the third session, while Ruth was, as usual, explaining Jerome to me, I noticed a far-away look on his face while his open hands made slow, rhythmic arcs in front of his chest. Noticing my noticing of this gesture,

Ruth told me that this was Jerome's way of negating what she was saying and of tuning her out. Explaining that I needed to conduct some research with Jerome, I motioned him to accompany me to the far end of the room where I invited him to repeat and vary the gesture. After experimenting with pushing away with open palms and short punches with closed fists Jerome cupped his hands and appeared to be stroking a spherical surface, reporting a connection to this movement. Half a minute after I asked him to associate to the gesture verbally he exclaimed, "Fortune-telling!" in a surprised but pleased voice. I instantly understood that Jerome's sphere was a crystal ball and that he had made a connection to the mind-reading and predicting the future features of Ruth's pronouncements; on second thought, I guessed it might be his evaluation of therapy as well. Turning to Ruth, I stated that I believed there might be a different way they could explore their problems.

After introducing them to some beginning improv exercises at the end of that third and during their fourth session, I set up a fortune-telling scene in which Ruth was "Madame Irene, the fortune-teller," and Jerome a client named "Victor." I instructed Madame Irene to read Victor's mind as well as to offer him advice and predict his future. In the scene that ensued, Madame Irene was oracular and verbose, intent on impressing Victor with her powers; Victor was openly skeptical, even rude in letting Madame Irene know he thought her a fraud. Of course, Jerome was blocking Ruth's offers, as I rather expected he would; I thought it of some use to give Jerome a pretext to express by proxy his hostility to being defined by Ruth's character. After letting this scene play for about one minute I interrupted and asked them to start the scene over. For this next take I asked Jerome to play Victor as an awestruck, credulous client, amazed that everything Madame Irene said was true. Aided by some coaching, the scene was humorous and good-natured, though with a slyly ironic undertone as Victor would gush lines like, "My God! Wonderful! How did you know?" Both of them really enjoyed this opportunity to play freely; Ruth was delighted and amazed (and only slightly more surprised than I was) at how lively, articulate, and expressive Jerome became during this scene. At the next session, Jerome had only to say "fortune-teller!" to halt Ruth from speaking for him; she grew to be far more cautious and respectful of his opinion in the therapy that followed.

About three weeks later, I had them reverse roles in a scene that had the "know-it-all stockbroker, Victor" financially advising "bewildered customer, Irene." What really seemed to help them was their discovery through the game that they enjoyed playing together and that Victor could act just as opinionated as Ruth. In discussion following these enactments, Jerome reported that he withdrew into himself when he grew angry and disgusted with Ruth's presumptiveness; for her part, Ruth had become lonely and anxious with his withdrawal from her at times when she needed intense conversation. They had evidently fallen prey to the kind of positive feedback loop patterning described by Haley in early strategic family therapy writings.

What worked so well in this case seemed to be that the fortune-teller metaphor emerged out of Jerome's problematic experience with Ruth, that Ruth had a sense of humor about her verbally expressive overfunctioning, and that both preferred the playful, interactive reality they discovered that they could cocreate.

Using Metaphor to Set the Stage

CASE 13   *Rehearsal for Seduction*

Lois and Henry, both in their early fifties, each with grown children from previous marriages, had been living together for the past two years when they entered couples therapy. Lois, verbal yet emotionally reserved, found herself shutting down when Henry insisted in having "feeling talk" conversations, a practice that appeared linked to times of his high anxiety. Henry, a semiretired salesman, complained that Lois was unsupportive of him when she distanced from his attempts to "communicate"; Henry was, however, reluctant to acknowledge his sexual difficulties in their relationship, along with his prior history of premature ejaculation and low sexual desire that appeared linked to performance anxiety.

Following six sessions of exclusively verbal psychotherapy I suggested an improvised role-play. Henry (eagerly) and Lois (reluctantly) agreed. I had them both stand up and move about while briefing them on the scenario. Henry was told that he was to play "Ivan," a trade official just arrived from an Eastern European country (the Cold War was then still in existence) while Lois's character, "Jennifer," was a 20-year-old fun-loving "California girl." They were further instructed that they were meeting in an American airport, and the scene was then turned over to them.

Ivan started by immediately asking for directions from Jennifer, gesturing emphatically and dominating the scene. I quickly interrupted, instructing Ivan that as a foreigner he needed an accent, not to be so fluent in English, and "reminding" Ivan that his superiors back home had warned him to be cautious, lest he become entrapped or compromised by American agents. Henry accepted direction well, and started over by fumblingly asking for directions in a heavily-accented, broken English, moving in a more constricted way. As he did so, Jennifer, who had been a virtual bystander up this point, "came to life" as a talkative and seductive young woman. They developed a scene in which the California girl coaxed a nervous, hesitant, foreign official into going to a motel with her. The dialogue was fast-paced, humorous, and contained numerous parallels to Lois and Henry's real-life problems.

Applauding their efforts, I ended the improvisation and invited them to discuss their experience. Both were happily surprised at the fluency and enjoyment they had gotten from cocreating this improv; Lois, in particular, was enthusiastic at the freedom she had felt from taking the social initiative and being seductive. While they could reconstruct the real-life parallels in their dialogue, neither reported being aware of any self-conscious irony during the scene.

In the session following this improvised role-play, Lois and Henry reported that they had used a shorthand version of their scene to successfully initiate love-making on two occasions. Evidently, the role-play had broadened their relational possibilities to include Lois as emotionally active and Henry as more relaxed and less verbally compulsive, a change that permitted a breakthrough in their sexual relationship.

My choices in setting the scene were guided by the vague intention to give Henry a character in which to explore being less self-assured and glib, while giving Lois the freedom to be more confident and "at home." I had no preconceived idea that they would develop a seduction scene; clients regularly develop scenes in which they solve their real-life problems, often in fantastic ways. In their case, the improv that emerged between Lois and Henry became a literal rehearsal for growth.

CASE 14   *Shifting the Burden*

Occasionally, a stage (performance) game can be adapted to clinical use. Marge, a chronically low-status-playing secretary, and her husband Fred, a mechanic, came into family therapy with their two sons: Michael, age 6, and Gary, age 9. Marge was resentful of her classically overburdened role as full-time housekeeper, full-time mother, as well as full-time employee. Verbal family therapy had, after four sessions, established the operation of a basic family pattern: Though somewhat aware of their work-load inequality, Fred minimized Marge's distress with consistent, cheerful coaching from the sidelines. At the same time that Fred encouraged Marge to have a better attitude, he maintained a distant, expert position on child-rearing, leaving Marge with the brunt of the responsiblity and labor. As everyone in their social network and extended family saw Fred as an excellent father and good husband, Marge was isolated in her perception of being overworked; indeed, at times she expressed doubts herself. The boys were quite in alignment with their father and while no one denigrated Marge or failed to acknowledge verbally her central contribution, no one seemed willing to alter the status quo.

Structural family therapists characteristically deal with these situations by putting father in charge of the children during the session, while strategic family therapists prefer to give a similar directive as homework between therapy sessions. In this case, Fred had no problem in organizing the boys during the session; they cooperated readily with him, which only added to Marge's demoralization. I next suggested that Marge select an "emergency" day on which she would announce in the morning that she would be unavailable to handle her household duties, thus requiring Fred to take over her usual domestic functions. Predictably, Fred's response was to turn Marge's unavailablity into an opportunity to let the housework go for the day, order in fast-food dinner, and allow the boys to stay up later than their scheduled bedtime. Marge, who had retreated to the bedroom following work, was dismayed to hear the lively goings-on in the rest of their apartment, as she realized that the next day she would face additional work from what had been neglected on her emergency day. It struck me that Marge was functioning as the "hands" of the family, that the others would wait until the hands were once again free to perform those "manual" tasks that, seemingly, could only be done by her.

While a more strenuous ordeal over a longer period of time might have altered the pattern, I was pessimistic, given the stuckness of the family status positions. Something else was needed. Advocating greater support for Marge, I sensed, would be counterproductive. A common occurence for beginning (and sometimes, experienced) family therapists is to attempt to redress the status imbalance encountered in a family immediately and directly, which usually takes the form of advocacy on behalf of the downtrodden one. The trap is not so much that the therapist loses neutrality by taking sides but that he or she then gets triangled into propping up the family members' new status positions.

Two sessions following this emergency day homework assignment, I remembered a stage improv game, *Torture a Teammate/Puppets*, that offered the possibility of "handing off" the work burden to Fred. I proposed that the family play a scene in which only Fred could move and in which statements of any of the other three that referred to action or movement would require Fred to move that person's body to another place and to perform that action for them. With a lot of initial confusion and active coaching, the following scene ensued. The scene was played in a shopping mall, with the characters being a family virtually identical to the players' own.

GARY [affecting a husky loud voice, signaling he was in character] Hey! They have Nintendo in there! [pointing to stage left]

THERAPIST Dad, pointing Gary's finger is your job. [Fred goes over to Gary and lifts his arm horizontally, arranging Gary's fingers into a point gesture]

MIKE Come on, Mom, let's go in. [starts to move to the left]

THERAPIST Hold it, Mike, let Dad move you! [Fred goes over to Mike, pushing alternatively against each leg to move Mike to the "store"]

MARGE [catching on] No, I'll go look at these sweaters in here. [looking toward stage right; Fred moves her legs, shuffling her to the oppisite side of the room]

THERAPIST Good! Fred, you're playing this scene, too. What is your character doing?

FRED I guess I'll go with the boys this time. [starts to walk toward Mike]

GARY Hey! I saw the store first! [Fred goes back to the center, moves Gary next to Mike]

THERAPIST [to Marge] What do you want to do in this store?

MARGE I'd like to try on that sweater in my size.

THERAPIST Indicate this.

MARGE I'm going to try on that green sweater.

THERAPIST Fred! [Fred crosses the room to stand by Marge, looking confused]

THERAPIST Move her to try on that sweater! [Fred moves Marge's arms, vaguely imitating pulling a sweater over her head]

THERAPIST Of course, the mirror's over *there*.

MARGE Yes, let me see how I look. [Fred moves her legs three steps over; holding her, he twists her torso from side to side]

THERAPIST Guys! What's going on in the toy store?

MIKE I want a water gun!

THERAPIST [walking over to Mike and looking up] Is that it on the shelf up there? [Mike nods. Therapist gestures to Fred. Fred crosses the room, lifts Mike's arms above his head and brings them back to chest level]

MARGE No, the beige looks better. [Fred rushes back to move her. Before he gets there . . .]

THERAPIST [waving his hand around stage left and saying to Gary] Where in this store can you try out that cartridge?

GARY Here's the screen and joystick. Over here, Dad! [Fred starts back to Gary]

MARGE I want to get out of this green sweater and try the beige one on now! [Fred rushes to seat Gary and get him to hold the game joystick; then it's off to Marge again to change sweaters. He's game, but getting frazzled]

By this point the others were all laughing—the boys at the absurdity of the situation (and seeing their Dad in a new [lower] status); Marge with appreciation at the mirror held up to her own real-life situation and with hope and relief at learning to use the demanding/waited-on/high-status helpless position of her stage role. I ended the game here.

The therapeutic shift was immediate and profound. Once the debriefing descriptions of the boys' experience in the game were over, Marge went directly into a state of heightened clarity and intensity as she pinpointed the now-seen-as-unacceptable role patterns of the family's domestic life. What was so striking was the contrast between Marge's prior and present status:

her previous uncertain, tense, and verbally-qualified statements contrasted with her concise and emphatic presentation; her previous rigid, chin-lowered, elbows-tightly-against-her side, low-status body posture, contrasted with her now-erect bearing. However he managed it, Marge told Fred, he was going to have to pitch in from now on, as she would no longer do, or be solely responsible for, such a disproportionate share of the housework.

Fred, too, had shifted position in the aftermath of the scene. He had reported being so involved in the frenetic dashing back and forth during the scene that he was unaware of the relevance of the game to their lives until the shock of hearing family laughter near the end of their scene. Then, he reported feeling bewildered and upset that no one else appreciated how hard he was working to make the scene work. For whatever reasons, Fred had become far more receptive to Marge's point of view. After she had had her say, his responses led into a bargaining session over implementing task-sharing. Gone was the cheery coach; Fred now displayed less self-assurance and spoke with a respect for Marge that was unprecedented in their therapy.

In the following session, Marge reported that everyone was now more involved in housework and that she and Fred had started to quarrel as status equals. From this point, the boys were excused from further therapy sessions and Marge and Fred proceeded in couples therapy to a satisfactory conclusion.

The factors that had brought this game to mind, I now believe, were: (1) the above-mentioned "hands" analogy; (2) a desire to enact a role reversal that altered Fred's and Marge's status positions; (3) the memory of this game as entertaining to audiences because of the comical overburdening of the mover. During the session, of course, there was no planning or calculation in this choice.

The way a clinical improv is created or selected can be understood after the fact as having occurred as the result of associations and metaphors that were made at the time. However, this is of little use in advance or at the time of creating an intervention. By analogy, deductive reasoning can be used to check a mathematical proof of a theorem once it has been constructed, but not to construct it in the first place.

CREATING NEW PARTNERSHIPS WITH CLIENTS' OTHER SELVES

One of the most fruitful methods of promoting change and growth in psychotherapy is to cocreate a new client character in session that can be expanded upon in the client's life outside of therapy. Although this is done

effectively in many ways within different schools or modalities, most therapies offer only a limited range of possibilities. The reason for this is that the
alternatives come down to only those modeled or taught by the therapist;
even where the therapist believes in the desirability of the client discovering
or fully manifesting his own unique self, the client can only draw upon the
offer of a present encounter with the therapist-in-role-as-himself in order to
locate a changed client-self. Moreover, a belief of the therapist in a core or
unitary self will likely create an unstated-yet-powerful demand for consistency and for the client to adopt a stance requiring the same of the therapist.

By contrast, the RfG therapist invites a character directly into being
through improv which (because of the play-context) is understood to offer
provisional, rather than permanent, alternatives to the client's ordinary
range of personae. In a relatively short time span a client can not only enact
a large range of role possibilities but also encounter a variety of other
players' roles, as well as experience the mutual influence that self and other
have on these choices. Consequently, the client vividly learns something of
the possibility of choice regarding whom one is capable of becoming, as
well as the limits or constraints of choice by which he or she habitually
operates.

Improv also offers clients an alternative sense of self by the transformation that occurs when one player gives attention to another player and
enters a new, shared reality. That is, the act of voluntarily attending to
another person's reality and living inside of it (which many therapists do as
a natural extension of their own personal style in therapy and hence take
for granted) is a novel experience for the many clients whose conscious
interpersonal experience is dominated by blocking the offers of others in
order to "be themselves." Improv actors are often advised to have their
character "fall in love" when a scene is in difficulty, since this intention will
help to shift the focus of attention away from self (which is likely to be the
reason the scene isn't working) and toward the "beloved."

Strangely, even clients whose pattern runs to the apparent opposite,
namely aligning themselves with others to the extent of having no opinions
and appearing self-effacing, benefit from improvising, since they gain practice in making offers to themselves and the other players in order to advance
the action. Both types of clients can be helped to integrate their improv
experience by means of retrospective analysis (especially when accompanied
by video feedback) of the choices made, as well as those avoided and
unthought-of.

The role of the therapist/director can shift across positions on the continuum described by Johnson to assist the development and exploration of
new characters. In order to explore verbally with the client the conceptual
shift necessary to assume a new character, the therapist/director can func-

tion as off-stage Director before or between enactments by pointing out, "Your character wouldn't want/isn't afraid of/doesn't know that." As a Sidecoach the therapist/director can make offers to advance the action, shape or guide avoided choices, or introduce novelty or unpredictability into the scene. Functioning as a Leader, the therapist/director may walk into a scene to become a confidante of a player's character, taking her aside to talk over or commiserate with for having to deal with other characters (this is particularly useful when the player is holding back from acting fully in character in a socially risky way). Occasionally, the therapist/director becomes a "double" of the player's character, alternating playing the role with the player in order to model clearer or more committed choices. In these cases it is important that the therapist/director does not get too far out in front of the client and take over the role (which many clients are only too ready to allow).

Immediately after enactments, and even during therapy sessions conducted later without enactment, the therapist/director may wish to reinforce features of new characters by invoking them by name or by calling them forth in new enactments (as occurred with Micky in Case 1, Chapter 10). While it is a great asset in therapy for the client to have had a transformative experience in-role (since it demonstrates the possibility of change to the client and to all who witnessed the enactment) more is usually necessary for the transformation in the moment to become incorporated into the client's life. In general, (a) further rehearsal with accessing the character, (b) restorying the dominant themes of the client's life, and (c) developing the character in-depth (by such means as everyday life practice and repeated RfG enactments) are needed.

What is involved in this process, ultimately, is the transformation of the therapeutic system, not just of the client's identity. Seen in this way, therapy becomes an antidote to the conservative patterning of social identity/storying formation and maintenence found in many families. In such families parents are typically slow and/or reluctant to acknowledge changes in their children (e.g., "You'll always be my little boy") with the result that even adult children with children of their own may find it difficult to own fully their maturity and autonomy when around such parents. In RfG therapy, by contrast, changes of social identity are far more readily experimented with by a therapist who is disposed to make a greater variety of offers and is willing to accept and be affected by the client's offers as well. Here, the therapist's own willingness and skill in giving character to the newly emergent client self are critical; creating rituals for making and confirming the transition to becoming a "new client" is one way the therapist helps confirm the shift of identity. Now, to participate in the cocreation of such a shift in identity, the therapist must believe sufficiently in the new client identity as *to be himself changed in its presence*. At first, the therapist may consciously be trying on the part of "one-who-is-changed," yet in time the therapist's reality must also alter to accomodate the transformation in order for it to "take." As Carl Whitaker (personal communication, 1988) has said, "I know the family has changed when I am changed." This is entirely different from the superficial tolerance displayed by a covertly judgmental therapist who accepts the client "as he is," which will be ineffectual at best and may well replicate a patronizing or manipulative patterning that led to the client's being mystified, limited, or demoralized in the first place. And, as should come as no surprise to the reader, improv training itself prepares the therapist to shift his or her social role to accommodate a client's new identity features.

IMPROV FROM THE INSIDE:
INTERVIEWS WITH IMPROVISERS

As noted in the Introduction, training in improvisation, and experience with performing theater improvisation, appears to benefit people. I conducted informal interviews with 42 improvisers who were trained in Keith Johnstone's approach, and who have been performing improvisation from 2 to 18 years. They are improvisers I know personally from having performed with or having attended improvisation training together; they range in age from 19 to 66; 26 are men and 16, women. Eight of them reside out of the United states, chiefly in Scandinavian countries. Twenty-eight regard theater as their work identity, although only 7 earn their livelihood primarily from that profession.

My intent in these interviews was to gain an impression of how improvising had affected their social skills and use of self in their off-stage lives. This took the general form of inviting them to compare their lives before and since coming to improvisation. Interviewees were first asked to address the question, "In what ways has improvising changed you as a person?" and next to respond to specific questions about each of the topics listed in Table 3. They were then encouraged to expand upon their answers and to give anecdotal examples. For example, following an affirmative response to the question, "Has improvisation increased your self-confidence?" I asked for a personal story relevant to self-confidence from both a time before and a time since coming to improv. Of course, since this investigation is methodologically quite loose, one should not view as conclusive the results obtained; still, they do suggest stongly that improvising is beneficial.

No statistical analyses on these data were performed, but it was possible to tell, by visual inspection, that women were more likely to report greater postimprov willingness to take risks (12 out of 16, compared with 11 out of 26 men) and that a slightly higher proportion of men attributed a broadening of emotional expression to improv (18 out of 26) than did women (8 out

TABLE 3 Reported consequences of theater improvisation

Number Agreeing (N = 42)	Percent of Total	Topic
41	98	Awareness of blocking in social interaction
38	90	Awareness of status transactions in social interaction
32	76	Lower interpersonal anxiety/Greater self-confidence and self-trust
32	76	Greater playfulness in everyday life
28	67	Greater willingness to take risks in interpersonal situations
26	62	Greater awareness of body movement and posture
18	43	Lessened anxiety concerning the future
15	36	Broader emotional expressiveness
07	17	Greater trust of others
04	11	Negative consequences (miscellaneous)

of 16). Of the 29 interviewees who did *not* characterize themselves as having been "class clowns" or "entertainment stars" within their families of origin, 20 reported greater playfulness since coming to improv; 12 of the 13 self-designated "class clowns" reported the same. This may be due to the "clowns" having found an expressive outlet for their playfulness that was previously unavailable to them.

An unexpected finding was that performance improvising increased interpersonal trust in only 15 of the 42 cases; follow-up questions revealed that trust of other improvisers as a group was no greater than that extended to people in general, although most respondents stated that improvising had brought them into close friendships with certain other performers. There were also 4 improvisers who reported negative consequences: 2 respondents reported having an unwelcome reputation as a "funny person"; 1 felt his self-esteem had been stressfully challenged by his failure to meet his own expectations as an improviser; 1 attributed a lack of career direction to improv's encouragement of present-centeredness. All 4 persons, however, stated their intention to continue performing, which pointed up that, at least in this sample, improvisers do not regard such drawbacks as outweighing the personal satisfactions of continuing to improvise.

How does one learn improvisation? The only answer is to ask another question: What is stopping us? Spontaneous creation comes
from our deepest being and is immaculately and originally ourselves. What we have to express is already with us, is us, so the
work of creativity is not a matter of making the material come,
but of unblocking the obstacles to its natural flow.

—Stephen Nachmanovitch (1990, p. 10)

The greatest potential for improvisation is as a means for the student to discover self in relation to his Art.

—James Hooker (cited in Sperber, 1974, p. 3)

CHAPTER 14

Improvisation in Clinical Training

FROM THE VIEWPOINT of social constructivism, the therapist and cli-
ent(s) are cocreating a reality within the framework of their social expectations regarding therapy. The major challenge and task for the therapist is
to interpret the role of therapist in a way that is clinically helpful to clients
while at the same time meeting her or his own personal needs (this last
element is underemphasized in most formal training programs). Professionalism is signified by the degree to which the therapist performs the therapeutic role as she or he fulfills both of these conditions. A therapist who
serves only her- or himself will be ineffectual, even damaging to clients in
the long run while one who ignores or suppresses her or his own needs
for very long will eventually burn out, becoming incapable of functioning
effectively as a therapist.

Even more influential than the theoretical ideas held and the techniques
employed are the beliefs that the supervisor/teacher holds toward the interpretation of the therapeutic role; these are the main influence on the training of therapists. This is inevitable and not a bad thing; we learn by imita-

239

tion. If the belief is that the therapist is an expert, she or he will instruct or
retrain client(s), challenging their irrational beliefs (rational-emotive therapy), or exposing their inauthentic games (transactional analysis); if the belief
is that the therapist is a paragon of psychological health, she or he will communicate understanding, warmth, and respect (client-centered therapy), or
establish a climate of emotional acceptance and expressiveness (Satir).
What gets taught, in effect, is how to use the self of the therapist. Thus,
psychoanalysts are trained to value a neutral mask and minimalist display
of the therapist's personality: Rogerians, to be warm, authentic, and nonjudgmental; Bowenians, to remain unanxious and stay out of familial fusion or triangulation; etc.

Whichever way therapists are socialized in their clinical training, the
result is a professional stance that may limit what the therapist-in-role is to
present, whether the limitation is in self-disclosure, emotional range and
intensity, or status position. An emphasis on diagnosing psychopathology
encourages a tendency to view difference as wrongness, regardless of
whether the source of that difference is contextually appropriate (e.g., cultural differences). An overemphasis on mastering theoretical knowledge
and technique sets up the trainee to assume an "expert" stance which both
increases social distance between therapist and client and subtly discourages
the use of spontaneity and imagination by either one. Assumption of the
professional role all too often focuses attention away from the trainee's
own unique personal abilities and encourages the creation and maintenance
of a facade (the professional mask), further hampering the fully effective
use of self. Lastly, much conventional training embodies a positive value
placed on the attainment of mastery as rapidly and painlessly as possible;
the result, rather than the process of becoming, counts.

By contrast, therapists take a more effective healing stance when they
put aside their tendency to objectify the client in terms of diagnostic descriptions. Often, trainees and beginning therapist cling to an overdistanced
stance in order to keep from feeling overwhelmed and to conceal their
nervousness at their felt incompetence. The following description articu-
lates a more effective position:

> You are immersed in the case itself, letting your view of it develop in context.
> You certainly use your training; you refer to it, understand it, ground yourself
> in it, but you don't allow your training to blind you to the actual person sitting
> in front of you. In this way you pass beyond competence to *presence*. To do
> anything artistically you have to acquire technique, but you create *through* your
> technique and not *with* it. (Nachmanovitch, 1990, p. 21)

ENHANCING EFFECTIVE USE OF SELF

Since I view the effective therapist as creating a context of change via
the use of self rather than by mere application of technique, improv can

become a means by which therapists in training cultivate and expand their capacity to use the self fully. Flexibility is a virtue in therapy; an effective therapist is one who can switch stances easily in order to maximize clinical effectiveness. In my own way of training therapists, I put considerable emphasis on the assumption of risk (which is mainly, though not exclusively, a willingness to experience emotional discomfort) as a necessary component of psychological growth. In the same way that improv stretches clients, improv used in training empowers therapists to experience risks personally, which leads to their empowering clients to take risks. While therapists need not experience precisely what they are asking a client to undergo, if they have not had some personal experience of risk-taking, their attempts to induce change by encouraging client risk-taking will lack authenticity and effectiveness. As noted before, it is a common experience in improv for players to avoid or push away even imaginary danger (e.g., to create a dragon off-stage rather than on-stage, or to have the dragon go to sleep rather than try to eat them), or to unthinkingly block offers that, upon retrospective analysis, entail greater personal risks than bargained for. It is not my intention to treat every limitation that surfaces in a trainee as an obstacle to be surmounted; as with therapy itself, I support people to work on what changes they themselves elect. It should also be added that the isomorphism of empowering risk-taking extends to the teacher's/supervisor's effectiveness as well; I play improv games with my trainees and frequently "fail" visibly!

The fundamental risk in improv is to experience and act in the moment fully and without reservation—to allow spontaneity that permits the imagination to work without censorship and the body to move uninhibitedly. A therapist trained in improv will not be spontaneous all, or even most of the time, but will be able to deploy greater imaginative use of her- or himself on behalf of the client in treatment. For instance, the therapist's being "stuck" is often a result of her or his having become fixed at a particular degree of interactive intensity, constant status position, or viewpoint regarding the client's problems, resources, or weaknesses. By attending to her or his imagination and shifting to a playful, fantasy context, the therapist may surprise her- or himself out of the stuckness.

Improv also sharpens the beginning therapist's grasp of the client's narrative themes, preparing her or him to devise enactments that offer alternatives. This is where the value of improv work on giving character (Chapter 6) has particular usefulness, since the client brings to therapy her or his own expectations for the therapeutic role. I also regard *Gibberish Encounter* (p. 82) as a vivid demonstration of how we persist in seeing what we have convinced ourselves is there. A less-recognized aspect of counter-transference is the therapist's not merely projecting feelings onto clients but actually becoming what the client trains her to be; it can be difficult not to give others what they want, at least on a subtle level.

Learning improv also enhances therapists' use of self by making manifest styles of learning and expression in response to the (at times) challenging requirements of games and exercises. When a therapist approaches improv with the committment to play full-out, she or he will, at times, unambiguously break down. One of the important attitudinal differences between persons that emerges from such inevitable improv breakdowns is in how they respond to their own mistakes or perceived failure. Often, people act as if in pain, demonstrating that they are to be viewed as suffering. Keith Johnstone (personal communication, 1986) speculates that such a performance (probably learned in the classroom) serves to ward off anticipated disapproval or punishmment, as if to say, "I am so miserable for having failed that this is punishment enough." Not only is the performer drawing attention to what didn't work in his enactment, he is also taking a low-status position that distances the onlooker from him and precludes any enjoyment of the performance.*

In order to develop the trainee's self, it is most necessary to have a safe and supportive training context within which trainees can risk making mistakes. Having been involved, either as trainee or as teacher/supervisor, with 14 clinical training programs during the past 24 years, I have personally and repeatedly witnessed the deleterious effects of inviting trainee self-disclosure while at the same time using this information to make evaluative judgments that damaged the trainees' reputation, career, trust, and self-confidence. In two cases in particular, the way trainees were treated was diametrically opposite to the professed values of that program's philosophy regarding the treatment of clients. I am confident that most readers can recollect similar experiences. Integrity in training demands, at the minimum, isomorphism between the supervisor/supervisee and the therapist/client relationship (see Liddle & Saba, 1985).

When mistakes and failures are allowed in the learning context, trainees and clients learn to forgive themselves, empowering themselves to take more chances and broaden their repertoires. We are all taught to fear, hide, or avoid mistakes. Yet, viewed differently, mistakes are attempts to learn and improve and can inspire further effort. "The power of mistakes enables us to reframe creative blocks and turn them around . . . The troublesome parts of our work, the parts that are most baffling and frustrating, are in fact the growing edges. We see these opportunities the instant we drop our preconceptions and our self-importance" (Nachmanovitch, 1990, p. 92). Or as Tom Watson, long-time CEO at IBM, put it: "Good judgment comes from experience. Experience comes from bad judgment."

My approach to training family therapists emphasizes the importance of

---

*Hence the emphasis on good-natured failure in Johnstone's training of stage-improvisers (as noted in Chapter 1).

(a) understanding one's position in current and past systems, (b) learning to use differences between self and others as assets, and (c) giving and receiving support to work effectively with systems. Improv training contributes to learning how one's family of origin position influences her or his functioning in the current system (during the improv game and within the training group). For example, a trainee who has difficulty playing either high or low status may use this discovery to explore its connection to family of origin issues, or conversely may use improv roles to go beyond her or his historically familiar range in current "real life." Improv's contribution to learning to value and utilize differences lies in demonstrating how the trainee blocks offers when threatened (often leading to a focusing on the trainee's underlying judgments) and in observing how other trainees approach comparable tasks in improv games. The most direct and valuable contribution of improv to teaching about self in systems lies in the basic experience of making the improv game work by putting the principles and objectives into action.

One versatile technique I have developed uses intentional status shifts by the trainee in-role as a therapist of a simulated beginning family therapy session. The training class first selects an actual clinical family (or invents one), and then assigns family roles to trainees. I then send the "family" out of the room to rehearse their interaction while I instruct the trainee who will play the therapist to select the status rankings she herself will play and those to be played toward family members. This is similar to *Hidden Pecking Order* (p. 117).

The "therapist" now greets the "family," ushers the group into the room, and begins the opening session. I usually sit or stand near the "therapist" to coach if needed. The interaction is usually very brief (three minutes at most), just long enough to establish the "therapist's" differential status treatment of the "family members." The scene is then halted and the "family members" are asked in turn, *still in-role*, how they experienced the therapist and the session. Following this, the "therapist" speaks. Usually the scene is repeated a few times with the "therapist" leaving the room with me to select a different set of status rankings between each scene. Following these enactments, the players (now out-of-role) and audience discuss the differences felt and observed.

What always happens is that the status choices, if played clearly, strongly affect the "family members'" individual perceptions of the "therapist," their degree of anticipated cooperation (highly correlated with the "family's" own status hierarchy when that hierarchy is unchallenged), and which member's viewpoint is expected to define the therapeutic issues addressed.

Another variation to this exercise is to have different trainees replace the original family cast members in successive reinactments of the initial

therapy session scene. This is particularly useful to heighten empathic identification with family members treated as low-status by the "therapist."
Conversely, by keeping the "family" constant, the "therapist" role can be
played by different trainees, each attempting to play the same status rankings. This adaptation of *Tag Improv* (p. 106) facilitates comparison of the
impact on families of stylistic differences across therapists or, when done
rapidly, distributes any pressure to be clinically competent across the training class. A *Crazy Eddie* (p. 106) version has the rest of the training class
poised and ready to jump in to tag out the therapist whenever she signals
she is at a loss. Incidentally, competitive feelings regarding therapeutic
competence are mitigated considerably by use of this version.

A further use of this role-playing format is to superimpose *Behavioral
Lists* (p. 137), particularly for the therapist role. Such lists, drawn up by the
training class, can include "To Be Thought Compassionate," "To Be Seen
as Totally Out of Touch," "To Be Regarded as Brilliant," and even "To
Induce a Cathartic Cure Within Five Minutes." My trainees once made a
videotape clip of a simulated family session and challenged me to say what
list the therapist was playing. The therapist on the tape appeared to be
doing a fairly good job except that his use of language was overly laced
with jargon, so I replied, "To Be Thought Learned." Laughing, they informed me the therapist had been quoting me from their notes taken at my
lectures!

LEARNING SYSTEMIC THINKING

Improv exercises accelerate the learning process of thinking systemi-
cally, a process that cannot be imparted by a purely conceptual approach.
Naturally, improv alone will not adequately convey systemic thinking, yet
it contributes in the following ways:

1. By participating in improv exercises, trainees experience first-hand
   the social construction of "character" and "reality."
2. By participating in improv exercises, trainees acquire narrative
   skills which prepare them both to formulate systemic hypotheses
   and to assess the family "game."
3. When directing clinical families in improvs, trainees observe the
   "family dance" and are in a position to try out interventions that
   stretch the family's reality and rules in a relatively safe way.
4. When participating with clinical families in improvs, trainees can
   experience the "pull" of the family system as well as the boundary
   of the family/therapeutic systems.
5. In varying their own emotional and status position in improvs,
   trainees experience with immediacy their own effectiveness and
   limitations, thereby learning the importance of changing context.

In order to facilitate systemic thinking, I use a variety of improvs, including *One Knows, The Other Doesn't* (p. 101), which directly illustrates a social construction process to develop character and relationship; *Gibberish Encounter* (p. 82), which illustrates how family members can be living in different realities; and *Exclusion* (p. 118), which demonstrates hierarchical formation and triangulation. I also make use of other, nonimprov action methods, notably sculpting.

Learning systemic hypothesis-formulation and testing these hypotheses is aided by simulations of clinical sessions in which the underlying premises of the trainee therapist/therapy team are enacted to test for congruence with the clinical data. Or, conversely, the therapeutic team or trainee-therapist leaves the room, whereupon the trainees acting the family roles are assigned status positions, behavioral lists, or other details consistent with an invented reality that the therapist/team endeavors to discover.

One technique I use to accomplish this is to give each of four trainees the roles of a nuclear family: mother, father, elder son, and younger daughter. I then set up an *Unknown Status* scene (described on p. 117 and used clinically in Case 8, Chapter 11), in which I give out cards that privately indicate to each player her or his status position relative to each of the other members. For example, Mother's card might read:

> You are the MOTHER in this family. Your SON is the *most* important member. Your HUSBAND is the *second-most* important member. You are the *third-most* important member. Your DAUGHTER is the *least* important member.

The players are asked to memorize the assigned status positions and to return the cards without revealing the contents to anyone else. A scene is played in which the family, in their home, discuss how to divide up household chores. The players are to play the family hierarchy given on their card.

The cards can be written so that varying degrees of status conflict are built into the family hierarchy. For instance, the cards might be written according to the plan in Table 4.

What usually will happen is that Mother will defer to both Father and Son, but will side with Son, who is of higher status to her than her husband. Son's attempts to elevate Mother's position will bring him in conflict with Father, whose treatment of both Mother and of him (Son) is unacceptable. Father will be faced with an oppositional coalition of Mother and Son with only Daughter to support him. Daughter will tend to be ignored as she attempts to get her Mother and Brother to heed Father. Occasionally one gets a player who is interested only in being treated "properly" by others and takes no interest in any incongruities that do not directly affect her- or himself. In the example above, Father may only be concerned with being deferred to by all the rest; how they treat one another will be of no concern

TABLE 4 Assigned status rank

Card Of	Mother	Father	Son	Daughter
Mother	3	2	1	4
Father	2	1	4	3
Son	1	3	2	4
Daughter	3	1	4	2

to him. Conversely, one might get a daughter whose interest may focus on the way Father and Son treat one another to the exclusion to her own treatment.

I usually let the scene play on long enough so that the patterns are established and then ask the trainees in the audience to describe the status conflicts and to reconstruct the status position diagram (this is excellent training for interactional observation). Then I ask the players to report on their experience of the scene and find out how they attempted to operate under the conditions given. Finally, I have them replay the same scene but with new cards reflecting a different status matrix. This demonstrates the importance of status and hierarchy, and the relative unimportance of content, in family therapy.

Initially, all trainees are encouraged to utilize improv principles and objectives in their clinical work, both as ways of establishing a playful context and (then) of utilizing improv for assessment. When they become sufficiently experienced as therapists, those trainees who take to improv and show some facility with it are encouraged to utilize improvs for making clinical interventions. Of course, as noted before, there is no clear-cut distinction between assessment and intervention, save in the intention of the therapist. Planning improv interventions and training to become skilled in the use of improv may appear to violate the objective of spontaneity, yet if the therapist genuinely establishes a playful context in the session, which must be created in the moment with clients and cannot be guaranteed to occur in advance, the improv can work, just as a class on improvisation may be planned and needn't, itself, be improvised.

USING IMPROV IN CLINICAL SUPERVISION

In all therapy training, supervision is enhanced when the trainee gets to observe the supervisor's work. When possible, I arrange live consultations in which the supervisor/trainer "sits in on" the session with the trainee therapist and the clinical family. In this arrangement, the supervisor neither takes over the session nor remains a passive observer in the room, but becomes a part of the therapeutic team whose function it is to support the trainee to do his job. While this may, at times, take the form of suggesting, directing, or participating in an improv, it more often results in the supervisor treating the trainee as a respected colleague, usually by raising the trainee's status in the presence of the family; often the supervisor leads the session into a playful context (see Case 7 in Chapter 11), or better still, empowers the trainee to do so.

Similarly, live supervision from behind a one-way mirror works best when the team and/or supervisor are not intent on devising interventions, but rather on supporting the therapist by creating a context of playfulness, support, and mutual high-esteem. Once supported, therapists are amazingly more competent; the team maintains the supportive atmosphere, occasionally makes a status observation, or asks the therapist's "expert" opinion on what it's really like in the room. As an aid to getting clinical teams to function more supportively, I use improv games (such as *Puppets* [p. 85] or *Slo-mo Commentator* [p. 107]) in which a player confidently poses as an authority or expert on an improbable subject. Since the subject is not one that anyone expects the player to be knowledgeable about, the player is free to spout nonsense and enjoy high status without having to "earn" it.

Another technique I employ in training and group supervision is improvised role play within simulated therapy sessions. Unlike role plays that aim to practice realistic clinical skills, the main function served here is to try out feared or forbidden responses as a way of helping the trainee detoxify those limiting, painful, or taboo reactions that arise in all therapists. Sometimes this takes the form of exaggerating the problematic feature of an actual case, such as confronting an absurdly conflictual couple; at other times, the premise is that the trainee is to respond as the "therapist from hell" with the most inappropriate technique imaginable. I find here, more than in most areas, that the trainees will take the plunge of attempting these improvs only when their trainers have taken the lead in modelling such risk-taking and when they trust in the integrity of the training class. I knew that one class trusted me when I returned from a break to find them performing a truly inspired "supervisor from hell" scene!

CONCLUSION

Theater improvisation is a play-inducing, creativity-releasing, growth-enhancing art that resonates to the heart of the therapeutic endeavor. Rehearsals for Growth offers personal growth and renewal for the therapist as well as techniques that aid clients to discover and experiment with other sides of themselves. I invite you to discover the truth of these assertions for yourself; come and play!

Improv Games and Exercises Described in This Book

I T SHOULD BE NOTED that the games and exercises listed below are the ones described separately in the text, although some might be considered as variations of others.

KEY

Column
number
1. Name (alternative names)
2. Game (G) or exercise (E)
3. Page number of description
4. Number of variations described
5. Minimum number of players (where "+" follows number, this indicates "or more," up to any number)

6.   Level of difficulty:
     1 easy; can usually perform without prior experience
     2 moderate; will prove challenging and/or need practice to perform
     3 difficult; requires skill and practice to perform
7.   Uses verbal skills (V), movement skills (M), or both (VM)
8.   Most important improv objectives learned by use:
     1 freeing the imagination
     2 expanding emotional range
     3 encouraging spontaneity
     4 breaking conventional logic
     5 giving up overcontrol
     6 getting others into trouble playfully
     7 using voice and body fully
     8 utilizing narrative skills in cocreating adventures
     9 attending to status (power) transactions

[1]	[2]	[3]	[4]	[5]	[6]	[7]	[8]
Accepting in Mime	G	70	1	2+	3	M	5,6,7
Arms-Through Puppets	G	85	1	2	2	VM	1,6,8
Backward Scene	G	81	0	2+	3	VM	4,8
Behavioral Lists	G	137	1	3+	2	VM	7,2
Blob, The (Speaking in One Voice)	E	84	1	3+	1	V	3,5
Blocking or Accepting Lists	G	74	0	2	1	VM	5
Blocking and Accepting Offers	E	64	7	2	1	V	5
Body Freezes	E	68	1	1	1	M	1,3
Body Offers (Blind Offers)	E	68	0	2	1	M	1,3
Boring Scene (Serious Scene)	G	87	0	2+	2	VM	1,7
Boris/Doris	G	72	2	2	2	VM	1,4,8
Calling Objects the Wrong Name	E	81	0	2+	1	V	1,4
Character Relay	G	136	2	2+	3	VM	2,7
Circle Gibberish	E	128	2	3+	1	V	2
Cooperative Storytelling	E	94	0	2	1	V	2
Combined Lists	G	138	1	3+	3	VM	2,7,8
Couples with Contrasting Emotions (Family Masks)	G	131	2	4	2	VM	2,5,7
Crazy Eddie	E	106	0	3+	2	VM	1,3,5
Directed Story (Options)	G	102	1	2+	1	VM	1,5,8
Dream Story	E	94	0	2	1	V	1,3,8
Dubbing	G	86	3	2+	2	VM	4,6,7
Emotional Lists	G	131	1	2	1	VM	2,7,8
Emotional Short-Circuit	E	81	0	1	2	M	4,2

[1]	[2]	[3]	[4]	[5]	[6]	[7]	[8]
Emotional Zones	G	131	0	2+	1	VM	2,7,8
Endowment Lists	G	101	0	2+	2	VM	1,6,7
Exclusion	G	118	0	3+	1	VM	9
Excuses	G	97	1	2	1	V	3,5,8
Family Legend	G	136	0	3+	1	V	2,1
Family Story	G	97	0	3+	1	V	3,5,8
Fortunately/Unfortunately	G	98	0	2	1	V	1,8
Freeze with a Line	G	71	2	2	1	VM	1,5,7
Freeze Tag (Space Jump)	E	71	1	3+	2	VM	1,3,7
Gibberish Emotions	E	128	2	2	1	V	2
Gibberish Encounter	E	82	0	2	2	M	1,3,6
Gibberish Group Story	G	129	0	3+	1	VM	2,7
Giving Character	E	100	1	2	2	VM	5,7
Hands Out	E	79	0	1	1	V	1
He Said/She Said	G	87	0	2	2+	VM	5,6,7,8
Hat Game	G	109	1	2	3	VM	3,6
Hidden Pecking Order	G	117	0	3+	1	VM	9
Hitchhiker	E	130	0	5+	1	VM	2,7
How We Met	E	103	1	2	1	V	8,5,1
Imposing Status	E	115	2	2	1	VM	9
Insults	G	132	0	2	1	VM	2,6,7
Inviting a Character	E	138	0	2+	2+	VM	2,1,7
It's Tuesday	G	133	1	2	1	V	2,5
Little Voice (Off-Stage Voice)	G	86	1	2	2	VM	1,5,6,8
Mantra	E	135	0	2	2	VM	7,2
Master/Servant Games	G	119	5	2	2	VM	9,6,5
Mirrors Exercise	E	69	1	2	1	M	5
Monsterpiece Theater	G	82	1	2+	2	VM	1
Moral Choices	G	104	0	1+	1	VM	1
Narrative/Color	G	98	0	2	2	V	1,5,8
No, You Didn't	G	74	0	2	1	V	3,5
Object Relations	E	68	0	2	1	M	1,5
One Knows, The Other Doesn't	E	101	0	2	2	VM	5,7,8
One Word at a Time	G	65	5	2	1	VM	5,3,8
Overaccepting	E	65	1	2	1	V	5,2
Overaccepting Together	E	65	0	2+	1	V	5,2
Play the Monster	G	139	1	2	2	VM	2,1,7
Poet's Corner	E	84	0	2	1	VM	2,5,8
Presents	E	105	0	2	1	M	1,3,5
Puppets	G	85	0	3	2	VM	1,5,6,8
River Exercise	E	95	0	2	2	VM	1,5,7,8

[1]	[2]	[3]	[4]	[5]	[6]	[7]	[8]
Simultaneous Leaving (3 Persons Leave the Stage for the Same Reason)	E	70	0	3	3	M	5,6,7
Slo-mo Commentator	G	107	3	2+	2	VM	1,2,7
Soap Scene	E	96	0	2	2	M	6,7,9
Sound and Movement	E	67	2	3+	1	M	3
Spoon River Game (Voices from the Grave) (Tapestries)	G	99	0	3	2	V	1,5,8
Status Conflict	G	116	1	2	1	VM	9
Status Party	E	118	0	4+	1	VM	9
Status Perception	G	117	1	2	2	VM	9,3
Status Transfer	G	116	3	2	2	VM	8,9
Status Triangulation	G	118	1	3	1	VM	9
Stop and Go	G	73	1	2	2	VM	4,5
Stories from Feelings	E	95	0	1	2	V	1,8
Tag Improv	E	106	0	3+	1	VM	1,3,7
Take One, Give Two	E	67	0	4+	2	M	3,7
Team Insults	G	133	1	4+	1	VM	2,7,6
Trial, The	G	99	0	3+	2	V	1,8
Truth Exercise	E	93	0	1	2	V	1,3,8
Torture a Teammate/Puppets (Moving People)	G	232	1	0	3+	VM	5,7,8
Tug-of-War	E	121	3	2	1	M	9,5,7
Unknown Status	G	117	0	3+	1	VM	9
Verbal Mirrors (Simultaneous Speech)	E	70	0	2	2	V	5
Volume Control	E	129	8	2	1	VM	2,7
Wallpaper Drama	G	134	1	4	2	VM	1,3
What Are You Doing?	G	72	1	2	2	VM	1,3
"Yes" Game	E	69	1	3+	1	M	3,7
You Will/I Won't	E	129	0	2	1	V	2,7

External Resources,
Devices, and Conditions

EXTERNAL RESOURCES

EXTERNAL RESOURCES are conventionally used in theatrical productions to heighten the dramatic effect for the audience. These resources include: music, sound effects, lighting, costumes, props, and sets. In RfG, we are more interested in the effect of using these resources on the players (clients) than on an audience.

Regarding the use of such resources, more is definitely not always better. Apart from the cost and inconvenience of employing such resources, their use may also distract players and, most significantly, limit and concretize imagination. (The difference in variety of play between a child using a stick and one using a commercial toy should make this clear.)

It is preferable to do without costumes altogether (save, perhaps, for a few hats) and without props or sets except for such nondescript furniture as a few chairs, a table, and perhaps a (movable) sofa. Other props can be mimed during the scene. Sound effects can be supplied by the therapist/ director or off-stage players. Music, on audio tapes, can occasionally be used to set the mood (it should then be faded out or turned off at or near the beginning of the scene). Music as an offer to the improvisers requires either an improvising musician (as is sometimes employed in playback theater) or a "sound person" supplied with a variety of prerecorded sounds and musical selections; this becomes too elaborate and complicating for clinical application in most settings. Lighting may consist simply of using an on-off switch to signal the beginning and ending of a scene; a dimmer switch adds the possibility of fading in or fading out the action. Having a few different colored lights may be used to set or change the mood, though again this is not necessary.

DEVICES

Devices are elements that define the game or exercise in ways other than the conditions outlined below. Examples include: imaginary players onstage (as in the game *Boris*); emotional doubling (where one or more players, onstage but in the background, mime the unexpressed emotion of a player in the scene); soliloquy and asides (in which players step out of the action on-stage but remain in character to deliver their thoughts to the audience); a voice of conscience off-stage and commentators (as in the game *Slo-mo Commentator*) on- or off-stage.

CONDITIONS

Conditions are specific instructions that may be added to an improv scene, most often before the scene begins. In some cases, conditions are sufficient to define the entire game; in others, they are offers that establish the orientation of the players for that particular scene only. Even when conditions are specific to one character the instructions are for all players in the scene, since players need to give one another character. The categories and examples given below are fairly comprehensive but not exhaustive and may be combined in many different ways.

I. *Endowments* establish the identity that the player assumes in the scene ("Who you are").
   A. *Basic identity*. Ordinarily, a player is assumed to be portraying a human being. However, the offer could be to portray an animal, inanimate object, alien creature, cartoon character, deity, or even an abstract force or concept.
   B. *Impersonation*. Infrequently used, this offer is of a famous person, or someone well-known to the players, to be imitated in all particulars.

C. *Social*. These endowments describe the character within a sociocultural context, and include such characteristics as: rank, power, fame, wealth, and occupation.

D. *Attitudinal/psychological*. These are thought of as traits rather than situational responses, such as: pessimistic, naive, aggressive, paranoid, irritable, etc.

E. *Emotional*. Blending somewhat with the previous category of endowments, these include: weepy, bitter, depressed, angry, cheerful, etc.

F. *Behavioral*. As characters display who they are to others through behavior, all endowments are accepted behaviorally; this category applies to specific gestures and mannerisms (such as: constantly picking lint off of clothing, frequently yawning, giving a military salute whenever first making eye contact with someone, etc.) that are suggestive of compulsions or intended to convey symbolic meaning.

G. *Physical*. These endowments are physical properties and functioning, such as: fat, having only one arm, smelling bad, walking with a limp, etc. As offers, physical endowments blend with limitations and powers (below).

H. *Relational*. These describe the way the characters stand in relationship to one another, and include: status (higher, equal, or lower), occupational (teacher-student[s]), social role (neighbors), familial (father-son).

II. *Limitations and powers* establish unusual rules for the conduct of one or all of the players ("What you can/cannot do").

A. *Speech*.
1. No speaking—mime only
2. Speech without words—using expressive sounds or gibberish
3. Using/omitting—having to use/not being permitted to use a letter of the alphabet, grammatical part of speech, etc.
4. Number of words—limiting the length of each turn of speech (e.g., three-word sentences)
5. Accent—speaking in a designated foreign accent
6. Rhyme/meter—speaking in verse or in rhyme (e.g., rhyming couplets)
7. Volume—regulating the loudness of speech according to instructions
8. Proxy—speaking for, or being spoken for by other players

B. *Movement*.
1. Proxy—moving all or parts of the bodies of others; players have other players move parts of or their entire bodies
2. Location—usually in conjunction with setting, entering certain areas of the stage is not permitted, or, upon entering a certain

area, changing the mode of movement (e.g., slow-motion, crawling, etc.)

   3. Tempo—varying the speed of movement; one player might move at a different rate of speed than another

  C. *Information.* One player posesses information that another lacks, usually based on information given out of earshot of the unknowing player (characteristic of a number of "parlor" games), or given in front of all; the scene is played as though others do not know the "secret."

  D. *Magical/supernatural powers.* While any improviser can "grant" him- or herself such powers, these offers are assigned, typically at the beginning of the scene.

III. *Setting* defines the environment; it is possible for players to be in a different location or time period from one another ("Where/when you are").

  A. *Location.* This setting defines the place, which may be geographically specific (e.g., atop the Eiffel tower), nongeographical (e.g., on a beach, in a kitchen), or conceptual (e.g., inside a computer, in Heaven).

  B. *Environmental features.* This setting is a mood combined with physical qualities, such as: intense heat, a messy room, a haunted house at midnight.

  C. *Historical period.* This can refer to the distant past (e.g., the French revolution), the recent past (e.g., a week earlier), the near future (e.g., an hour later), or the far future (e.g., the twenty-fifth century). Historical culture is usually specified at the beginning of the scene while time jumps are usually performed during the scene.

  D. *Orientation.* Gravity may be suspended or attract from a direction other than "down" to the audience (which may lead to a "sideways scene" in which the back wall of the stage area is "down" for the players).

IV. *Style* specifies the tone, manner, and genre of the enactment. Players may play identical or contrasting styles ("In what manner you act"). *Styles* may be literary (Shakespeare, Beckett) or musical (salsa, Mozart); *genres* may be literary (modern poetry, detective fiction) or musical (opera, rock-n'-roll). Other fields that may be varied in style and genre include movies, radio or TV shows, magazines, and newspapers.

V. *Theme* sets forth a topic about which the scene is constructed, such as: love, death, illness, greed, food, God, pets, horror, art, jealousy, lying, etc.

REFERENCES

Aloff, M. (1993, July). Beautiful theories. *Atlantic Monthly, 272*(1).

Anonymous (1989). *Quotable Women.* Philadelphia: Running Press.

Anderson, H. D. (1992). C therapy and the F word. *AFTA Newsletter.*

Aponte, H. J. (1977). The anatomy of a therapist. In P. Papp (Ed.), *Family therapy: Full length case studies* (Chapter 6). New York: Garden Press.

Atwood, J. D. (1992). Using therapeutic metaphors. *The Family Psychologist, 8*(4), 15–17.

Barragar-Dunne, P. (1993). *The narrative therapist and the arts.* Self-published.

Bateson, G. (1972). *Steps to an ecology mind* (Chapter 5). New York: Ballantine.

Belt, L., & Stockley, R. (1989). *Improvisation through Theatre Sports.* Seattle: Thespis.

Berne, E. (1964). *Games people play.* New York: Grove.

Blatner, A., & Blatner, A. (1988). *The art of play.* New York: Human Services Press.

Boal, A. (1992). *Games for actors and non-actors.* London: Routledge.

Bretherton, I. (1984). *Representing the social world in symbolic play: Reality and fantasy.* New York: Academic.

Bruner, J. (1986). *Actual minds, possible worlds.* Cambridge, MA: Harvard University Press.

Carlson, B. W. (1973). *Let's pretend it happened to you.* Nashville: Abingdon.

Chasin, R., Roth, S., & Bograd, M. (1989). Action methods in systemic therapy: Dramatizing ideal futures and reformed pasts with couples. *Family Process, 28*(1), 121–136.

Colapinto, J. (1991). *Structural family therapy.* In A. S. Gurman, & D. P. Kniskern (Eds.), *Handbook of family therapy Vol. 2.* New York: Brunner/Mazel.

Coles, R. (1990). *The spiritual life of children.* Boston: Houghton Mifflin.

Couch, A., & Kenniston, K. (1960). Yeasayers and naysayers: Agreeing response set as a personality variable. *Journal of Abnormal Social Psychology, 60,* 151–174.

Daintith, J., Egerton, H., Fergusson, R., Stibbs, A., & Wright, E. (1989). *Macmillan Dictionary of Quotations.* New York: Macmillan.

de Shazar, S. (1985). *Keys to solution in brief therapy*. New York: Norton.

Duncan, N. (1962). *Communication and the social order*. New York: Oxford University Press.

Efran, J. S., Lukens, R. J., & Lukens, M. D. (1988, September/October). Constructivism: What's in it for you? *The Family Therapy Networker*, 27–35.

Efran, J. S., & Clarfield, L. E. (1992). *Constructionist therapy: Sense and nonsense*. In S. McNamee, & K. J. Gergen (Eds.), *Therapy as social construction*. London: Sage.

Fineman, J. (1962). Observations on the development of imaginative play in early development. *Journal of the American Academy of Child Psychiatry, 1*, 167–181.

Fluegelman, A. (1976). *The new games book*. Garden City, NY: Doubleday.

Fluegelman, A. (1981). *More new games!* Garden City, NY: Doubleday.

Freud, S. (1904). Freud's psychoanalytic method. In P. Rieff (Ed.), *Freud's therapy and technique*. New York: Macmillan.

Friedman, E. (1984). The play's the thing. *The Family Therapy Networker, 8*(1).

Gergen, K. (1991). *The saturated self*. New York: Basic Books.

Gilligan, S. (1993). Therapeutic rituals. In S. Gilligan, & R. Price (Eds.), *Therapeutic conversations* (pp. 237–252). New York: Norton.

Goffman, E. (1959). *The Presentation of self in everyday life*. Garden City, NY: Doubleday.

Goffman, E. (1974). *Frame analysis*. New York: Harper & Row.

Grainger, R. (1992). Dramatherapy and thought disorder. In S. Jennings (Ed.), *Dramatherapy: Theory and practice 2*. London: Tavistock/Routledge.

Harris, T. A. (1969). *I'm OK – You're OK*. New York: Harper & Row.

Heilbrun, C. G. (1988). *Writing a woman's life*. New York: Norton.

Herzka, H. S. (1986). On the anthropology of play: Play as a way of dialogical development. In R. van der Kooij, & J. Hellendoorn (Eds.), *Play, play therapy, play research*. Berwyn, The Netherlands: Swets, North America.

Hodgson, J., & Richards, E. (1966). *Improvisation: Discovery and creativity in drama*. London: Methuen.

Holt, D. (1992). Enactment, therapy and behavior. In S. Jennings (Ed.), *Dramatherapy: Theory and practice 2*. London: Tavistock/Routledge.

Hothman, R. (1965). *Strasberg at the actors studio*. New York: Viking.

Howes, C. (1988). Sharing fantasy: Social pretend play in toddlers. *Child Development, 56*, 1253–1258.

Howes, C. (1992). *The collaborative construction of pretend*. Albany, NY: S.U.N.Y. Press.

Hubert, Judd, D. (1991). *Metatheater*. Lincoln: University of Nebraska Press.

Huizinga, J. (1949). *Homo ludens: A study of the play element in culture*. London: Routledge & Kegan Paul.

Imber-Black, E., Roberts, J., & Whiting, R. (Eds.). (1988). *Rituals in families and family therapy*. New York: Norton.

Jacobus, L. A. (1989). *The Bedford introduction to drama*. New York: St. Martin's Press.

James, R., & Williams, P. (1984). *A guide to improvisation: A handbook for teachers*. Oxon, England: Kemble Press.

Johnson, D. R. (1981). Drama therapy and the schizophrenic condition. In G. Schattner, & P. Courtney (Eds.), *Drama in therapy 2*. New York: Drama Book Specialists.

Johnson, D. R. (1992). The dramatherapist in-role. In S. Jennings (Ed.), *Dramatherapy: Theory and practice 2*. London: Tavistock/Routledge.

Johnstone, K. (1981). *Impro*. London: Methuen.

Johnstone, K. (1987, July). *Keith Johnstone's Theatresports and Life Game Newsletter*.

Johnstone, K. (1988, June). *Keith Johnstone's Theatresports and Life Game Newsletter*.

Johnstone, K. (1990, May). *Keith Johnstone's Theatresports and Life Game Newsletter*.

Johnstone, K. (1992, June). *Keith Johnstone's Theatresports and Life Game Newsletter*.

Johnstone, K. (1993, April). *Keith Johnstone's Theatresports and Life Game Newsletter*.

Keeney, B. P. (1991). *Improvisational therapy*. New York: Guilford.

Keith, D. V. (1987). The use of self in therapy: A field guide. In M. Baldwin, & V. Satir (Eds.), *The self in family therapy*. New York: Haworth.

Koestler, A. (1964). *The act of creation*. New York: Dell.

Kopp, S. B. (1972). *If you meet the buddha on the road, kill him!* Palo Alto, CA: Science and Behavior Books.

Kopp, S. (1977). *This side of tragedy: Psychotherapy as theater*. Palo Alto: Behavioral Science Press.

Laing, R. D. (1970). *Knots*. New York: Random House.

Laing, R. D. (1972). *The politics of the family*. New York: Vintage.

Landy, R. J. (1986). *Drama therapy: Concepts and practice*. Springfield, IL: Charles C. Thomas.

Landy, R. J. (1991). The dramatic basis of role therapy. *The Arts in Psychotherapy, 18*, 29–41.

Lankton, S. R., Lankton, C. H., & Mathews, W. J. (1991). Ericksonian family therapy. In A. S. Gurman, & D. P. Kniskern (Eds.), *Handbook of family therapy, Vol. 2*. New York: Brunner/Mazel.

Leacock, S. B. (1981). *The Penguin Stephen Leacock*. New York: Penguin.

Lewis, J. M. (1993). Childhood play in normality, pathology and therapy. *American Journal of Orthopsychiatry, 63*(1), 6–15.

Liddle, H. A., & Saba, G. W. (1985). The isomorphic nature of training and therapy. In J. Schwartzman (Ed.), *Families and other systems*. New York: Guilford.

Lutfiyya, M. N. (1987). *The social constitution of context through play*. Lanham: University Press of America.

Luthe, W. (1976). *Creativity mobilization technique*. New York: Grune & Stratton.

Madanes, C. (1981). *Strategic family therapy*. San Francisco: Jossey-Bass.

Mahoney, M. (1990). *Human change process*. New York: Basic.

Millar, S. (1972). *The psychology of play*. Baltimore: Penguin.

Miller, S. (1973). Ends, means and galumping: Some leitmotifs of play. *American Anthropologist, LXXV*, 88–99.

Minuchin, S., & Fishman, H. C. (1981). *Family therapy technique*. Cambridge, MA: Harvard University Press.

Moreno, J. L. (1934). *Who shall survive?* Beacon, New York: Beacon Press.

Moreno, J. L. (1983). *The theatre of spontaneity*. Ambler, PA: Beacon House.

Myerhoff, B. G. (1977). We don't wrap herring in a printed page: Fusion, fictions and continuity in secular ritual. In S. F. Moore, & B. G. Myerhoff (Eds.), *Secular ritual*. Amsterdam: Van Gorcum.

Nachmanovitch, S. (1990). *Free play*. Los Angeles: Tarcher.

Naranjo, C. (1968). Contributions of Gestalt therapy, Otto. In A. Herbert, & J. Mann (Eds.), *Ways of growth* (pp. 128–146). New York: Viking.

Neill, J. R., & Kniskern, D. P. (Eds.). (1982). *From psyche to system: The evolving therapy of Carl Whitaker*. New York: Guilford.

Nerin, W. F. (1986). *Family reconstruction: Long day's journey into light*. New York: Norton.

Novello, M. C. (1985). *Theater games for young performers*. Colorado Springs: Meriwether.

Nye, C. H. (1993). Screen memories. *Readings, 8*(2), 12–17.

O'Hanlon, W. H. Commentary. In S. Gilligan, & R. Price (Eds.), *Therapeutic conversations*. New York: Norton, 1993.

Ouspensky, P. D. (1971). *The fourth way*. New York: Vintage Books.

Papp, P. Staging reciprocal metaphors in couples groups. *Family Process, 21*, 1982.

Partington, A. (Ed.). (1992). Oxford Dictionary of Quotations (4th ed.). New York: Oxford University Press.

Piaget, J. (1962). *Play, dreams and imitation in childhood*. New York: Norton.

Pirandello, L. (1951). *Six characters in search of an author*. E. Storer (Trans.). New York: Meridian.

Riebel, L. (1992). On with the show. *Family Therapy Networker, 16*(5), 32–35.

Roberto, L. G. (1991). Symbolic experiential family therapy. In A. S. Gurman, & D. P. Kniskern (Eds.), *Handbook of family therapy, Vol. 2*. New York: Brunner/Mazel.

Roberts, J. (1988). Setting the frame: Definition, functions and typology of rituals. In E. Imber-Black, J. Roberts, & R. Whiting (Eds.), *Rituals in families and family therapy* (pp. 6–46). New York: Norton.

Roberts, J. (1994). *Tales and transformations*. New York: Norton.

Roth, S., & Chasin, R. (1994). Entering one another's worlds of meaning and imagination: Dramatic enactment and narrative couple therapy. In M. Hoyt (Ed.), *Constructive therapies*. New York: Guilford.

Salamon, E., Grevelius, K., & Andersson, M. (1993). Beware the siren's song. In S. Gilligan, & R. Price (Eds.), *Therapeutic conversations* (pp. 330–343). New York: Norton.

Salas, J. (1993). *Improvising real life*. Dubuque, IA: Kendall-Hunt.

Satir, V. (1987). The therapist story. In M. Baldwin, & V. Satir (Eds.), *The use of self in therapy* (pp. 17–25). New York: Haworth.

Scheff, T. J. (1979). *Catharsis in healing, ritual and drama*. Berkely: University of California Press.

Schwartz, R. C. (1992). Rescuing the exiles. *Family Therapy Networker, 16*(75), 33–37.

Schorr, J. E. (1972). *Psycho-imagination therapy*. New York: Intercontinental Medical Book Corp.

Seeman, H. (1976). *A comprehensive bibliography on affective-humanistic education*. Unpublished.

Seeman, H., & Wiener, D. J. (1985, Winter). Comparing and using psychodrama with family therapy: Some cautions. *Journal of Group Psychotherapy, Psychodrama and Sociometry,* 143–156.

Shaffer, J. B. P., & Galinsky, M. D. (1974). *Models of group therapy and sensitivity training*. Englewood Cliffs: Prentice-Hall.

Shepher, B. (1992). Theatre as community therapy: An exploration of the interrelationship between the audience and the theatre. In S. Jennings (Ed.), *Dramatherapy: Theory and practice 2*. London: Tavistock/Routledge.

Singer, D. G., & Singer, J. L. (1990). *The house of make-believe*. Cambridge, MA: Harvard University Press.

Sonne, J. (1973). *A primer for family therapists*. Morristown, NJ: Thursday Press.

Spence, D. P. (1987). *The Freudian metaphor*. New York: Norton.

Sperber, M. (1974). *Improvisation in the performing arts*. Unpublished doctoral dissertation, Teachers College, New York.

Spolin, V. (1963). *Improvisation for the theatre*. Evanston, IL: Northwestern University Press.

Stravinsky, I. (1942). *The poetics of music*. Cambridge: Harvard University Press.

Sweet, J. (1987). *Something wonderful right away*. New York: Proscenium.

Telander, M., Quinlan, F., & Verson, K. (1982). *Acting up! An innovative approach to creative drama for older adults*. Chicago: Coach House Press.

Vygotsky, L. S. (1978). *Mind in society*. Cambridge, MA: Harvard University Press.

Watts, A. W. (1961). *Psychotherapy east and west*. New York: Pantheon.

Watts, A. W. (1966). *The book: On the taboo against knowing who you are*. New York: Collier.

Watts, P. (1992). Therapy in drama. In S. Jennings (Ed.), *Dramatherapy: Theory and practice 2*. London: Tavistock/Routledge.

Waters, D. (1993). Family therapy as an excellent adventure. *Family Therapy Networker, 16*(5).

Watzlawick, P., Bavelas, J. B., & Jackson, D. D. (1967). *Pragmatics of human communication*. New York: Norton.

Whitaker, C. A., & Keith, D. V. (1981). Symbolic experiential family therapy. In A. S. Gurman, & D. P. Kniskern (Eds.), *Handbook of family therapy* (pp. 187–224). New York: Brunner/Mazel.

White, M. (1993). Deconstruction and therapy. In S. Gilligan, & R. Price (Eds.), *Therapeutic conversations*. New York: Norton.

White, M., & Epston, D. (1990). *Narrative means to therapeutic ends*. New York: Norton.

Whiting, R. (1988). Guidelines to designing therapeutic rituals. In E. Imber-Black, J. Roberts, & R. Whiting (Eds.), *Rituals in families and family therapy*. New York: Norton.

Wiener, D. J. (1991). You wanna play? *Journal of Feminist Family Therapy, 3*(1, 2), 213–219.

Wiener, D. J., & Maddox, G. J. (1992). The voyeur and the exhibitionist: Comparing improvisation for therapists and actors. In D. J. Wiener (Ed.), *The Rehearsals! for Growth Newsletter, 1*(2), pp. 11–14.

Wilshire, B. (1991). *Role playing and identity: The limits of theatre as metaphor*. Bloomington: University of Indiana Press.

Winnicott, D. W. (1951). *Collected Papers* (pp. 229–242). New York: Basic Books.

Winnicott, D. W. (1971). *Playing and reality*. London: Tavistock.

INDEX